132 THE GREENING OF EUROPE by Ed Gallagher, Chief Executive of the Environment Agency

138 THE DEVELOPING WORLD: IMPROVING THE EU'S EFFECTIVENESS by The Rt. Hon. Clare Short MP, Secretary of State for International Development

142 SHAPING THE FUTURE: RESEARCH AND DEVELOPMENT, EDUCATION & TRAINING by Dr Howard Machin, Director of the European Institute at the London School of Economics

148 RECONNECTING EUROPE WITH ITS CITIZENS by Charles Grant, Director of the Centre for European Reform

152 BRITAIN'S SUCCESSES IN THE EUROPEAN UNION 1973-98 by Anthony Teasdale, former Special Adviser to Chancellor of the Exchequer Kenneth Clarke and Foreign Secretary Sir Geoffrey Howe

161 THE SINGLE CURRENCY: PRACTICAL CONSIDERATIONS FOR BUSINESSES by Vernon Ellis, Managing Director for Europe, The Middle East, Africa and India, Andersen Consulting

166 IN THE MARKET FOR FLEXIBILITY by Adair Turner, Director-General of the Confederation of British Industry

168 ACCELERATING DRUG APPROVAL IN EUROPE by Fernand Sauer, Executive Director, European Agency for the Evaluation of Medicinal Products

177 WHY EUROPE MATTERS by The Rt. Hon. Lord Howe of Aberavon CH, QC, former Deputy Prime Minister

Commissioning Editor and Editor, Maurice Fraser, is Visiting Fellow at the London School of Economics and Political Science. A former Special Adviser to Foreign Secretaries Douglas Hurd, John Major and Sir Geoffrey Howe, he is a regular writer and broadcaster on European affairs and a consultant on EU strategy.

FEATURE ARTICLES

16 RECLAIMING VAT ON SERVICES WITHIN THE EU by Jane E. Holmberg, General Manager, United Cash Back (Holding) Ltd.

136 BBC MPM: MAKING A DIFFERENCE TO PEOPLE'S LIVES by Joan Connolly, BBC MPM Ltd.

174 MAKING CANCER HISTORY by Professor J. Gordon McVie FRCP, Director-General, Cancer Research Campaign

PUBLISHED BY:
Strategems Publishing Limited
40 South Audley Street
Mayfair
London
W1Y 5DH
Tel: 0171 495 8662
Fax: 0171 409 0229

Editor — Maurice Fraser

Publisher — Anthony J Mullarkey

Sub-Editor — Mark Hollingsworth
Art Editor — Tian Mullarkey
Production Manager — Melissa Alexander
Advertising Sales — Aspect Publishing
New Era Publishing
Daniel Slack
Tony Oaklands

Reprograhics & Pre-Press:
Red Repro
Tel: 0181 533 1118
Fax: 0181 533 1119

Printing:
Acorn Web Offset Limited
Tel: 01924 220633
Fax: 01924 890623

Telegraph Colour Libary: Front cover, pp34, 36, 38, 44, 46, 70, 71, 86, 102, 118, 139
Corbis: pp24, 26, 30 (Delors & Thatcher), 47, 52, 74, 75, 77, 136.
Tony Stone: pp10, 72, 80, 114, 132
Popperfoto: pp18, 56, 91, 128
Hulton Deutsch: p30 (Howe & Cockfield)

The London School of Economics and Political Science

▌path-breaking theoretical and empirical research on Europe

▌unrivalled expertise in economics, accountancy, information systems, management, politics, gender, public policy, law, communications, international relations, risk analysis, industrial relations, contemporary history, welfare states, sociology, finance, anthropology and social psychology

▌a truly international research environment - with top faculty and 1000 research graduates from all parts of Europe and the rest of the world

▌in-depth specialists on the European Union and on the economies, societies and states of Europe - including France, Germany, Italy, Spain, Greece, Britain, Poland, Hungary, Sweden, and Russia

▌Europe's largest social science library, with a full EU European Documentation Centre, extensive specialist collections on Europe and excellent on-line services

▌experience of working in close cooperation with businesses, associations and governments in all parts of Europe and the European Commission on contractual research

▌advanced European Masters and Doctoral programmes in all the social sciences

▌specialised teaching and organisation of post-experience short courses, summer schools, professional conferences and executive seminars in all parts of Europe

▌successful teamwork in research networks, development projects (PHARE and TACIS), staff and student exchanges (Council of European Management Schools, Socrates) and in partnership with the British Council in its European Networking Programmes

For more information on LSE, its European interdisciplinary Doctoral and Masters programmes (European Political Economy, Nationalism, European Studies, the Political Economy of Transition in Europe, Russian and Post-Soviet Studies), and about research groups, networks and short courses on Europe please contact:

The European Institute, LSE, Houghton Street, London. WC2A 2AE
Telephone: (44) 171 955 6780; E-mail: m.clark@lse.ac.uk
Website: http://www.lse.ac.uk/depts/european/

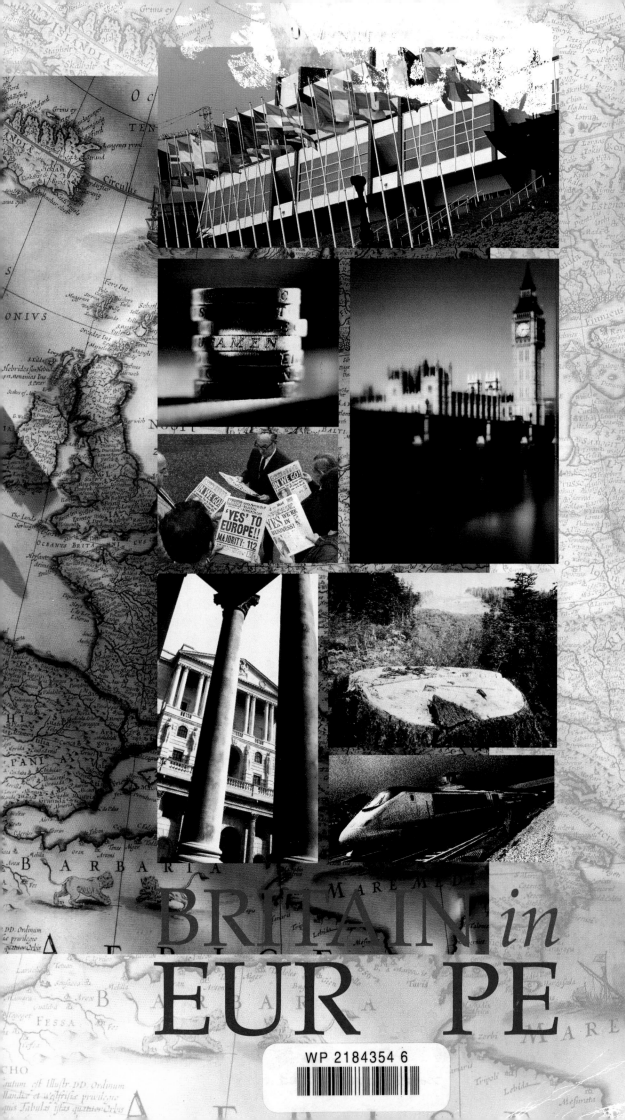

BRITAIN in EUROPE

Contents

5   FOREWORD by the Prime Minister, The Rt. Hon. Tony Blair MP

6   PRIORITIES FOR THE UK PRESIDENCY: BUILDING A EUROPE FOR THE PEOPLE by The Rt. Hon. Robin Cook MP, Secretary of State for Foreign and Commonwealth Affairs

10   BRITAIN AND EUROPE: HISTORY OF A RELATIONSHIP by Stephen Woodard, Director of the European Movement

18   THE EUROPEAN UNION IN THE WORLD: A FORCE FOR FREE TRADE by The Rt. Hon. Sir Leon Brittan QC, Vice-President of the European Commission

24   THE UNITED KINGDOM AND THE EUROPEAN UNION: LIGHT ON THE RELATIONSHIP by Vernon Bogdanor, Professor of Government at Oxford University

30   POINTING THE WAY: HOW THE SINGLE MARKET CAME ABOUT by Michael Welsh, Chief Executive of the Action Centre for Europe

34   LONDON: FINANCIAL CENTRE OF EUROPE by Judith Mayhew, Chairman of the Policy and Resources Committee, Corporation of London

40   THE BBC: AT EUROPE'S CUTTING EDGE by John Birt, Director-General of the BBC

44   THE EU & NATO: REWRITING OUR CONTINENT by Lord Wallace of Saltaire, Reader in International Relations at the London School of Economics

50   EU ENLARGEMENT: COSTS AND OPPORTUNITIES by Heather Grabbe and Dr Kirsty Hughes, Royal Institute of International Affairs

56   MAKING EUROPE SAFER: FOREIGN POLICY AND DEFENCE by The Rt. Hon. Lord Hurd of Westwell CH, CBE, former Foreign Secretary

62   THE EU COMMISSION: WHY WE NEED IT by Geoffrey Martin, Head of the European Commission Representation in the United Kingdom

68   THE EUROPEAN PARLIAMENT: WHAT IT DOES by Martyn Bond, Head of the European Parliament Office in the UK

72   EUROPE ON THE MOVE: THE TRANSPORT AGENDA by The Rt. Hon. Neil Kinnock, Member of the European Commission

80   A COMPETITIVE EUROPE by Frank Vibert, Director of the European Policy Forum

86   PARTNERS IN URBAN REGENERATION: A PERSONAL REFLECTION by Duncan Hall, Chief Executive, Teesside Development Corporation

98   ECONOMIC & MONETARY UNION: PROSPECTS, PROBLEMS AND OPPORTUNITIES by Lord Currie of Marylebone, Professor of Economics at the London Business School

102   PREPARING THE CITY FOR THE EURO by Eddie George, Governor of the Bank of England

109   THE TREATY OF AMSTERDAM by Dr Timothy Bainbridge, Author of The Penguin Companion to European Union

114   MAKING EUROPE SAFER FOR THE CITIZEN by Dr Matthew Sowemimo, Director of Research, the European Movement

120   CITIZENSHIP OF THE EUROPEAN UNION by Professor Elizabeth Meehan, The Queen's University, Belfast

126   THE BRITISH COUNCIL: PROJECTING THE NEW BRITAIN by Sir Martin Jacomb, Chairman of the British Council

128   EUROPE & ITS REGIONS by Dr Robert Leonardi, Jean Monnet Fellow at the European Institute, London School of Economics

FOREWORD BY THE PRIME MINISTER

January 1998 marks the beginning of the United Kingdom's Presidency of the European Union. It is fitting that our Presidency should start on the 25th anniversary of our membership of the European Community. That membership has registered real successes, but it has also been a story of missed opportunities. For too long we gave the impression that we were less than fully committed to the success of Europe's leading enterprise. We never made up the ground we had lost by failing to join the European Community at its inception. Our influence suffered accordingly, with real damage to our national interest.

That is set to change. Our Presidency of the European Union is a unique opportunity to rebuild Britain's standing. We want to channel more of Europe's energies into those things which most matter to ordinary people, like jobs, crime, the war on drugs and the quality of our environment. At the same time, we will use our Presidency to make sure that the Single European Currency is built on solid foundations. And we want to make sure that the next round of EU enlargement gets off to a flying start.

Britain in Europe is a timely initiative which explains in a clear and accessible way the main issues we need to address at this critical point in the history of our continent. It sets Britain's European role in the positive perspective which it deserves, and will, I hope, help to meet the public demand for more information on the European Union.

The better we understand our role in Europe, the better placed we will be to bring about what we all want to see: a real People's Europe.

Tony Blair

PRIORITIES FOR THE UK PRESIDENCY:
BUILDING A EUROPE FOR THE PEOPLE

BY THE RT. HON. ROBIN COOK MP,
SECRETARY OF STATE FOR FOREIGN AND COMMONWEALTH AFFAIRS

"As Presidency, we will promote the basic principles of economic reform necessary to make Europe competitive in future. This will run through a number of fronts, including a more effective Single Market, boosting the Union's competitiveness and a greater emphasis on creating jobs"

INTRODUCTION

In recent years, the European Union has moved too far from the hopes and aspirations of its peoples. Too often it has appeared concerned with institutional change for change's sake, and unconcerned about real issues. The people need to be reconnected to the EU their governments are trying to create. Our mission as Presidency of the European Union is to create a Europe for the people.

We seek in the longer term to build a Europe which brings practical benefits and genuinely responds to the people's concerns: more open, more transparent and free from the burden of unnecessary regulation.

Britain's six-month Presidency of the European Union's Council of Ministers (January-June 1998) is an exciting opportunity to bring this vision closer, by engaging people's interest and enthusiasm.

Six months is a comparatively short time. Much of the Presidency will involve careful management of the inherited agenda, running EU business impartially in the interests of the Council as a whole. Our European partners will judge us by the competence and drive with which we take it forward. But the Presidency also offers the chance to bring out some key issues affecting people's everyday lives.

These include economic reform and the fight against unemployment; a tougher approach to crime; the search for a healthier environment; the challenge of EU enlargement and associated policy reform; and a co-ordinated, coherent external policy. The most momentous decision will be the Council's decision on which countries should enter Stage III of EMU.

THE MAIN CHALLENGE: ECONOMIC REFORM AND UNEMPLOYMENT

As Presidency, we will promote the basic principles of economic reform necessary to make Europe competitive in future. This will run through a number of fronts, including a more effective Single Market, boosting the Union's competitiveness, and a greater emphasis on creating jobs. We want to combine economic dynamism with social justice.

Finding and keeping a job is the people of Europe's greatest concern. One in ten among its young people is jobless. Long-term unemployment is another cause for acute concern. The modern economy is stimulating for those with the skills to flourish – they can change jobs, even careers, several times in their working lives. But many feel threatened by it, others entirely excluded. Government must make sure that the economy is inclusive of all sectors of society. The UK Presidency will therefore focus on four main goals:

❖ *Employability*. We must help people acquire the skills to get and then keep jobs. Without education and skills, people risk permanent exclusion.

❖ *Flexibility*. Companies must be able to adapt to a fast changing market without red tape, while ensuring decent minimum standards for workers.

❖ *Entrepreneurship*. To allow Europe's creativity and innovation to translate into jobs, we must nurture small businesses – so important in this respect – by reducing their non-wage costs and encouraging investment in new companies.

❖ *Equal Opportunities*. All who want to work must be given the chance, regardless of sex, age, race or disability.

The European Council convened last November to address unemployment is a launch pad for putting Europe back to work. In the Presidency, we aim to agree guidelines that will help member states determine and pursue their own policies and targets for reducing unemployment in 1998; make EU policies more job-productive; and learn from the best of employment policies across the Union.

But the Union will only create jobs and increase sustainable growth by being more innovative and more competitive – another of our central themes. The role of smaller companies in the European economy will be central to the first formal debate on competitiveness held in the Industry Council during the UK Presidency.

Closely tied to competitiveness is an effective Single Market. Only a genuine Single Market, free of hidden barriers and unfair state aids, can produce a Europe fully capable of working for the people. The UK is already co-operating with the preceding and succeeding Presidencies, Luxembourg and Austria, on priority items in the Commission's Action Plan. These include better enforcement of existing Single Market legislation, correct use of EU legislation in national law, more simplification and better regulation, and tighter control of state aid.

We must also develop the EU's trade policy. A strong, outward-looking Europe is pivotal in the world's economy: the stronger its trade, the better the prospects for growth and jobs. Our Presidency should enable the EU to play a leading role in laying the groundwork for comprehensive WTO negotiations at the turn of the century on further trade liberalisation. Major trade-related events of the Presidency will include the second WTO Ministerial Conference in May; the second Asia-Europe Summit; and EU summits with Japan, the USA and Canada. The Partnership and Co-operation Agreements with Russia and Ukraine are also likely to enter into force.

WHAT THE EU CAN DO FOR THE CITIZEN

Crime is a further source of serious public concern. We want to use the Presidency to reinforce cooperation between Europe's police forces against drugs and organised crime. We will prepare the way to get Europol up and running. Governments across Europe must work more closely together if we are to counter the highly integrated international drugs trade. We must also stem the flow of drug supplies at source by carrying forward the EU's initiatives with governments in the Caribbean and Central Asia.

The UK is not a party to the Schengen Agreement on the abolition of border controls. But one of the UK Presidency tasks will be to take forward the detailed work required for the incorporation of Schengen, including the association of Norway and Iceland, into the EU Treaties.

We also need to improve our citizens' knowledge of their rights in the internal market. Too often, people are simply unaware of what these are, hidden as they can be behind unnecessary bureaucracy. The next stage of the Citizens First programme should be a help here. The UK Presidency will also seek better Europe-wide consumer protection, through stronger enforcement of present laws and by pushing for new measures on minimum consumer guarantees.

We shall work to improve EU regulation, ensuring it is simple, fair and helpful to business and citizens. Too often red tape strangles innovation and job creation. There will also be opportunities to build on advances made by the Amsterdam Treaty on openness and transparency.

Reduction of waste and a stepping-up of the fight against fraud are further targets. People need to have confidence that their taxes are being properly and responsibly administered. Measures here involve following up the Commission's Sound and Efficient Management (SEM 2000) initiative designed to improve the management of Community finances.

The people of Europe care deeply about living in a healthier environment. Enhancing the EU's contribution to this has high priority, including action to improve air and water quality. The main business will fall to the Environment Council. But our Presidency will also work to ensure that environmental considerations feature in other Community policies. Food and other agricultural production, along with energy and transport policies, for example, all have an important effect on the environment. We must work to make them more environmentally responsive.

Internationally, the EU is already giving an important lead – for example, in the UN negotiations on clean water and sanitation for all the world's population and on managing the world's forests. The British Presidency will maintain that lead. We also want to build on the conclusions of December's important Kyoto meeting on climate change.

INHERITED AGENDA

At a special Council of the Heads of State or Government in Brussels over the weekend of 1-3 May, the EU will take the momentous decision on which countries should participate in a Single Currency from 1 January 1999. The Chancellor of the Exchequer made clear last October that the Government is in principle in favour of UK membership

> "The enlargement process has to be like a pipeline – with all the applicant countries in it, moving at their own speeds towards the same goal. To underline that this is an inclusive process, we propose to establish a European Conference, during our Presidency, in which all the applicants and members will take part"

of a successful currency, and sees no constitutional bar to it. However, we shall not join in 1999 nor, barring a fundamental and unforeseen change in economic circumstances, will it be realistic to take a decision to join during this parliament. The Government is now preparing intensively, so ensuring that Britain will be able to join, should the Government and the people in a referendum so wish, early in the next Parliament.

As Presidency, we shall do all we can to get the Single Currency off to a successful start, devoting all the necessary time and energy to facilitating decisions on EMU, and rigorously demonstrating our constructive approach to Europe. As an impartial chairman, the United Kingdom will discharge its Presidency responsibilities to the highest standard, both over the important decisions on membership and over the considerable volume of technical legislation which will also have to be agreed in ECOFIN.

Another memorable event will be the Union's next enlargement. A successful opening of negotiations with those countries ready to join the EU is a key Presidency objective. Here we have an historic opportunity to bring the people of Europe peace and prosperity. Enlargement will help create a self-confident, outward-looking Union and give a huge boost to all our economies. The Commission presented its Opinions on the Central European applicants' readiness for membership to the General Affairs Council in July (the Council had already agreed to start negotiations with Cyprus six months after the IGC). It will fall to the UK Presidency to launch the enlargement process in line with the decisions at the Luxembourg European Council.

It is essential that countries which do not open accession negotiations remain fully engaged in the enlargement process. We must avoid leaving them disappointed and disillusioned. The enlargement process has to be like a pipeline – with all the applicant countries in it, moving at their own speeds towards the same goal. The Commission's proposals for reinforcing the pre-accession strategy are thus particularly important. To underline that this is an *inclusive* process, we propose to establish a European Conference, during our Presidency, in which all the applicants and members will take part.

Enlargement is part of a wider project – modernising the EU to meet the challenges of the next century. Central to this is the Agenda 2000 package of Community policy reforms of the CAP and of the Structural and Cohesion Funds; and the EU's post-1999 financing arrangements. Giving effect to the Luxembourg European Council's guidance on how this complex package should be handled over the following six months is set to form one of our Presidency's leading areas of activity.

Nationally, the Government strongly supports the Commission's recommendation to maintain the current ceiling on Own Resources at 1.27% of GNP throughout the next financial period at least. On CAP reform, Commission thinking on the long-term process of reform represents a good starting point. It recognises the importance of reducing production support, enhancing the rural environment, tackling consumer concerns about food safety, and sustaining rural communities. Simultaneously, the Government seeks reform of the Structural and Cohesion Funds, so that the new demands of enlargement can be met, while ensuring a fair and efficient distribution of the available resources to Europe's regions according to needs. On each of these dossiers, the UK Presidency will want to start discussion of detailed Commission legislative proposals as soon as these are available.

The British Presidency is also a chance to restore the people's confidence that the EU can speak for them in the world, and co-ordinate its EU foreign policy effectively. Priority areas are likely to include:

❖ *Asia.* The second Asia-Europe Summit, to be held in London in April, will be a means to forge stronger ties between two economic powerhouses which between them account for 50% of world GDP.

❖ *USA.* The UK will host an EU/US Summit in May – an opportunity to underline the importance of the transatlantic relationship.

❖ *Lomé V.* The EU mandate for negotiations with the 71 countries of Africa, the Caribbean and the Pacific should be agreed largely during the UK Presidency.

❖ *Arms Exports.* We will press for an EU Code of Conduct setting high common standards to govern arms exports from all Member States.

CONCLUSION

Our benchmark will be how policies impact on the peoples of Europe. They must reflect the concerns of the people, not the preoccupations of the politicians or the bureaucrats. The Government has worked hard on the careful preparation required. But, throughout, the Government's particular objective will be to help to restore the people's faith in the European project. We cannot complete the task in six months. But we can make a start on some important new priorities; and in doing so, help establish a Europe for the people. ☆

Are all your talents working in concert?

An impressive range of skills can be found in almost every organisation. The challenge, of course, is getting them to perform harmoniously.

Andersen Consulting works to help synchronize all of your vital components: strategy, technology, process and people.

With vast experience in each of these areas, we can help you seamlessly blend individual strengths with collective goals. Because these days, organisations don't perform. Unless they perform together.

ANDERSEN CONSULTING

Visit our web site at www.ac.com

*"After the end of the Second World War, Europe
looked to Britain for a leadership which was not
forthcoming. In the 1950s we stood aside from the
moves to create a more united Europe and when
we finally decided to join we were kept out by
President de Gaulle. Since joining in 1973 we have
too often behaved as a semi-detached member"*

BRITAIN & EUROPE:
HISTORY OF A RELATIONSHIP

BY STEPHEN WOODARD, DIRECTOR OF THE EUROPEAN MOVEMENT

The new Government is committed to British leadership in Europe. It will clearly take some time for this to be established. The Government starts, however, with the advantage of a large majority in the House of Commons in favour; the agreement of the leaderships of all major political parties that Britain must be a full member of the European Union; and a broad consensus across the political establishment and in public opinion that membership is vital to our national interests.

The tragedy is that this was not established sooner. In the 1940s and 1950s leadership was there for the taking. After the end of the Second World War, Europe looked to Britain for a leadership which was not forthcoming. In the 1950s we stood aside from the moves to create a more united Europe and when we finally decided to join we were kept out by President de Gaulle. Since joining in 1973 we have too often behaved as a semi-detached member.

This article looks back at the story of Britain's relations with Europe over the past fifty years to see what lessons can be drawn for the future.

LEADERSHIP REFUSED 1945-61
Winston Churchill was one of the earliest and foremost advocates of European unity. In a series of speeches between 1946 and 1948 he set out a vision of Europe which inspired a generation to build a new kind of Europe. Addressing the problem of Europe after the War he declared in Zurich in 1946 that the need was "to re-create the European Family, or as much of it as we can, and provide it with a structure under which it can dwell in peace, in safety and in freedom".

This speech, made just a little over twelve months after the end of the War, had an electrifying effect on the European debate. Within two years a Congress of Europe, bringing together supporters of European unity, including many leading political figures of the day, had taken place in The Hague, leading to the creation of the Council of Europe.

The British government was a reluctant participant in these developments. Ernest Bevin, the Labour Government's Foreign Secretary, was pursuing an Atlanticist agenda, aimed at keeping the Americans involved in Europe, ignoring perhaps conveniently that the Americans were strong supporters of European unity. He was indifferent to these attempts to unite Europe, and disliked the fact that the two main supporters of unity seemed to be Churchill and the French. Britain joined the Council of Europe as a founder member but refused to take the lead in developing closer ties.

Supporters of European unity soon found the Council of Europe too inflexible and unambitious to be the focus of future attempts to unite Europe. They looked for an alternative. Jean Monnet, a senior French official, proposed a plan to the then French Foreign Minister, Robert Schuman, to create a supranational community to oversee the management of the coal and steel industries in Europe. Economically this would involve organising investment to encourage production after the devastation of the World War and creating a freer market in those materials. Politically it would control the means to make war and would unite in common institutions France and Germany and other European nations. Germany, Italy, Belgium, Luxembourg and the Netherlands responded positively; the British government hesitated before deciding against participation. The Labour government had only recently nationalised the coal and steel industries and was not prepared to see control pass to a common European institution. Dean Acheson, US Secretary of State, described this decision as "the great mistake of the post-War period".

The success of the ECSC led the supporters of European unity to think ahead to the next step forward in European integration. A plan was drawn up to organise a European Defence Community to deal with the threat from the communist Soviet Union and the need to incorporate West Germany into Western defence policy. A treaty was agreed and signed. Five of the six ratified it. France held back, partly because of British reluctance to follow. Following the death of Stalin and a general election in which anti-Europeans did well, France voted against ratification.

Supporters of European unity soon looked for alternatives. The six member states of the ECSC agreed in principle to investigate developing the Community in two new areas: the development and use of nuclear energy; and economic co-operation in a new customs union to promote trade and economic growth. A conference of the six Community members was organised to prepare a new treaty. Britain was invited to participate but its response was unenthusiastic: it sent a lowly official from the Board of Trade who, under instructions to make no commitments, left early.

These moves came at a confusing time for British foreign policy, struggling to come to terms with Britain's position in a changing world. Regrettably the then British Prime Minister Anthony Eden was unable to deal with these challenges. He had consistently opposed European unity as he still believed in Britain's imperial role, launching the doomed attempt to take military control of the Suez canal following its nationalisation by Egypt. The attack brought condemnation the world over, isolating Britain more than ever before. Nearly all the Commonwealth opposed it and the United States undermined it. Eden, failing to appreciate the significance of the developing momentum in favour of European integration, kept Britain out of the European Community at exactly the moment when the Empire was becoming independent and the special relationship with the United States was weakening. It was a colossal strategic error.

Eden proposed that, instead of developing a new European Community, a looser free-trade area be established. Ten years earlier this proposal might have been welcomed but now it no longer matched the scale of Continental ambitions. Once it was clear that this scheme of deflecting the Six from creating a fully-fledged customs union in favour of a free-trade area had failed, Britain went ahead with a free trade area of seven other European countries (EFTA). Although it was successfully established it was soon seen as second best. Harold Macmillan, succeeding Eden in 1957, initially pursued the policy he had inherited. Over the next four years, however, he was to conclude that the policy was failing and ought to be abandoned.

LEADERSHIP REJECTED 1961-72
By 1961 Macmillan recognised that Britain needed to find a new place in the world. The old white dominions were increasingly autonomous, the Indian Empire had become independent fourteen years previously, and now the "winds of change" were sweeping Africa as the territories of the Empire were prepared for independence. The days of the British Empire were over. Dean Acheson famously commented that Britain had "lost an Empire but not yet found a role". Macmillan was determined that a *new* role would be found for Britain as a leading member of the European Community. By working with our near neighbours, Britain would be able to defend its interests and maintain its influence: the alternative was increasing political and economic isolation.

On 31 July 1961 Macmillan announced to the House of Commons that "after long and earnest consideration, Her

> "By 1961 Macmillan recognised that Britain needed to find a new place in the world. The old white dominions were increasingly autonomous, the Indian Empire had become independent fourteen years previously, and now the 'winds of change' were sweeping Africa as the territories of the Empire were prepared for independence"

Majesty's Government have come to the conclusion that it would be right for Britain to make a formal application . . . with a view to joining the Community".

Macmillan recognised the historic proportions of the decision. In a pamphlet published to promote the case for membership he wrote: "It seems certain that the policies adopted by this powerful Community in Europe will have a decisive effect on the future history of the world and on our own fortunes here in Britain. We are faced with a tremendous issue. This is no time to bury our heads in the sands of the past and take the kind of parochial view which regards Europe with distrust and suspicion." (*Britain, the Commonwealth and Europe*, Conservative Political Centre, 1962)

The Labour Party hesitated before coming out against membership. Hugh Gaitskell, its leader, decided to oppose membership for reasons of loyalty to the Commonwealth, fear of the constitutional consequences and, perhaps, a little political opportunism.

The application was an historic step, but it was made five years too late. De Gaulle had come to power in France in 1958. Initially opposed to European unity as a threat to the nation state, he now appreciated it was in fact a way for Europe's nation states to advance their common interests together. But he was suspicious of Britain, which he saw as a potential rival to French leadership in Europe and too closely wedded to the United States. To Macmillan's consternation, he vetoed the application. Macmillan's administration had made a bold attempt to reorientate Britain's place in the world in the light of changing circumstances: to decolonise the Empire, to understand the evolving nature of the special relationship with the United States following the Suez crisis, and to make Britain a leading player in the European Community. He felt he had failed.

The new Labour Government elected in 1964 soon came to share Macmillan's conclusion that entry was the best option for Britain. In 1966 Harold Wilson decided to pursue Macmillan's vision and re-applied for British member-

Bridging the gap.

Hyder, a modern, technologically advanced company with worldwide commercial interests has grown rapidly over the past five years.

A company of considerable financial strength and stability, Hyder provides infrastructure services for many aspects of modern life.

And with offices on every continent, the Hyder group is using the combined skills and experience of its 9,000 employees to offer an essential service to business and society. One that covers the engineering and operational needs of the electricity and water industries, transportation, including roads and tunnels, railways, ports and airports, and all matters environmental.

Hyder

Infrastructure for life

Hyder plc • PO Box 295 • Alexandra Gate • Rover Way • Cardiff • CF2 2UE • UK
Tel: +44 (0)1222 500 600   Fax: +44 (0)1222 585 600

ship. Labour had changed its mind but de Gaulle had not; on 22 November 1967 he vetoed the application for a second time.

An uncertain member 1973-83

In 1970 yet another membership application was lodged. De Gaulle was no longer President of France and his successor, Georges Pompidou, indicated he was favourable towards British membership. Originally planned by the Labour Government, the new application was submitted by Edward Heath following the Conservative election victory in the 1970 election. The negotiation was successful and the vote in the House of Commons on the principle of membership was 356 in favour and 244 against.

But membership was to start on the wrong foot. Labour, which had prepared the application in government, now decided to oppose membership "on Tory terms". Following the parliamentary ratification of the membership treaty, the Labour Party remained bitterly split, subsequently patching together a compromise: to renegotiate the terms of membership and put these to a referendum. Returned to power in 1974, the Labour Government pursued this renegotiation – a move hardly likely to win friends amongst Britain's new partners. The renegotiation resulted in revised terms which contained a few improvements but was seen – correctly – as largely a cosmetic exercise to justify a political U-turn. The referendum was called for June 1975. The result was an overwhelming victory for continued membership, by a margin of two to one.

For a short time this verdict seemed to resolve the issue. But by the early 1980s doubts were again being expressed. The Labour Party, in opposition since 1979, came out against continued membership. The Conservative Government was grappling with the difficult issue of Britain's contribution to the European Community budget which was becoming manifestly unfair. After years of rapid development and growth the European Community seemed to have lost momentum.

A new consensus? 1983-88

The atmosphere changed dramatically after the 1983 election. The budget problem was solved in 1984 and, following its election defeat, the Labour Party abandoned its policy of withdrawal. The European Community embarked on a new initiative: the creation of a single internal market where all hidden barriers to trade within the Community would be abolished. It was put together by the President of the European Commission, Jacques Delors, and the British European Commissioner Lord Cockfield, with the enthusiastic support of the British Government. To make it happen, and to implement other reforms, changes in the rules of the European Community were agreed in a new treaty, the Single European Act.

In Britain all these changes were welcomed; it seemed a new consensus was emerging. Unfortunately, this positive debate about Britain's future in Europe did not endure.

Second thoughts 1988-97

As the rules of the Single Market started to impinge on people's daily lives, anti-Europeans began to exploit such stories – real or invented – to undermine support for membership. When the member states of the Community began working on the details of a single currency, the Conservative Party started to get nervous about the reference to monetary union which the Government had agreed could be included in the Single European Act. The Government also started to worry about the implications of the social dimension to the internal market: the commitment in the Single European Act to protect the health and safety of workers. As Labour was becoming more enthusiastic about Europe, so tensions in the Conservative Party, which had prided itself for a generation as Britain's "Party of Europe", grew more acute. The consensus seemed to be holding, however, and John Major declared it a key aim of his administration when he took office in 1990 to put Britain at "the heart of Europe".

Dealing with these concerns about interference by Brussels, the single currency and the social dimension dominated the debate during the preparation of the Maastricht Treaty in 1990-91. At the Maastricht Summit, John Major agreed on a new treaty which emphasised decentralisation and "subsidiarity", left Britain outside its Social Chapter and reserved Britain's position on a single European currency. It was welcomed by most of the Conservative Party at the time but Labour decided to abstain in order to register its opposition to the "opt-out" from the Social Chapter. Initially it seemed that the consensus about the principle of our membership of the European Community (which the Treaty renamed the European Union) was going to hold. But when in June 1991 the Danish people voted against the treaty, the Eurosceptics seized the opportunity to launch a counter-attack. The subsequent ratification debate was dominated by a Eurosceptic minority inside the Conservative Party supported by allies in the press. The Labour opposition front bench had no reason to help the Government to overcome this small back-bench rebellion by helping with procedural motions; but in refusing to do so they helped prolong the Eurosceptic domination of press coverage which distorted the national debate about the Treaty and our membership of the European Union – to damaging effect on public opinion.

Despite the overwhelming support for Europe in Parliament, business, the trade unions, local government and many social sectors, the debate developed into a frenzy, fuelling the attempts by some to turn the 1997 general election into an anti-European referendum. The electorate, however, firmly rejected this at the ballot box.

A new opportunity? 1998

For fifty years Britain has had a choice: to build a new world role for itself based on our full and active membership of Europe, or to face a future of increasing isolation and impotence. At times we *have* led and achieved results, but too often it has been a story of missed opportunities, of half-heartedness and late decisions which have damaged our interests. As we build a new relationship in Europe based on commitment and leadership, these are lessons we should not forget. ☆

BP encourages European students to analyse road safety.

Road safety is of European concern and so was a natural as a new topic in BP's Science Across Europe programme.

This helps participants from secondary schools throughout Europe to understand their environment better by looking at issues from a more scientific angle.

So in this new unit students talk to experts, such as traffic police, and analyse local road safety factors. Then via fax and the Internet they compare their results with those of schools in other parts of Europe.

This sharing of results internationally extends the opportunities for scientific comparisons and opens up an understanding of varied social circumstances.

Developed in partnership with the Association for Science Education, BP's Science Across Europe helps students discover that although scientific methods may be the same the world over, patterns of human behaviour, on the roads as everywhere else, can be very different.

Science Across Europe is a partnership project between BP and the Association for Science Education. If you'd like to find out more about it, contact: ASE, College Lane, Hatfield, Herts AL10 9AA, UK. Tel: UK 44 (0) 1707 267411. Fax: UK 44 (0) 1707 266532 email: sae@bp.com web: http://www.bp.com/saw

RECLAIMING VAT ON SERVICES WITHIN AND OUTSIDE THE EU

by Jane E. Holmberg, General Manager, United Cash Back (Holding) Ltd.

All VAT registered companies have the right to reclaim VAT incurred on services abroad in all European Union (EU) countries and in many others too.

Companies need to be aware of these possibilities so that they can get back what they are entitled to as easily and quickly as possible.

First, the facts. In 1982 the then EEC decided that in order for companies within the EU to compete on equal terms VAT legislation applying to local companies should also apply to foreign companies when conducting business in their country.

Consequently the EU's 8th VAT Directive was implemented to allow businesses registered for VAT in one member state to recover VAT incurred in another member state.

In 1988 the EU's 13th VAT Directive was implemented: this extended the possibility for companies domiciled outside the EU to reclaim VAT within the EU.

Today several European countries outside the EU, including Hungary, Iceland, Norway and Switzerland, also refund VAT to foreign companies. The Czech Republic and Poland will follow suit in 1998 and this trend is set to continue outside Europe. The reason for this is that VAT, as a form of tax, is growing in popularity with governments around the world: more and more countries are starting to charge VAT on goods and services. However, VAT is intended to hit only the end consumer. For this reason, and in order to promote trade, fiscal authorities will be compelled to refund these taxes to both local and foreign companies.

So the opportunities for businesses to reclaim VAT are set to increase. The existing potential is already huge: as long ago as 1991, an American Express survey concluded that European businessmen were spending approximately £100 billion on travel and entertainment. However, despite the fact that many companies successfully reclaim their VAT, there are millions of pounds are left unclaimed from the various fiscal authorities each year. Information received from some of the fiscal authorities in Europe brings this out. In 1995 the UK tax authorities paid out a total of £70 million to foreign companies, the German authorities DEM 40 million, the Swedish authorities SEK 383 million and the Dutch authorities approximately NLG 50 million. They all acknowledge that this is just a small portion of the actual VAT amount foreign companies are eligible to reclaim.

Evidently there is still a lack of awareness about the possibilities of reclaiming VAT. There is also reluctance within companies to retrieve what they are entitled to due to a misunderstanding regarding the ease of reclaiming and the value of their entitlement.

The red tape involved is indeed enormous, with each country in Europe having different tax legislation and varying rates. Couple that with the need to fill in application forms and provide documents in the local language: it is hardly surprising that companies are deterred from reclaiming what is rightly theirs.

But there is no need for companies to go to this trouble. For only a small fee, Cash Back, with in-house VAT experts in ALL European countries and offices around the world, can reclaim VAT without the claimant having lifted a finger.

In order to maximize the recovery of VAT which a company has incurred on business expenses, Cash Back will:

- ✦ come and sort and retrieve all eligible invoices.
- ✦ alternatively, for those companies who wish to handle their own invoices, Cash Back will provide on-site training of company staff and provide assistance in setting up procedures compatible with the company's existing systems.

Upon receipt of the company's invoices, Cash Back do the rest. They will:
- ✦ double check the validity of the invoices;
- ✦ complete the VAT Reclaim Application Form
- ✦ tensure all other relevant forms are authorized and attached to the claim;
- ✦ give each claimant and each claim its own code number and enter all details of the claim in their in-house computer software programme;
- ✦ provide a reporting system to the claimant, advising them of the date the claim was submitted and the exact value of the claim;
- ✦ continue to update the claimant throughout the process until successful completion and repayment of the VAT application;
- ✦ advise you of the reason for any rejections;
- ✦ update clients regarding all new VAT regulations, possibilities, deadlines etc through their regular news bulletins

In summary, Cash Back provide companies with a local

service for managing their foreign VAT claims. Cash Back's offices throughout Europe and the world employ local VAT specialists, ensuring that they are close to their clients and their local authorities, in terms of both proximity and understanding.

Cash Back is one of the founder VAT Reclaim Agents, established in 1988. With its years of experience and its international network, it has developed the technical expertise which guarantees outstanding hit rates and superior customer service.

Through Cash Back's client protected account at Svenska Handelsbanken in Luxembourg, clients' VAT refunds are transferred to the claimant. Cash Back provide the claimant with the authority's notification of acceptance showing the date and amount refunded. All claimants can therefore be assured of a quick and full refund by Cash Back.

In addition to their basic VAT reclaim package, Cash Back's local sales offices can provide companies with a tailor made service and after sales support package to suit the individual companies corporate needs including:

✦ free and accurate information and advice regarding VAT issues sourced through their regular meetings and liaisons with the tax authorities;

✦ pre-purchasing of invoices through our finance partner;
✦ advice and assistance regarding registering for VAT in a foreign country;
✦ assistance in making VAT declarations in another country where the customer is already VAT registered;
✦ the service of their staff to assist companies with queries they may have regarding other business requirements in a country where Cash Back is represented.

Cash Back only take a percentage of a successful refund: it is worth all companies using their services.

Even if the VAT industry and systems are getting more complicated and the process tougher, the opportunity to refund VAT is still there and it is Cash Back, not the claimant, who needs to manage these complexities. That is why companies should take advantage of the services of Cash Back – a company with years of experience and a founder member of the International VAT Association.

The table below gives an indication of the most common services on which VAT can be reclaimed. ✳

VAT in Europe

Countries	VAT	Normal Taxation	Hotel	Restaurant Meals	Business Entertaining	Conferences	Travel	Transportation	Petrol	Diesel	Exhibitions Trade Fairs	Marketing	Consultants	Car rental	Lawyer's Fees	Telephone
Austria	•	20%	•			•	•	•			•	•	•		•	•
Belgium	•	21%				•	•	•	x	x	•	•	•	x	•	•
Denmark	•	25%	x	x						•	•	•	•		•	•
Finland	•	22%	•			•	•	•	•	•	•		•	•		•
France	•	20,6%				•		•		•	•	•	•		•	•
Germany	•	15%	•	•	•	•	•	•	x	x	•	•	•			•
Great Britain	•	17,5%	•	•		•	•		•	•	•		•		•	•
Greece	•	18%							x	•	•	•	•		•	•
Hungary	•	25%	x	•		•	•	•	•	•	•	•	•	•		•
Iceland	•	24,5%	•			•	•	•	•	•	•	•	•		•	•
Ireland	•	21%				•			•	•			•			•
Italy	•	20%				•		•	x	x	•	•	•			x
Luxembourg	•	15%	•	•	•	•	•	•	•	•	•	•	•	•	•	•
The Netherlands	•	17,5%	•			•	•	•	•	•	•	•	•	•		•
Norway	•	23%						•	x	x	•	•	•	x		•
Portugal	•	17%				•				x	•	•	•		•	•
Spain	•	16%	•	•	•	•	•	•	•	•	•	•	•		•	•
Sweden	•	25%	•	x	x	•	•	•	•	•	•	•	•	x	•	•
Switzerland	•	6,5%	•	x		•	•	•	•	•	•	•	•	•	•	•

Examples of items for which VAT may be refunded
•= Refundable x= Partly Refundable

THE EUROPEAN UNION IN THE WORLD:
A FORCE FOR FREE TRADE

BY THE RT. HON. SIR LEON BRITTAN,
VICE-PRESIDENT OF THE EUROPEAN COMMISSION

"Trade is the lifeblood of the EU's economy. As the world's largest exporter, the EU's economic welfare is dependent on the existence of open markets around the globe"

1998 is not only the 25th anniversary of the UK's entry to the European Union: it also marks two other important anniversaries. First, 1998 is fifty years since the foundation stone of today's world trading system – the General Agreement on Tariffs and Trade (GATT) – came into being. It was the establishment of the GATT which set the world on its trade liberalisation course, leading to the establishment of the World Trade Organisation (WTO) three years ago. Second, 1998 is the 40th anniversary of the decision by EU member states to share responsibility in trade matters by establishing the Common Commercial Policy. As a result of these developments, Europe has become a global economic power and the major force for international trade liberalisation.

GLOBALISM

Economic activity today is an intricate spider's web of cross-border activities, involving foreign direct investment, international financial transactions, and multinationals operating all over the world. Across the globe, economies are increasingly linked. To meet the challenges of this globalisation, the world trading system has had to embark on a much broader based process of liberalisation than in the past.

Interdependence is not new, but in the age of globalisation it has assumed new characteristics. In the past, nation states, through co-operation, were able to a large degree to regulate international economic activity. This is no longer possible in a world where up to a third of international trade takes place within transnational corporations. Recent turbulence in financial markets worldwide has shown that no economy can remain insulated from the global marketplace.

The challenge today is to win public support for such an open free trading system – and to make clear the benefits it brings. There is rising concern in Europe and elsewhere about the relationship between worldwide economic activity and its social and environmental consequences. Many fear that global free trade does nothing to stop exploitative employment practices such as forced or child labour and environmental destruction. Others are concerned about the effect of a liberalised global system on developing countries. In advancing the cause of opening up trade, Europe needs to be responsive to these concerns, but wary of allowing them to be used as a pretext for new protectionism.

THE EU'S ROLE IN GLOBAL LIBERALISATION

Trade is the lifeblood of the EU's economy. As the world's largest exporter, the EU's economic welfare is dependent on the existence of open markets around the globe.

The EU has played a crucial role in forging this liberal, multilateral world economic order. In recent months, in negotiations on telecommunications, information technology, and, most recently, financial services, it has been the EU which has been in the forefront, pushing for greater liberalisation. And it is consumers in the high street who benefit from these deals – with lower prices and more choice.

From its establishment 40 years ago, the EU's external trade policy – officially called the Common Commercial Policy – has become one of the keystones of the European Union. As a result member states have benefited from being part of the largest trading bloc in the world, strengthening their hands in negotiations and enabling them to deal as an equal partner with the other major trading powers in the world. If any EU member state negotiated on its own behalf it would have no more influence in international negotiations than a middle-size country. In contrast, through the Common Commercial Policy, the EU has exerted crucial influence over the last four decades on the elimination of trade barriers, in both multilateral and bilateral negotiations with third countries.

MULTILATERAL TRADE: FOWARD FROM THE URUGUAY ROUND

Multilateral trading arrangements have blossomed in the post-War period, and the EU has played a crucial role in their development.

Two years after the end of the Second World War, the GATT was set up, leading to a series of negotiations that successively reduced trade barriers from the 1960s onwards. The most ambitious of these was the Uruguay Round, one of the largest treaties ever signed. The Final Act adopted in Marrakech in 1994 not only led to the dismantling of barriers to international trade but also gave birth to a stronger supervisory body for global trade, the WTO. The EU played a crucial role in mak-

Federal TRUST

THE FEDERAL TRUST is an independent charity working through education and research towards the widening and deepening of the European Union as well as to enhance the European policy of the United Kingdom.

Founded in 1945 under the auspices of William Beveridge, the Trust has made a powerful intellectual contribution to Britain's European policy.

Drawing on a wide network of specialist knowledge, the Trust conducts major inquiries, organises seminars and conferences, and publishes a variety of research and educational material.

Its current work programme involves studies on the emerging issues of European integration and on the future of the European Parliament. The Trust is also engaged in the production of teaching materials on European citizenship.

'The Federal Trust plays an important part as a specialist in the debate on European unity issues, not only by bringing these issues firmly into the public domain but also by pushing forwards the frontiers of that debate.' SIR LEON BRITTAN

RECENT FEDERAL TRUST PUBLICATIONS

Federal Trust Report, *Britain's Agenda in Europe: the UK presidency of the Council of the European Union*, December 1997. £5.00; 32 pp; ISBN 0 90157 368 X

Ian Davidson, *Jobs and the Rhineland Model*, Federal Trust Report, December 1997. £12.95; 85 pp; ISBN 0 90157 364 7

Andrew Duff (ed.), *The Treaty of Amsterdam: Text and Commentary*, October 1997. £12.95 (paperback); 362 pp; ISBN 0 90157 365 5. £45.00 (hardback); 362 pp; ISBN 0 90157 367 1

Raymond Plant and Michael Steed, *PR for Europe: Proposals to change the electoral system of the European Parliament*, May 1997. £10.00; 24 pp; ISBN 0 90157 366 3

Andrew Duff, *Reforming the European Union*, February 1997. £12.95; 210 pp; ISBN 0 90157 361 2

Graham Bishop, José Pérez and Sammy van Tuyll (eds), *User Guide to the Euro*, December 1996. £9.95; 208 pp; ISBN 0 90157 362 0

Harry Cowie, *Private Partnerships and Public Networks in Europe*, Federal Trust Report, October 1997. £15.95; 110 pp; ISBN 0 90157 371 X

For up-to-date news about Federal Trust activities, find us on www@fedtrust.co.uk or write to the Director, Andrew Duff, at Dean Bradley House, 52 Horseferry Road, London SW1P 2AF tel 0171 799 2818; fax 0171 799 2820.

<u>Book orders from:</u> Sweet & Maxwell Ltd
Cheriton House, North Way, Andover SP10 5BE
From UK — tel 01264 342899; fax 01264 342723
From non-UK — tel + 44 1264 342906; fax + 44 1264 342706

ing these achievements possible, acting as a motor for liberalisation. In the Uruguay Round, it was the EU that pushed for services to be included in the world free trade system for the first time. The EU was also in the forefront of moves to ensure that rules on intellectual property did not become obstacles to free trade.

The WTO

The establishment of the WTO led for the first time to the creation of a binding dispute settlement procedure for trade conflicts – replacing the rule of the jungle with the rule of law. The new system is based on the voluntary acceptance by governments of common rules. It allows penalties to be imposed on those countries who are not willing to play by the increasingly complex range of rules which govern international trade. In many cases the mere existence of such a mechanism has acted as an effective deterrent. Moreover it has limited the right of trading nations to take the law into their own hands on trade matters.

The next challenge for the WTO is to expand its membership, so that its rules will apply *throughout* the global economy. The most important candidates to join are China and Russia.

China's growing economic weight makes its participation vital both in China's and the world's interest. Membership will lock China into a book of rules designed to keep markets open, root out protectionism and settle disputes fairly. This is the kind of certainty that will encourage European businesses to take the plunge and increase their presence in the Chinese market. The EU has pushed continuously for Chinese membership of the WTO for many years on the basis of China's acceptance of the basic rules and its readiness to open up its economy. Europe has an abiding interest in seeing that the expansion of WTO membership goes ahead smoothly and on the right terms.

In the case of Russia, membership will help bolster economic reform by opening markets, introducing effective disciplines and creating a more stable climate for companies to invest in Russia.

Towards the Millennium Round

The other major challenge for the world trading system will be the launch of another comprehensive set of liberalisation talks: a so-called "Millennium Round". Europe has been at the forefront in setting out the case for such a Round.

This idea is gathering speed. There are many subjects such as services and agriculture on which fresh negotiations are set to start in January 2000, according to the timetable already agreed at the end of the Uruguay Round. There are other subjects such as industrial tariffs which, while not forming part of the WTO's so-called "built-in" agenda, are obvious areas for further liberalisation. And there are also a variety of reviews of existing WTO agreements. If you put all these together, and add new issues such as the relationship between trade and competition policy, and between trade and investment, there is ample scope for a fresh set of global negotiations. Such a new round would provide a further boost to the world economy.

The European Union's bilateral relationships

But the EU has not just relied on multilateral arrangements in its work for global liberalisation: *bilateral* deals are also important.

The United States is by far the most important political and economic partner of the EU. The transatlantic economic relationship remains the biggest in the world and there is little sign of the huge trade and investment flows diminishing. The establishment of the New Transatlantic Agenda has provided a regular framework of meetings and an agenda for co-operation across a wide range of issues. This has had some very important practical results, most notably in the negotiations of a Mutual Recognition Agreement in the area of standards and certification of products.

With the world's other great economic power, Japan, Europe has played an active role in the process of deregulation, especially the opening up of Japanese distribution networks. With so much attention focused on the growth and potential of China, it is too easy to forget that Japan remains by far the biggest Asian economy, and that the value of Japanese exports to and imports from the EU is more than twice as great.

The future

Trade policy is not just a technical subject: it is of vital concern to *all* of us, not just to the experts who grapple with it. Despite the often technical vocabulary, trade policy is a vital part of economic policy and a means of creating the jobs and prosperity that we demand.

In May, leaders from around the world will gather in Geneva to celebrate the 50th anniversary of the GATT and the worldwide free trading system. This meeting takes place against a backdrop of concern about threats to free trade. The setback to the US fast-track procedure for negotiating trade deals is an example of how public hostility to global liberalisation is growing, with trade unions and environmental groups in the forefront of opposition. The Asian currency turmoil may also lead to greater caution in this field.

The Geneva meeting provides the opportunity for world leaders both to reaffirm their commitment to multilateral free trade, and to restate the benefits it offers people around the world.

In late spring, another important meeting will take place, this time in London. The issue on the table will be who is going to participate in the single currency. The euro will have a far reaching impact on international trade. The introduction of the single currency will equip the world's largest trading area with a powerful international currency to match its economic weight. With the euro as a major world currency, more investment, debt and trade will be dominated in euros.

The single currency will transform global trading and political relations, allowing Europe to punch its true weight in the global economy. It will mean in the future the EU will be able to play an even more pivotal role in global liberalisation. ☆

What every go ahead company should have behind it.

Us.

The Impact of the EU – the Lawyer's Perspective

Easy Access to Europe

by Jonathan Guest, Head of Commercial Department, Eversheds, Leeds & Manchester

The EU has benefited enterprise in Britain more than it has helped any other member state.

For US and Japanese businesses Britain has become the easy access point to the European market. Eversheds has spent much of the last decade advising North American and Far Eastern players on their strategies for Europe in their continued drive for globalisation. Entry to the EU can take many forms: strategic alliances, joint ventures, acquisitions, agency or distribution networks, franchising and/or green field sites. It is the ability to take strategic advice in the relatively friendly and stable UK eco-political environment from sophisticated advisers like Eversheds that is attractive.

Employment: Will Change Help the UK Workplace?

by Peter Norbury, Head of Employment, Eversheds, Leeds & Manchester

Over the past twenty years the employment and social policies of the European Union have had an increasingly significant influence on domestic UK employment law and practice, probably the first major influence being the introduction of the Transfer of Undertakings (Protection of Employment) Regulations 1981 (TUPE) as the UK Government's response to the Acquired Rights Directive. Whilst the development of the principles behind TUPE over the past 16 years has been one of the more obvious influences of EU policy, there have been other notable features arising from EU Directives and ECJ case law, for example:

• the abolition of the maximum limit on compensation for discrimination claims

• the enforced consultation on transfers and redundancies.

Whilst the previous UK Government fought a rearguard action to minimise the impact of EU Social Policy in the UK, the present Government has indicated a willingness to take a more open and inclusive approach towards Europe. There is a clear difference of emphasis between what the other members of the UK would see as necessary regulation within the workplace and the UK Government's view of the need to create an environment which encourages job promotion.

As the UK presidency of the EU commences, the attack on unemployment and the means to create work are part of the UK Government's key initiative. Many commentators have highlighted the contrast between the high level of unemployment in the EU member states with the low levels of unemployment in the USA. Of the EU member states the UK's unemployment record is among the best.

Over the next few years some of the key areas for UK employment law are likely to be:

• how the Working Time Directive is implemented

• how the Labour Government achieves the introduction of mandatory trade union recognition

• the role of Works Councils

• the impact of the national minimum wage

• the impact of any further Directives under the Social Chapter.

It will be interesting to see whether within the UK, acknowledging the Government's stated intentions on employment policy and the acceptance of the EU Social Chapter, a balance can be achieved. The aim will be to preserve the perceived flexibility in the workplace and a culture of job creation whilst accommodating the more regulated types of framework for employment regarded as being necessary by other EU member states.

The lessons of the 1970's and early 1980's suggest that a policy of enforced union recognition was unpopular and unsuccessful. How far has the UK employment scene moved on in order to make such a prescriptive policy more acceptable? How does the policy interact with those UK companies which have voluntarily embraced the EU initiative on Works Councils?

Given that the UK has on the face of it been more successful in tackling unemployment and job creation than the other EU member states, the success of this balancing act cannot be taken for granted.

Intellectual Property: The Impact

by Rex Parry, Head of Intellectual Property, Eversheds, Leeds & Manchester

Europe has had a major effect on intellectual property rights in recent years. The clients Eversheds advises have seen this through:
- the introduction and growth of the Community Trade Mark
- the development of a database directive governing use of personal data
- the creation of legislation dealing with lending and rental rights
- the development of the law dealing with parallel imports
- the technology transfer block exemption (governing patent and know-how licences).

In addition, we at Eversheds highlight the following as further areas to watch:
- further draft directive on the protection of personal data and privacy in the telecommunications industry
- the amendment of the draft directive on industrial designs and models which re-instates uniform design protection for vehicle spare parts
- anticipated EU legislation to provide increased copyright protection over the Internet (including protection of digital signatures and cryptography)
- a uniform European approach to software patents
- directive on legal protection of biotechnological inventions.

We see our mission as helping business assimilate Europe-driven change quickly and commercially.

Competition & Regulation: The UK in the EU

by Adam Collinson, Head of EC & Competition, Eversheds, Leeds & Manchester

Regulatory authorities throughout Europe have acquired or developed the ability to control mergers and have toughened their stance towards restrictive practices and anti-competitive behaviour. As a result, competition law (anti-trust) has come to play an increasingly important role in business life.

Within the UK there has been a competition law regime in place for the last 40 years. Until now, it has been an essentially benign system which has not afforded the authorities sufficient powers of investigation or enforcement to create a deterrent against cartels or other undesirable practices. Shortly after its election, the Labour Government committed itself to reforming UK competition law. It did so as a means of ensuring the long-term competitiveness of UK PLC. If our own companies become attuned to conducting their business within the confines of an effective competition law, they will (the argument runs) begin to look longer term in planning their business strategy, improving the prospects for the country's economy in world markets. The Government has taken the EC regime as its model for reform and this is a further example of the huge influence which EC law has had on firms conducting business in the UK.

Eversheds has a wealth of experience in EC and UK competition law. We also have a strong track record in using that experience to help clients achieve their business aims in a way that is acceptable to the authorities. We know how the authorities think, and who to talk to. Furthermore our previous experience has given us an in-depth understanding of many different industry sectors and how competition works in those sectors. This enables us to provide the highest quality advice in the shortest possible timescales.

For further information, please call:

Freephone 0500 994 500

EVERSHEDS
The Business Lawyers

Eversheds, Cloth Hall Court, Infirmary Street, Leeds LS1 2JB. Tel: +44 (0)113 243 0391
Eversheds, London Scottish House, 24 Mount Street, Manchester M2 3DB. Tel: +44 (0)161 832 6666

London ● Birmingham ● Bristol ● Cardiff ● Derby ● Ipswich ● Jersey ● Leeds
● Manchester ● Norwich ● Nottingham ● Teesside ● Brussels

"All too often we have been seen as the 'bad boy' of Europe, reacting, sometimes rather negatively, to initiatives proposed by others. It is high time that we adopted a more constructive approach"

THE UNITED KINGDOM AND THE EUROPEAN UNION: LIGHT ON THE RELATIONSHIP

BY VERNON BOGDANOR, PROFESSOR OF GOVERNMENT AT OXFORD UNIVERSITY

Britain was a late entrant to the European Community, forerunner to the European Union. This was because, until the 1960s, most of our political leaders did not see our relationship with the continent as fundamental.

In the 18th century, when British identity, in the view of historians such as Linda Colley and Gerald Newman, was being formed, we believed that we had found a path of political development radically different from, and superior to, that of our continental neighbours. This belief was reinforced by the fact that we did not experience the upheavals associated with the French revolution and we were not invaded by Napoleon. We looked instead to Empire, turning our back on the continent for much of the 19th century.

In 1947, however, when India achieved her independence, we voluntarily relinquished our Imperial role. In the 20th century, we have twice been compelled to go to war to preserve the European balance of power, to prevent Europe from falling under the domination of a single state.

"The English," George Orwell wrote in an essay published in 1947, the year of Indian independence, "must stop despising foreigners. They are Europeans and ought to be aware of it. Perhaps the period between the late 18th century and the mid-20th century should be seen as an aberrant period in our long history during most of which the fate of Britain and that of the continent have been intertwined."

Sadly, however, British governments in the immediate post-war period did not heed Orwell's advice to become aware of Europe. We failed to enter the European Coal and Steel Community, the precursor of the European Community, in 1951. We failed to enter the European Economic Community, the "Common Market", in 1957; indeed, we did not join until 1973, after two failed applications. This has meant that much of our time as members of the European Communities and of European Union has been spent trying to make up for lost time. All too often we have been seen as the "bad boy" of Europe, reacting, sometimes rather negatively, to initiatives proposed by others. It is high time that we adopted a more constructive approach.

If, however, we are to be able to influence Europe, we have first to understand it. This is not easy to do, since the European Union is quite different from any other international organisation to which Britain belongs. Most such organisations, such as the Commonwealth and NATO, are *intergovernmental* in nature. They cannot bind individual states against their will. Some European Union activities, it is true, are carried out in an intergovernmental way. Under the Maastricht Treaty, two intergovernmental "pillars" were set up, under which a common foreign and security policy (CFSP) and co-operation in the field of Justice and Home Affairs could be established. Under the Treaty of Amsterdam of 1997, this intergovernmental pillar was reduced so as to cover just police and judicial co-operation in criminal matters. In these areas, member states cannot be bound without their own specific consent.

"If Europe united is to be
a living force, Britain will have
to play her full part as a member
of the European family"

For most European Union matters, by contrast, the key characteristic is *supranationalism*. The European Community was not merely a contract between member states but creates a new legal order, which creates rights and imposes obligations upon individuals and organisations. In a landmark judgement in *Van Gend en Loos* (1963), the European Court of Justice held that: "Independently of the legislation of Member States, Community law . . . not only imposes obligations on individuals but is also intended to confer upon them rights which become part of their legal heritage."

The law of the European Union, then, has a *direct effect* upon the individuals and organisations which it regulates. The rights and obligations which it creates must be upheld by the domestic courts of the member states. This requirement was achieved in Britain by means of section 2(1) of the European Communities Act of 1972, which provides as follows:

"All such rights, powers, liabilities, obligations and restrictions from time to time created or arising by or under the Treaties, and all such remedies and procedures from time to time provided for by or under the Treaties, as in accordance with the Treaties are without further enactment to be given legal effect or used in the United Kingdom shall be recognised and available in law, and be enforced, allowed and followed accordingly; and the expression 'enforceable Community right' and similar expressions shall be read as referring to one to which this subsection applies."

Moreover, European law not only has *direct effect*, but also *primacy*. This means that it is superior to domestic law. Primacy was established in the case of *Costa v E.N.E.L.* (1964) in which the Court of Justice ruled that: "The law stemming from the Treaty . . . [cannot] be overridden by domestic legal provisions . . . The transfer by the States from their domestic legal systems to the Community legal system of the rights and obligations arising under the Treaty carries with it a permanent limitation of their sovereign rights against which a subsequent unilateral act incompatible with the concept of the Community cannot prevail."

In Britain, Parliament gave effect to the primacy of Community law in section 2(4) of the 1972 European Communities Act. This provided that: "Any enactment passed or to be passed . . . shall be construed and have effect subject to the foregoing provisions of this section." The "foregoing provisions" include section 2(1) which, as shown above, provided for European Community law to be given direct effect in British law.

A simple example of judicial recognition of the primacy of Community law can be found in the treatment by the courts of the Sex Discrimination Act of 1975 which provided that a compensation order must not exceed a specified limit (£6,250 at the material time). The discrimination in question was also, however, a breach of Community law, and Community law requires adequate financial recompense. Such adequate financial recompense could, in the view of the Community, exceed the limit laid down by the Act. Therefore, British courts, where necessary, have been prepared to disregard the upper limit which Parliament imposed on their powers.[1]

The doctrine of the primacy of European law conflicts, however, with that of the sovereignty of Parliament. For the sovereignty of Parliament implies that Parliament can do what it likes. Under this doctrine, Parliament is both omnicompetent and paramount. A continental jurist, de Lolme, once said that Parliament can do anything except turn a man into a woman and a woman into a man. But, if Parliament were to declare that a woman were a man, then, from the point of view of the law, women would be men! It follows from the doctrine of parliamentary sovereignty both that no court in Britain can question the legal validity of an Act of Parliament and also that no lawmaking body, whether within Britain or outside, can be superior to Parliament.

From the point of view of the British legal order, Parliament is supreme; from the point of view of the European legal order, Parliament is subordinate to European law. There is, therefore, scope for conflict between the doctrine of the supremacy of European law and that of the sovereignty of Parliament.

Is Parliament, then, still sovereign? This question arose in the *Factortame* cases in 1990 and 1991.[2] These cases dealt with the claims of Spanish fishing companies who believed that the Merchant Shipping Act of 1988 prevented them obtaining access to the British fishing quota. In one of the cases, the British government accepted that:

"With regard to legislation, the courts did not have the right, under the British Constitution, to nullify an Act of Parliament. It was otherwise in the case of legislation which was contrary to Community law since section 2(1) and (4) of the European Communities Act 1972 empowered the courts to uphold the primacy of rights arising from Community law."

In the House of Lords, the ultimate court of appeal, Lord Bridge declared: "Under . . . the Act of 1972 it has always been clear that it was the duty of a United Kingdom court, when delivering final judgement, to override any rule of national law found to be in conflict with any directly enforceable rule of Community law."

Parliament, then, can no longer do what it likes if its enactments are now to be construed in accordance with European Community law. The implication of section 2(4) of the European Communities Act is that any law which cannot be so construed must be declared void. That implication, however, has yet to be accepted by the British courts. It would amount to a constitutional revolution for a British court to strike down or refuse to apply legislation duly passed by Parliament.

Parliament presumably did not intend to breach European law in the Merchant Shipping Act. Therefore, it could be argued that the courts, in refusing to apply the relevant provisions of the Act, were merely giving effect to the explicit wish of Parliament in 1972 that the primacy of European law be accepted. Suppose, however, that Parliament were *intentionally* to breach European law? What would the courts do then? It is not clear whether, in such circumstances, they would uphold the doctrine of the sovereignty of Parliament; or alternatively whether, by refusing to apply the statute in question, they would uphold the doctrine of the supremacy of Community law.

Such a case has not yet arisen and perhaps may never do so. Nevertheless, it would be in accordance with Lord Bridge's dictum, quoted above, to argue that Britain now lacks the legal authority to legislate in direct conflict with Community law. Thus, unless and until Parliament expressly repeals the European Communities Act, the courts must assume that it did not intend to legislate in this way, and refuse to give effect to such provisions as could not be enforced consistently with Community law. On this view, Parliament, by passing the European Communities Act in 1972, voluntarily yielded its sovereignty.

As well as fundamentally altering the British Constitution, our entry into the European Community in 1973 also posed problems for our system of parliamentary government. It has not proved easy for Parliament to scrutinise European legislation, for Westminster is geared to scrutinising legislation only when it reaches a near final form. By the time that legislation comes before Parliament, it will normally have been drafted and redrafted many times, following consultation with various interested parties, and the backing and prestige of the government will be behind it.

European legislation is produced in a quite different way: a legislative proposal put forward by the Commission and a subsequent decision taken in principle by the Council of Ministers is subject to considerable amendment as it goes through the legislative process.

Moreover, the House of Commons is fundamentally a debating chamber, which is generally dominated by two main parties. It is adversarial in nature and its procedures are geared more to informing the electorate of issues in dispute between a Government and an Opposition, than to effective scrutiny of legislation.

European legislation, however, is not being promoted by a government nor attacked by an opposition. It is difficult, therefore, to accommodate European legislation within the House of Commons which has to struggle to assimilate an entirely different legislative process into its traditional procedures. It is not surprising, then, that the most effective consideration of European legislation occurs, not in the House of Commons, but in the House of Lords, whose Select Committee on the European Communities has developed, arguably, the most effective scrutiny procedures in any of the member states of the European Union. The Lords, unlike the Commons, is not composed primarily of professional politicians, but contains, through the system of nominating to life peerages men and women of eminence, experts in almost every field – lawyers, economists, agriculturalists – covered by Community activity.

"England," Disraeli once said, "is governed not by logic but by parliament." Europe, however, imposes upon us the need to adjust our parliamentary institutions. But, if we have much to learn from Europe, we also have an important contribution of our own to make because of our long history and understanding of the operation of parliamentary institutions. We must, in particular, try to make the non-elected European Commission more accountable, perhaps by making it responsible to the European Parliament. We need also to make the European Parliament more accountable to

the people of Europe. Above all, we must use the forthcoming enlargement of the Union to reform and rationalise its institutions, for institutions originally developed for a Community of six are unlikely to be appropriate for a Union of over 20 members.

The constitutional relationships between Britain and the European Union may seem mysterious and arcane. They reflect, however, matters of enormous importance for every citizen. Why, after all, did we decide in 1973, after 12 years of debate, to join the Community? Why indeed was the Community created in the first place?

It is worth remembering what Winston Churchill, prescient as always, said in a speech at the Royal Albert Hall in May 1948. "Europe," he said, was "a rubble-heap, a charnel-house, a breeding-ground of pestilence and hate. Are the States of Europe," he went on to ask, "to continue for ever to squander the first fruits of their toil upon the erection of new barriers, military fortifications, tariff walls and passport networks against one another? . . . Are we all, through our poverty and our quarrels, for ever to be a burden and a danger to the rest of the world? If [however] the people of Europe resolve to come together and work together for mutual advantage, to exchange blessings instead of curses, they still have it in their power to sweep away the horrors and miseries which surround them and to allow the streams of freedom, happiness and abundance to begin again their healing flow. [Moreover] if Europe united is to be a living force, Britain will have to play her full part as a member of the European family."

Britain, Churchill believed, had a special contribution to make in Europe. What is that special contribution? Let us return to Orwell again. In his essay *The English People*, published in 1947, from which we have already quoted, he predicted: "In a world of power politics the English would ultimately dwindle to a satellite people, and the special thing that it is in their power to contribute might be lost. But what is the special thing that they could contribute? The outstanding and – by contemporary standards – highly original quality of the English is their habit of *not killing one another*."

Twice this century, British lives have been lost in European quarrels. If British membership first of the European Community and now of the European Union has helped to enable our troubled continent to progress towards prosperity in peace and freedom, then it has more than justified itself. ☆

References

1. Marshall v Southampton and South West Hampshire Area Health Authority (No. 2) 1993, and R v Secretary of State for Employment ex p. Equal Opportunities Commission, 1994.

2. R v Secretary of State for Transport, ex p. Factortame Ltd, 1990; R v Secretary of State for Transport, ex p. Factortame Ltd, (No. 2) 1991; and R v Secretary of State for Transport, ex p. Factortame, (No. 3) 1991.

Results.

Why So Many Companies Try Other Firms.
But Turn To Us.

You've heard their buzzwords. Read their books. Attended their seminars. But are you seeing any results?

At Thomas Group, we deliver what you're seeking. Improved customer responsiveness. Accelerated R&D. Liberated cash. Bottom-line impact. Results. We stake our reputation and compensation to them.

If you're tired of speaker-circuit lingo, we're ready to talk about the only buzzword that matters. Call us at +49 (0)69 665 38 0 or +44 (0)171 872 5575.

Dallas • Frankfurt  Detroit • Singapore

International Headquarters: 5215 North O'Connor Boulevard Suite 2500 Irving, Texas 75039 USA 1-800-826-2057
European Headquarters: Hahnstrasse 43 60528 Frankfurt am Main Germany +49(0)69 665 38 0 www.thomasgroup.com

"The 1992 programme demonstrated that, given a clear-cut common objective and the right kind of leadership, the European partners were capable of rising above the internal squabbles and short termism of everyday Community life and embarking on a process of dynamic reform"

POINTING THE WAY:
HOW THE SINGLE MARKET CAME ABOUT

BY MICHAEL WELSH, CHIEF EXECUTIVE OF THE ACTION CENTRE FOR EUROPE

In 1983 the American Commerce Secretary, Malcolm Baldridge, made a speech in Venice in which he described a phenomenon he termed Euro-sclerosis, which was undermining Europe's ability to compete with the US, Japan and the fast growing economies of the Pacific rim. Euro-sclerosis was evidenced by the use of various devices to protect domestic industries from imports; generous government subsidies to prop up inefficient state-owned industries; and labour market rigidities flowing from a cast of mind that placed more emphasis on job protection than beating competition. The European Community, said Mr Baldridge, was manifestly living beyond its means and was evidently incapable of taking the hard decisions necessary to modernise its economy. This criticism, which was much resented at the time, was no less than the simple truth.

The European Parliament, directly elected for the first time in 1979, was casting around for a role and quickly took an interest in the obstacles to free movement which prevented the EC from realising its trading potential. Two of the British members, Basil de Ferranti and Sir Fred Catherwood, were instrumental in raising the issue of trade barriers to the top of the Parliamentary agenda. De Ferranti, a Minister in the Macmillan Government and former Chief Executive of JCL, used his extensive business contacts to mount a campaign to raise public awareness pointing out that, in spite of the existence of a common market, lorries still queued for days at a time at customs posts waiting for documents and cargoes to be checked to ensure conformity with national regulations. With two German MEPs, Karl von Wogau and Dieter Rogalla, a former customs official, he founded the Kangaroo Group whose regular monthly lunches became a platform for denouncing non-tariff barriers and enlisting business support for their removal. *Kangaroo News*, which achieved a wide circulation among big corporations, contained detailed case studies of the ways in which national authorities were abusing the system to protect domestic suppliers from competition, and did much to discredit the practice. Catherwood, a former Director General of NEDDY and Director of the British Overseas Trade Board, persuaded the President of the Parliament, Piet Dankert, to commission a report into the incidence of trade barriers by two distinguished economists, Professor James Ball of the London Business School, and Michel Albert, a former *Commissaire General du Plan*.

The Ball-Albert Report, published in 1983, contained a detailed analysis of what it termed "the costs of non-Europe", estimating that the abolition of frontier delays alone could add 2% to the Community's GDP. They highlighted the dangers of "balkanisation" of the European economy in ways which prevented companies from operating efficiently and the absence of a common market for capital and financial services. The Parliament set up a special Committee on European Economic Recovery to consider the Ball-Albert findings; Catherwood played an important role in shaping the Committee's conclusions which in many respects foreshadowed the legislative programme which was to create the Single Market. The Committee Chairman, Jacques Moreau, was a French trades unionist with close connections to Jacques Delors, at that time President Mitterrand's Minister of Finance. Through Moreau, Delors kept closely in touch with the Committee's work and took an active part in a meeting it held in Paris. When he assumed the Presidency of the Commission in January 1985, the concept of a barrier-free market was firmly established in his mind as the "big idea" with which he would galvanise the Community.[1]

When Jacques Delors arrived in Brussels in January 1985 the European Community was in a sorry state. In addition to the economic stagnation and drift identified by Baldridge at Venice, the escalating costs of the Common Agricultural Policy had brought the Community to the verge of bankruptcy and no progress was possible until the debilitating dispute with Margaret Thatcher's government over the size of the British budget contribution could be resolved. Negotiations to admit Spain and Portugal to membership were blocked and the three institutions – Council, Commission and Parliament – were locked in a seemingly endless and demoralising dispute over the size of the Community budget. Delors found the way out of the morass by reinventing the method pioneered

> *"Margaret Thatcher, Geoffrey Howe and Nigel Lawson had the courage and insight to put trade liberalisation and the abolition of barriers to free movement at the top of the European agenda, even when this seemed to conflict with some of their deeply held beliefs about national independence"*

by Jean Monnet: seeking collective solutions to common problems through co-operation between the member states and the Community institutions rather than confrontation, and persuading them to sign up to explicit targets by which progress could be measured. As Delors put it:

"Experience has shown that, on any given aspect of progress towards the internal market, the Commission's proposals get lost amid a welter of discussion by groups of experts and there comes a point when political sanction and political will are needed. We must therefore be able to refer to the political commitment of the Heads of State or Government in order to make progress on these dossiers at the appropriate time."[2]

Preparation of a White Paper setting out the Commission's detailed proposals was entrusted to the newly appointed British Commissioner, Lord Cockfield. Arthur Cockfield had been Secretary of State for Trade in Mrs Thatcher's Cabinet after a distinguished career in both private and public sectors. He was the kind of practical man of affairs who appealed to the Prime Minister and she enthusiastically backed him in his mission to create that "real Common Market" which seemed the obvious way to apply Thatcherite ideas at the European level. Cockfield was by temperament and experience the ideal choice to draft the Single Market White Paper and he threw himself into the task with all the zeal of a recent convert, personally drafting the introduction.[3]

The White Paper listing 300 legislative measures required to achieve a Single European Market based on the free movement of goods, services, people and capital by the end of 1992 was duly endorsed by the European Council meeting in Milan in May 1985. Its central objective was the removal of all physical and technical barriers to trade, abandoning the previous policy of harmonisation in favour of a new approach based on approximating national product standards. This was based on the decision of the Court of Justice in the *Cassis de Dijon* case[4] which established that any product lawfully manufactured and put on sale in one part of the common market could not be barred from being imported into any other. The new approach involved the adoption of framework directives setting out general principles and guidelines for the approximation of national standards. Alternatively, the adoption of Community standards by European trade associations and other competent professional bodies was applied to services using a minimal co-ordination of national rules as the basis for mutual recognition and supervision; detailed prescriptions by the authorities were to be replaced by the free play of market forces. Frontier posts were to disappear, any residual formalities such as health checks or the collection of excise duties and VAT would be carried out at the destination. The absolutism of Cockfield's approach is caught by the following quotation on the removal of customs posts:

"The objective is the total removal of barriers – not just their reduction . . . It is not enough to reduce the number of controls currently carried out at frontiers. So long as there is any reason for requiring people and goods to stop and be checked, the main objective will not have been reached . . . and there will be still no real Community."[5]

At Milan, the Italian Presidency, overriding objections from Denmark, Greece and the United Kingdom, announced that an Intergovernmental Conference would be convened to draw up the amendments necessary to entrench the principles underlying the Single Market in the Treaty and to reform the decision-making procedures of the Council of Ministers so as to make adoption of the necessary legislation possible. These changes were delivered in the form of the Single European Act of 1987 which made the attainment of the Single Market a Treaty objective[6] and provided that majority voting in the Council would apply for all Single Market legislation so that the programme could not be obstructed by the use of the national veto.[7]

The coming into force of the Single European Act was the signal for a period of intense legislative activity. There were inevitable set-backs and unforeseen difficulties: Cockfield's elaborate proposals for centralising the collection of VAT were never adopted and the state monopolies in fields such as energy, telecommunications and air transport have fought long and hard to preserve their privileges. Governments proved dilatory in passing implementing legislation and lax in enforcing Single Market regulations, but in spite of all the obstacles, by the end of 1992 the legislative programme set out in the White Paper had largely been delivered.

Lord Cockfield was not appointed to the second Delors Commission which took office in 1989, but his successor Sir Leon Brittan was to carry on the good work. As Commissioner responsible for Financial Institutions he was responsible for piloting the crucial Directives on Banking and Insurance through the Council, thus making a reality of the Single Market for Financial Services. It was Brittan who developed the principle of home state supervision so that the authorities in one state became responsible for licensing an institution to offer services throughout the Single Market.

In 1996 the independent policy studies network, Action Centre for Europe, established an Inquiry Panel, chaired by Lord Sheppard of Didgemere, to look at the operation of the Single Market from the standpoint of the businessmen who had to make it work, through a series of hearings in which they took evidence from representatives of different industrial and financial sectors on a systematic basis. The Sheppard Inquiry into Competitiveness and the Single Market[8] concluded that while most of the legislative framework was in place, there was some way to go in establishing the spirit of the Single Market as an active ingredient in the competitiveness of European business. The report contained an action agenda of eight specific proposals:

✦ Legislation to secure improved market access and more competition in key economic sectors such as energy, telecoms, transport and financial services, where the process of liberalisation is far from complete.

✦ Revised rules on public procurement to provide greater transparency and a more efficient use of public resources.

✦ A new initiative with the support of Heads of Government to eliminate remaining state aids and unofficial subsidies.

✦ Reform of Competition Policy to clarify the respective competences of the the Commission and national authorities and to provide a speedier reaction to market developments.

✦ A fast-track procedure for investigating complaints, making greater use of national courts.

✦ The Commission to produce an action plan to remove remaining barriers to free movement of persons.

✦ Re-examination of the case for a European Company Statute to ensure equal access for companies across the Single Market regardless of their nationality.

✦ Closer co-operation between the European authorities and business so that the dynamics of competitiveness are better understood by all concerned.

These recommendations, which were warmly welcomed by the Commission and the Labour Government, were very similar in tone to a Commission paper published by Commissioner Monti. In 1997, it is time for the Commission, Council and Parliament to mount a combined effort to put them into practice.

Although the process of liberalisation has some way still to go, we should not blind ourselves to the remarkable achievement of the years 1985-93 when the bulk of the Single Market programme was delivered as promised; few of those who listened to Jacques Delors' inaugural speech in 1985 would have given it a chance. The 1992 programme demonstrated that, given a clear-cut common objective and the right kind of leadership, the European partners were capable of rising above the internal squabbles and short termism of everyday Community life and embarking on a process of dynamic reform. As a result the facts of business and economic life have fundamentally changed. Our major businesses no longer think of themselves as British, French or German but as European. Individuals now expect to spend substantial portions of their working lives in countries other than their own. It is normal for British students to study and acquire recognised qualifications in universities across Europe and their parents now own property and retire in France, Spain, Portugal and Italy as well as Great Britain. Citizenship of the Union has become a reality not a mere concept, and the global competitiveness of European business has been massively enhanced. Nor is this a process

that can now be reversed: even the late Sir James Goldsmith accepted that Britain would need to remain part of what he termed "Europe's Common Trading Area".

The 1992 project acted as a catalyst for the resolution of a number of intractable problems which seemed at the time to have permanently stalled the process of integration. The enlargement of the Community to include Spain and Portugal was finally achieved, opening the way for further enlargement in the future. As a result of the Single Market initiative and all that went with it, the second half of the decade was a period of remarkable progress.

As we look forward to the British Presidency of the European Union in the first half of 1998 there are some compelling parallels with 1984. Then as now there was a sense of stagnation and under-achievement, of intractable problems that could not be resolved, competing national interests that could not be reconciled. Then as now it was widely felt that Europe had lost its way and would never be able to rise to the challenge of competition from the Far East and the Pacific; that the European institutions had lost the confidence of the citizens and with it their own self-confidence. Yet with the launch of the 1992 programme everything changed. In a twinkling of an eye there was a new vision, new inspiration and suddenly the impossible became possible again. History will record that it was the French socialist, Jacques Delors, who provided the clarity of vision and dynamic leadership that made this transformation possible, but he had a lot of help from the British – Arthur Cockfield, Leon Brittan and, at a Parliamentary level, Boz Ferranti and Fred Catherwood. Margaret Thatcher, Geoffrey Howe and Nigel Lawson had the courage and insight to put trade liberalisation and the abolition of barriers to free movement at the top of the European agenda, even when this seemed to conflict with some of their deeply held beliefs about national independence. The Single Market, which has transformed the economic face of Europe and contributed significantly to the prosperity and well-being of her citizens, was a very British project; perhaps the time has come to repeat the trick. ☆

Footnotes
1 The author was present at a meeting between Sir Fred Catherwood and Francois Lamoreux, one of Delors closest collaborators, in December 1995 when he gave him an extensive briefing on the Special Committee's main recommendations.
2 Speech to the European Parliament March 12th 1985 – Debates of the EP 2/324 page 5
3 In 1983, the author accompanied Basil de Ferranti to the Department of Trade to lobby for a Commission proposal to replace the multiplicity of national customs documents with a Single Administrative Document (SAD). We were given short shrift by the Secretary of State who assured us that the proposal was quite impracticable and there was no prospect for the foreseeable future of tried and tested British Customs procedures being overridden in this way. The Minister was none other than Lord Cockfield.
4. Case 120/78
5. Statement at the Milan council, Bulletin EC 6-1985, 1.32.2
6. "The internal market shall comprise an area without internal frontiers in which the free movement of goods, persons, services and capital shall be ensured in accordance with the provisions of this Treaty." (Article 7a)
7. Article 100a
8. Action Centre for Europe, May 1997.

*"London is the international financial
centre for Europe. Global financial activity is
concentrated in just a few major centres,
and London is the international financial
capital for the European time zone"*

LONDON: FINANCIAL CENTRE OF EUROPE

BY JUDITH MAYHEW, CHAIRMAN OF THE POLICY AND RESOURCES COMMITTEE, CORPORATION OF LONDON

The City of London is Europe's international financial centre. It generates over £20 billion a year for the EU economy, and has a more than enviable share of world markets.

The City is the bridge into Europe for worldwide firms, particularly those from the Far East, the Middle East and Latin America. Unusually among European financial centres, much of the business is international, not derived from the domestic economy; indeed, it has around twice as many non-EU banks as Paris and Frankfurt combined. The Bank of England has recently recorded that there are over 540 banks represented in London – more than any other city – and around 170 securities houses. It brings to Europe a high volume of business which would otherwise go to the United States or Japan.

In addition to being the bridge into Europe, the City is also the bridge out of Europe for European firms wishing to trade globally; indeed, it does the bulk of its business in the Far East, the Americas and the Middle East. UK banks invest more capital than those of any other country, accounting for 17% of external bank lending globally.

London also has the world's largest foreign exchange market, accounting in 1995 for 30% of global turnover, an average daily turnover of $464 billion – more than the turnover of New York and Tokyo combined. London also leads in international equity trading, and has half of the world turnover in non-local equity trading. The City has an estimated two thirds of the primary market and approximately three quarters of the secondary market in international markets. Just as the Eurobond market began in London in 1963 and the first bonds denominated in ECU were dealt in London, so London's wholesale markets will be ready to trade the euro from the first day of European Monetary Union.

In addition, London is the global clearing centre for gold forwards trading and financing, and the Baltic Exchange is the world's largest shipbroking market. London is also the world's largest international insurance market, with net premiums of £10 billion in 1993, equal to 28% of marine and 38% of aviation risks.

After Tokyo, the City is the second largest fund management centre, with over $750 billion of institutional equity holdings. It ranks second to the US in exchange traded futures and options, and the volume of derivatives traded per day on the LIFFE market averages 650,000 contracts with a nominal value of £150 billion. It outstripped the Chicago Board of Trade in September 1997.

The value of futures contracts traded in London in 1995 was $49 billion. London ranks second to the US in exchange traded financial futures and options. Its share of the world market has increased from 7% in 1988 to 17% in 1994. The London Metal Exchange saw a turnover of 47.2 million lots in 1995, representing over 1 billion tonnes of metal, valued at $2,500 billion.

"The Bank of England has recently recorded that there are over 540 banks represented in London – more than any other city – and around 170 securities houses. It brings to Europe a high volume of business which would otherwise go to the United States or Japan"

So the City of London offers Europe diversity, strength and depth. The clustering of markets allows key executives to have regular, face-to-face contact with each other. It offers international organisations economies of scale in running their businesses. They also gain access to large professional services firms, and to high quality workforces. In addition, the City offers international organisations access to state-of-the-art telecommunications and to back office space in Canary Wharf, east London.

It is a misconception to think that what is London's gain is somehow to the detriment of Europe. There is no distinction between the City and Europe in my mind: rather, London is the international financial centre for Europe. Global financial activity is concentrated in just a few major centres, and London is the international financial capital for the European time zone.

Will London's pre-eminence be damaged if the UK is not part of the first wave of countries to participate in EMU? We firmly believe that the City's attractions will be preserved with the advent of the euro, whether the UK is on board or not. That London continues to thrive in the age of the euro is vital not just for London, but for Europe – and the City's attractive openness to businesses of all nationalities will be undiminished. The City will also retain the advantage of the English language, and English contractual law. In addition, it will continue to boast advanced information technology. The beginning of automated trading on the London Stock Exchange (20 October 1997) is only the most recent IT development which the City offers international businesses.

In addition, the City of London has a dedicated authority, the Corporation of London, a non-party political authority which supports and promotes the City around the world. It does not take London's pre-eminence for granted, having an established an Economic Development Unit – a team of specialists dedicated to maintaining the City's prestigious global position.

The Corporation prides itself on being user-friendly, unbureaucratic and apolitical. These qualities are universally appreciated, said Mr Peter Berger, President of the Foreign Bankers' Association and General Manager of Commerzbank in London, in a recent article.

"It is important to have a political structure that supports your business, providing help on practical issues such as telecoms, electricity or building permits," he said. "In my experience, the Corporation has been quite excellent at providing that help: you get a very quick response, which isn't the case in other cities."

Guided by the Bank of England, the City of London is preparing vigorously for EMU. I am confident that London will be a highly competitive place in which to do business related to the euro; indeed, it aims to be the international financial centre for the euro.

In its arrangements for wholesale payments, the Bank of England is planning to take part in TARGET (Trans-European Real Time Gross Settlement Express Transfer). The Bank will use it as a high-volume, cheap system of choice for wholesale euro transfers throughout the EU. Testing of TARGET began in mid-1997.

Banks operating in the UK will have access to an efficient RTGS (Real Time Gross Settlement) facility. It will enable them to settle both domestic and cross-border transactions; and, importantly, it will be able to make payments in euro as cost-effectively as in sterling.

The clearing company CHAPS (Clearing House Automated Payment System), which owns and runs the current sterling system, is committed to offering its members and their customers a competitive and efficient service for euro payments. To that end it is building a network for payment settlements

LIFFE

THE WORLD CENTRE FOR EURO DERIVATIVES TRADING AFTER EMU

BY JACK WIGGLESWORTH, CHAIRMAN, LIFFE

Every day, on the trading-floor of Europe's largest futures and options exchange, the London International Financial Futures and Options Exchange (LIFFE), traders stand in pits buying and selling thousands of futures and options contracts denominated in Italian lira and German Deutschmarks, worth billions of dollars.

In other financial markets, such as foreign exchange and bond trading, the scene is much the same. The language is English, the location is London, but what the traders buy and sell is international.

Today London is the undisputed leading financial centre of Europe, ranked alongside New York and Tokyo. LIFFE itself is typical of the whole of the City in its European and international outlook. We are not primarily British – being less than 30% UK owned. Well over half our members are based in Europe. In that sense we are a European exchange and we are challenging the Americans – in September having usurped even the mighty Chicago Board of Trade to become the largest exchange in the world.

Economic and Monetary Union (EMU) poses a challenge and offers an opportunity to LIFFE. Our ambition is to be the world centre for Euro derivatives trading post-EMU. We recognise the challenge from our European competitors – particularly the recently announced link-up between the German, French and Swiss futures exchanges. However we have developed a strategy to achieve our ambition. This strategy focuses on extending and adapting our product range; developing our trading platforms and enhancing our regulatory standards.

LIFFE's trading volumes continue to increase dramatically. We are breaking records day after day, month after month. We offer the broadest range of contracts of any exchange in Europe and the greatest liquidity. The consensus of market opinion is that there will be one short term interest rate contract post-EMU. And LIFFE has total dominance in short term interest rate futures, holding over 80% of the market share of trading in these contracts. For delivery months after January 1999, this rises to 90%.

The Euro is already trading at LIFFE. LIFFE now lists post-January 1999 Three Month ECU futures. If EMU goes ahead as anticipated, these contracts will be denominated in Euros with a simple "one to one" contract conversion. However investors will be given a choice. Our existing German, Italian and UK short term interest rate contracts will continue to trade side by side with our ECU/EURO contracts. LIFFE will be providing special conversion and trading facilities for investors who choose to convert their short-term futures and options contracts to Euros.

LIFFE has already strengthened its product range by introducing the five-year German Government Bond futures and options and will be launching a new five-year UK Government Bond futures contracts to add to its wide range of financial instruments.

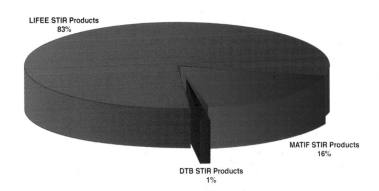

LIFEE STIR Products 83%

DTB STIR Products 1%

MATIF STIR Products 16%

We are making a substantial investment – over £100 million – to enhance the efficiency of our trading platforms. This investment will substantially increase the efficiency of member firms' operations and will reduce their costs.

LIFFE is reinforcing its own regulatory standards by achieving better surveillance through upgraded video logging and has undertaken an extensive Rules Review to increase efficiency and reduce the time taken to complete disciplinary proceedings. The new Financial Services Authority (FSA) is designing an environment which is safe for investors and yet allows the markets to be as innovative as is necessary to meet continued market needs.

Our partnership with the London Clearing House, which provides common clearing across all London derivatives exchanges, already provides our users with substantial savings and a high degree of confidence.

Looking into the future, we believe that both London and LIFFE are well positioned to meet the changing needs of the market and the challenges posed by EMU. ✫

> *"Guided by the Bank of England, the City of London is preparing vigorously for EMU. I am confident that London will be a highly competitive place in which to do business related to the euro; indeed, it aims to be the international financial centre for the euro"*

able to become full members of CHAPS. A bank joining on this basis would have a share in the ownership of CHAPS and a say in how it is run and developed.

The London Stock Exchange (LSE) will be ready for the introduction of the euro. Unusually among European stock exchanges, the LSE already organises a multi-currency trading platform in 36 currencies. It therefore has the ability to offer listing and trading in more than one currency. As a result, whether or not the UK joins the single currency, the LSE could support trading in both sterling and euro for individual securities, should the market wish.

The Bank of England is well aware of the importance of redenominating shares. Among other things, it has suggested that the qualifying share capital for companies registered in the UK should be changed from £50,000 to either £50,000 in sterling or its equivalent in foreign currency.

In derivatives, LIFFE is working on the changes it needs to make, and has already adapted the current short-term interest rate contract to euro interest rate settlement.

On the financial markets and exchanges, screen providers are preparing for the need to provide information about the price history of the euro on screens. They are aware of the need to create data from the former national currencies.

which will enable its members to make payments in euro within the UK and across the EU via TARGET. They in turn will be able to provide a full payment service in wholesale payments in euro to their customers.

CHAPS is the largest existing RTGS system in Europe, with daily flows averaging nearly 70,000 payments and daily turnover averaging £150 billion. The UK's experience in building a reliable, high-volume system has proved invaluable in our assistance at the European Monetary Institute in the development of TARGET.

CHAPS treats foreign and domestic banks equally with regard to its criteria for membership. Banks wishing to operate only in CHAPS's service for euro payments will be

The Bank of England is also working with the European Monetary Institute (EMI) and other EU National Central Banks to prepare for the introduction of the euro. The Bank is promoting discussion between the EMI and National Central Banks about issues such as the redenomination of securities in national currencies and market conventions for securities denominated in euro.

These vigorous preparations across the full variety of London's financial markets mean that the City of London has every chance of remaining Europe's international financial centre. Indeed, London will continue to be the leading international financial centre not merely *in* Europe, but *for* Europe. ☆

IN NOVEMBER 1922, THERE WAS AN
INCREDIBLE STORY
ON THE
BBC RADIO NEWS.
THE BBC RADIO NEWS.

"Good evening. The time is six o'clock, this is 2LO with the British Broadcasting Company wireless news."

Ever since the BBC made its first crackly transmission from a room in Marconi House, London, it has continued to set the standard in news broadcasting. The BBC World service for example, which was introduced in 1932 is today available in 45 different languages and boasts the largest international audience for a news service anywhere in the world. More recently, the BBC has also launched 'News Online', a live news service available to the millions of World Wide Web users. And, thanks to the unique way the BBC is paid for by you, the British public, the news is delivered in many other ways. From Radio 5 Live and Ceefax, through to 'BBC News 24', a round-the-clock current affairs channel. The BBC has also pioneered Digital Radio, on which you will soon be able to hear a rolling news service in CD quality sound, no matter where you are in the country.

It'll sound almost as incredible as those very first words 75 years ago.

BBC
You make it what it is.

THE BBC:
AT EUROPE'S CUTTING EDGE

BY JOHN BIRT, DIRECTOR-GENERAL OF THE BBC

"We are about to face the broadcasting big bang. Digital technology means that the imminent explosion in choice will be bewildering, almost uncontainable"

It is easy to get apocalyptic about the technological revolution that is about to transform our lives. Ever since we learnt how to transmit radio and television programmes, we have been used to a steady incremental growth in the number of channels available. First we had to build enough transmitters; then the Government had to set up and license broadcasters. There was only limited and tightly controlled availability of spectrum. The growth of analogue cable and satellites has allowed more channels to develop, but there have still been significant capacity constraints. Now, 75 years after the BBC was founded, we are about to face the broadcasting big bang. Digital technology means that the imminent explosion in choice will be bewildering, almost uncontainable. Yet, used aright, it has the enormous potential to make people's lives better – better informed, better educated, better able to choose – by putting power where it belongs: in the hands of the people.

Not only will there be practically no restriction on the number of channels available, but you will be able to determine how and when you watch whatever you choose. Sitting in front of your home screen you will have access to television and radio stations all over the world, including a whole range of new specialist channels offering exactly the combination of interests that appeal to you. You will instantaneously be able to order up the episode of the latest drama series that you couldn't watch on Thursday because it was your children's Parent Teachers' Association evening; or an old episode of *Horizon* to help you get that article right for Tuesday's edition. For news junkies you'll be able to catch the latest, 24 hours a day, or get tonight's edition of the *Nine O'Clock News* if you get home late; or you could compile your own bulletin that would contain just the news items that relate to your interests – local stories, sports news, economics, arts or politics. It will be an era of news on demand in which the broadcasters with the strongest news-gathering team will be able to offer the greatest choice. Broadcasters will no longer be able to rely on traditional channel loyalties. Branding (both of image and of values) will become ever more important. Those brands that stand for quality, honesty and accountability will shine like diamonds in the rough.

It will also be an era in which the old barriers between banking, shopping, broadcasting, computing and publishing will break down. Already a few financial institutions are offering on-line banking facilities, and supermarkets are trying out home shopping, but as the digital era becomes a reality it will become impossible to differentiate between a television programme and an educational computer file being downloaded on to your home PC. Moreover, this is technology that works. Channels are already being transmitted on the Internet and one British Member of Parliament in the last general election published five thousand letters to constituents on e-mail for all of four pence.

The effects of this new digital revolution will be so far-reaching that it is vital we have a clear idea of the key role that public policy will have on the development of these converging industries, and of the factors which should shape that policy. At the very heart of all public policy, at both European and British levels, should be the deliberate goal of providing the maximum amount of choice for consumers whilst maintaining the greatest possible plurality of producers. Arguably, with the virtual abolition of spectrum scarcity, greater choice is the inevitable result of the new technology. However, just as there are enormous benefits to the digital revolution, it also poses serious threats.

The first of these is obvious. For digital technology to succeed it needs to offer real choice – not just a reheated, homogenized serving of global culture, but genuinely exciting programming that reflects the fullest possible diversity – because most people's tastes are not narrow but eclectic. They want programmes that are useful and entertaining. They want natural history, sports, science, films and drama as well as game shows and the best of transatlantic imports. And we need to serve the needs and feed the aspirations of all.

This means maintaining the vitalising cultural diversity of European programming, not least because we have already gone a long way towards the wholesale globalisation of culture. Baseball caps have become so all-pervasive that even cricketers (and politicians) wear them and fast-food burger stalls now stretch from the Rockies to the Urals.

But I do not agree with the fanatical anti-yankeeism of some commentators. One of the main reasons that American broadcasting sells so well across the world is that the US has produced extraordinarily affecting cinema and some of the most beguiling of television programmes. Its popular music is characterised by great energy and innovation and, above all, people *enjoy* it.

But there are limits. We do not live in one "global village" – we live in hundreds of global villages, linked to each other but separate and proud of their own identity. And every sensible global broadcaster – the BBC included – knows that they have to match their output to what local viewers are interested in. That is why it would be futile to resist global forces with an instrument as blunt as broadcast quotas. People themselves will choose diversity without it being imposed. There is no market for homogeneous broadcasting, which is precisely why we need strong local and regional broadcasting production centres to give expression to our cultural diversity.

Clearly this is the responsibility of all our national cultural institutions. Our theatres and orchestras, and other arts institutions, which constantly feed their talent through into television and radio, are vital. But the most effective bulwark against wholesale cultural homogeneity is that particular mixture of artistic creativity and political common sense that is public service broadcasting. Britain's confident response to the globalisation of culture has been to accept the best from abroad whilst developing our own strong production centres based on shared creative values. So we have welcomed US films, but at the same time we have grown the strongest national television production base, outside the US, anywhere in the world. As the British saying has it: "If you can't join them, beat them." And we have embraced music from across the world whilst giving constant encouragement to home-grown talent. The BBC has become the main showcase for the most successful music industry per head anywhere in the world. The BBC, through its phenomenal newsgathering team, its regional production base and its local radio stations, has been able to compete with the best and to foster genuine talent from across the country. We are proud to be the biggest exporter of audio-visual material in Europe and within Britain to be the only broadcaster that is a net exporter.

A public service broadcaster cannot be preserved in aspic. It is no use repeating what has been done for years. That would be just as harmful an influence on national culture and regional diversity as global cultural uniformity. Much modern British culture has sprung not from the offices of multimedia corporations, but from the street and from the people, and it is vital that a public service broadcaster reflects this and retains its cutting edge. Similarly the BBC needs to move into the new digital era with bold steps. That is why we have committed both money and creative energy to bringing new digital services to the public as soon as possible. Digital Audio Broadcasting was launched last year and a new public service channel – BBC News 24 – is also now up and running. The BBC Learning Channel and BBC Online are on the way, along with four new commercial channels and new digital television services.

Public Service Broadcasting also acts as a vital counter to the inevitable fragmenting effect of increasing choice. Social cohesion depends on what we all know that we all know. If

> **"We are proud to be the biggest exporter of audio-visual material in Europe and within Britain to be the only broadcaster that is a net exporter"**

our shared national experiences, most notably our great political and sporting events, are relegated to pay-per-view channels, they will lose all their cohesive potency and we shall have dismantled any sense of a genuinely *national* experience. If we are not all able to see a football cup final on free to view television, can it really be considered a national event – and without shared national events what happens to our sense of national identity?

My biggest worry about the effects of digitisation is "who guards the gate to the digital world?" When I switch on my television or on-line computer, what will I see and where will it point me? And if there is more than one set-top box on the market, will they be interchangeable or will a programme provider be able to monopolise the market by making their access system indispensable for those who want their programmes? These are big questions for European policy and for anti-trust legislation in the USA.

Clearly if there is only one guardian of the gate and he also sells services, whether they are television programmes or computer systems, it is likely that he will want to sell his services above anyone else's. Which is why it is desirable that the people and the organisations that control the gateway should not also be providers of services on the other side of it. Otherwise the temptation to indulge in anti-competitive practices, completely distorting the market and giving unimaginable power to single organisations, will be irresistible.

This is particularly true when one considers that the amount of economic activity that passes down these lines will – within the next 10 years – become a very significant part of the national output. To have such a distorting monopoly and the threat of market dominance hanging over the whole arena of European economic activity would be immensely damaging. Strong European legislation to prevent the abuse of dominant market position and to provide a level playing field for all broadcasters is vital. This means fighting the battles over gateway dominance to a successful conclusion so that no one person or corporation determines how all Europe watches television, does its home shopping or surfs the Internet.

Finally, although received wisdom states that the all-singing all-dancing digital era may still be a decade away, this is a very fast-moving environment. BSkyB did not even exist eight years ago and fifteen years ago Microsoft was still in its infancy. The BBC is proud to be one of the most vibrant and creative organisations in the world, but its future depends on the cultural diversity of both Britain and Europe – a diversity we constantly seek to enhance and portray in all its richness. Wholesale cultural globalisation and gateway dominance threaten this rich, variegated world; but with strong legislation and healthy public service broadcasting across Europe we should be able to channel the forces of the digital big bang into ever more creative avenues, and above all bring people the choice and richness to their lives that they deserve. ☆

Soon broadcasters will be able to wish

As the world embarks upon a new era of economic growth and development, so it will witness an exciting new era for audio broadcasting.

WorldSpace is about to bridge the gap between the information rich and the information poor of the world with the launch of its new Digital Sound Broadcasting Service. Three European built and launched geostationary satellites, transmitting to 122 countries, will enable broadcasters to fulfil the growing need for information, education and entertainment to 4.5 billion people throughout Africa, the Middle

another 4½ billion people good morning.

East, Asia and Latin America. With a reception area of 14 million square kilometres the WorldSpace Service will take advertisers and broadcasters where they've never been before.

If you would like to say good morning to over 4 billion people in 20 different languages, contact us now.

WorldSpace 2400 N Street, NW, Washington, DC 20037-1153, USA.
Tel: 1.202.969.6000. http://worldspace.com

WORLDSPACE

Digital Broadcasting for the 21st Century

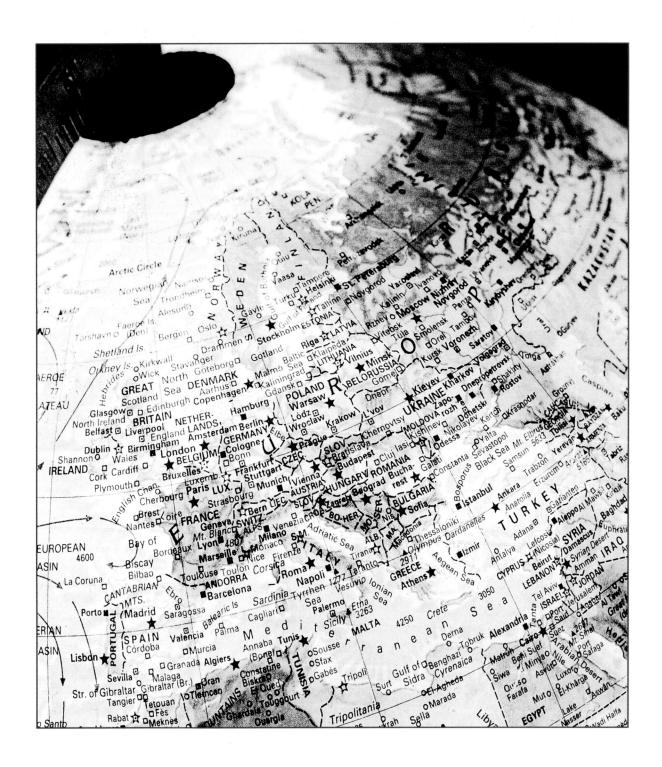

"Even more than the early years of West European integration, this is a journey to an unknown destination"

THE EU & NATO: REWRITING OUR CONTINENT

BY LORD WALLACE OF SALTAIRE, READER IN INTERNATIONAL RELATIONS AT THE LONDON SCHOOL OF ECONOMICS

Eastern enlargement will transform European institutions over the next 10-15 years. Both the European Community and NATO were designed for a divided Europe. Extending their boundaries east and south-east to bring in the former socialist states between Germany and Russia will unavoidably alter their structure, their policy priorities and their internal balance. If we get the double enlargement of the EU and NATO right, we will over the next ten years create the political and economic framework for a secure, prosperous and democratic European order for the 21st century.

The process of enlargement is well under way. In July 1997 the NATO Council agreed to negotiate terms of entry with Poland, the Czech Republic and Hungary, planning to welcome them into the alliance as full members in April 1999 – the fiftieth anniversary of the signing of the Atlantic Treaty. In May, NATO and its member governments had already signed association agreements with Russia and Ukraine; the NATO-Russia "Founding Act" committed the signatories to a pattern of consultation, including permanent Russian representation at NATO headquarters, that could conceivably develop into effective half-membership. The Alliance assured disappointed applicants from Romania, Slovenia and the Baltic states that there would be further rounds of enlargement, with the next group to be considered as soon as the current group joins in 1999.

The European Union has been moving – sometimes reluctantly – towards accepting former socialist states as new members since it negotiated the first "Europe Agreements" with Poland, Hungary and (then still united) Czechoslovakia in 1990-91. Three years later the number of Europe Agreement countries had grown to ten, with southern EU members pressing the claims of Cyprus and Malta. The Essen European Council in December 1994 upgraded the developing relationship into a "pre-accession strategy", with increased financial and technical assistance to potential applicants and regular multilateral meetings between current and future members.

The Inter-governmental Conference (IGC) of 1996-97 was intended to grapple with institutional reforms needed before the EU expanded beyond 15 members to 20 or more. Successive European Councils committed the EU to open negotiations with those candidates capable of meeting the obligations of membership within six months of its conclusion. Once the Treaty of Amsterdam was agreed, the European Commission in July 1997 published *Agenda 2000*, its assessment of the readiness of each of the applicants to join and of the adjustments in existing Community policies needed to make enlargement a success. Negotiations with those the European Council has approved as ready for membership will open under the British Presidency in January 1998: to work through the complexity of hard details and compromises will take two years or more, with a further 12-18 months required for ratification before the successful candidates are welcomed into the EU at some point between 2001 and 2005.

Even more than the early years of West European integration, this is a journey to an unknown destination. The number of potential extra members of NATO and the European Union stretches towards twenty. Behind the ten Europe Agreement states – Poland, the Czech Republic, Hungary, Slovakia, Romania, Bulgaria, Slovenia, Estonia, Latvia and Lithuania – and the three potential Mediterranean members – Cyprus, Malta and Turkey (this last already a NATO member) – stand other poorer and less stable south-east European states: Croatia, the Former Yugoslav Republic of Macedonia, Albania, the Federal Republic of Yugoslavia, and Bosnia and Herzegovina. These coun-

"All Western Europe's eastern and southern neighbours, from Morocco to Russia, depend upon the EU for markets, foreign investment and financial and technical assistance. Most also have depended on Western Europe to absorb a proportion of their rising populations, with young people still struggling to find ways into the EU against tighter and tighter controls on immigration"

mass of its population, or whether the wider public within Western Europe could ever be persuaded to accept this predominantly Muslim country into a Community defined by common acceptance of Western values. There are however already two million people within the EU of Turkish descent, most of them still Turkish citizens. The security of south-eastern Europe and of the eastern Mediterranean depends upon a stable and friendly Turkey. Whether or not within the next 10-20 years a Turkish government will gain full membership of the EU, West European governments must pursue the closest possible association with Turkey in the interim.

Implicitly at least, the eastern boundaries of our intended wider Europe have been drawn along the borders of Finland, Poland and Romania; leaving Russia, as well as Belarus and Ukraine, outside. Developing an economic and political partnership with Russia is therefore also a vital concern in constructing a wider European order. The German government and the US Administration have so far led in this endeavour: the former providing the lion's share of Western financial assistance, the latter dominating negotiations on security issues. The NATO-Russia Founding Act is too recent to allow for considered assessment of its potential development; much still depends on how constructively both sides build on what has been agreed. The EU has signed trade and co-operation agreements with both Russia and Ukraine, full implementation of which depend on further progress in those states' economic transition. Both NATO and the EU have also developed technical assistance and training programmes with the newly-independent states of the Caucasus and Central Asia, conscious that stability within Russia itself and stability across the territories of the former Soviet Union are closely linked.

tries between Italy and Greece are unavoidably dependent on their richer neighbours for hopes of prosperity. The period since 1989 has sharply demonstrated how immediately domestic disorder spills over into international concern, with flows of refugees and disruption of European transport. Whether or not the governments of Western Europe eventually admit them to their institutions there is little choice but to accept institutional responsibility for their future.

Then there are the neighbours who may not be admitted, but with whom a wider institutionalised Europe will have to manage intense economic and political relationships. All Western Europe's eastern and southern neighbours, from Morocco to Russia, depend upon the EU for markets, foreign investment and financial and technical assistance. Most also have depended on Western Europe to absorb a proportion of their rising populations, with young people still struggling to find ways into the EU against tighter and tighter controls on immigration.

The relationship with Turkey – a member of NATO for 45 years, associated with the EEC since 1963 – is most ambiguous. The EU remains formally committed to eventual acceptance of Turkey as a member, against firm opposition from Greece and silent denial from almost all other member states. Behind current reservations about the Turkish political system, its treatment of political and ethnic minorities, and the underdeveloped character of its economy, lie deeper reservations about the capacity of the EU to absorb a country with a population rising rapidly towards 100 million and with borders which touch on Iraq and Iran. Some also doubt whether the European commitment of Turkey's secular elite will ever spread to the

The Strait of Gibraltar is half as wide as the Strait of Dover. The EU's southernmost territories, Italian Lampedusa and Greek Crete, are further south than Algiers and Tunis. The countries of North Africa, all at one time occupied by European powers, depend overwhelmingly on European markets for economic growth. For Spain and France, Italy and Greece, stability in the Mediterranean is necessarily a more direct concern than EU enlargement to states which border the Baltic. Under the Spanish EU Presidency in November 1995 a conference of EU and Mediterranean governments in Barcelona pledged to develop a strategy for Mediterranean partnership in parallel with eastern enlargement, including the commitment of 4,500 million ECU over five years to support economic development in southern Mediterranean countries. Domestic politics within states going through rapid population explosions as well as industrial and agricultural revolutions do not allow for an easy multilateral dialogue. But here again the economic dominance of Western Europe in the Mediterranean, and the potential impact on the EU's southern members of disorder on the opposite shore, impose responsibilities.

"The Clinton Administration has driven NATO enlargement forward since 1994 as the key to continuing American engagement in Europe and to the projection of American power into Eurasia and the Middle East"

eventual framing of a common defence policy, which might in time lead to a common defence". Some optimists saw NATO as a Cold War alliance, which would slowly fade away once the Soviet threat had gone. Ex-socialist regimes, preoccupied with more immediate security concerns and seeking an American security guarantee, nevertheless pressed their case to join both the EU and NATO.

The future balance between a wider NATO and a wider EU will depend on the future relationship between the US and its West European allies. The Clinton Administration has driven NATO enlargement forward since 1994 as the key to continuing American engagement in Europe and to the projection of American power into Eurasia and the Middle East. The majority of NATO members are also members of the EU. In principle the two processes should therefore move in parallel, carefully concerted by governments, by the European Commission and the NATO secretariat, towards an end point in which the European members of both coincide. In practice NATO enlargement is moving much faster. Austria and Finland, as well as Romania and Slovenia, are mentioned as potential candidates for a second round which might well be completed before the EU has ratified terms of entry with its first group of applicants. Ratification of NATO enlargement should not, however, be taken as a *fait accompli*: there will be many critical questions posed within the US Senate in the spring of 1998 about transatlantic burden-sharing – about why the Europeans cannot pay for and organise their own defence.

It is difficult to explain to American voters why an institutionalised Europe of 370 million people, with a GNP substantially larger than that of the US, still remains dependent on the US for political leadership and security protection. It will be still more difficult after the first round of EU enlargement to explain why a wider Europe of 430 million – some 20 states concentrated into a region less than half the extent of the continental USA – should remain dependent on the United States. The habits of American leadership and of European followership which were institutionalised in NATO are hard to break, in spite of rhetorical commitments to build a European Security and Defence Identity within NATO and to provide American resources and equipment to joint European task forces in future emergencies. Fundamental issues lie underneath the process of dual enlargement once the question of the future balance between NATO and EU is addressed: of how much longer American public opinion will be willing to support the active commitment to European security which their foreign policy elite still believe essential; of how to balance the USA's military contribution against the far larger financial contribution which EU members are making to east European transition; and of whether a wider EU will find it easier or more difficult to develop a coherent foreign policy.

The hopeful applicants from central and eastern Europe are pressing to join the Western institutions they admire, to "rejoin the West" from which they were shut out for 40

The 12-member European Community of the mid-1980s was often described as "an economic giant but a political dwarf". Strategic questions of foreign and defence policy were scarcely addressed by the EC as an entity, even after 15 years of meetings of foreign ministers and their officials under the umbrella of European Political Co-operation. Policies towards the Soviet Union and the Warsaw Pact, the Middle East and the Arab-Israeli conflict, were managed under American leadership within the Atlantic framework of NATO. In the immediate aftermath of the revolutions of 1989-91 the European Community was restructured, under the Maastricht Treaty, into the broader European Union, which declares amongst its new commitments the establishment of a common foreign and security policy, "including the

years. Enlargement on this scale cannot however leave either the EU or NATO unaltered. The EU attempted to grapple with the institutional reforms needed to prepare for an expanding membership during the 1996-97 IGC; governments found the trade-offs so difficult that many issues were postponed until a future IGC. NATO in contrast has hardly considered how far expansion will (and must) transform an organisation which was designed to hold together the United States and a group of West European states under the clear and present danger of the Soviet threat. There is an underlying ambiguity between the American perception of NATO as a framework for the projection of allied power throughout and beyond Europe and the European perception of a wider NATO as a security framework for the European region itself. That ambiguity can only be resolved by a more coherent dialogue among the European members of NATO and between them and their American sponsor and partner.

The British Government's first response to the transformation of Central Europe and to the pressures from ex-socialist states to join the EU was to welcome the prospect of a Community which would become looser as it grew wider. It is now clear both that this widening Europe will be more diverse in its political and economic interests, and that in key areas more coherent common policies and policymaking capabilities will be required if the EU is successfully to manage its new responsibilities. The trade-offs between rich countries and poor, agricultural and industrial interests, will be much more complex. Greater skill and diplomacy will be needed to hold together the common interests of Finland, preoccupied with developments in Russia, of Greece preoccupied with Turkey and the eastern Mediterranean, of Spain and Portugal preoccupied with Morocco, the southern Atlantic and the Mahgreb. Above all, the weight which a wider EU will carry in international political and economic negotiations – most probably strengthened by the emergence of a common European currency – will necessitate a far more concerted approach to the American Administration and the US Congress than the EU has dreamed of so far.

Step by step, without looking too carefully where they are going, West European governments are moving towards the creation of a post-Cold War European order. The stakes are high. Success in integrating the former socialist states will extend the security community under which Western Europe has stabilised its democracies and fostered economic growth across the rest of the European region. Successful economic

transition within these states will also raise economic growth in Western Europe. The institutionalised order which will emerge will be one of the world's most important political and economic players. Failure to build efficient institutions for this wider Europe, or to integrate east-central and south-eastern Europe with their western neighbours, would marginalise the European region in a global economy increasingly oriented towards the Asia-Pacific, and leave the EU itself dependent on continued American benevolence for its security and political direction.

We have already come a long way. Underneath the frustrations of the Maastricht and Amsterdam treaties, the slow and hard-fought negotiations on Europe Agreements and pre-accession arrangements, the economies of central and eastern Europe have already turned round towards West European markets; several are now growing rapidly. Their governments have learned the new skills of multilateral negotiations; their political parties formed links with counterparts across the EU. Their military forces now regularly exercise with NATO partners, and their police forces benefit from Western exchanges and training. But the hardest is yet to come. An alliance designed for a world which we have happily lost, a Community created for six states huddled together in the heart of Western Europe, must be transformed to accommodate the diverse needs of a large group of countries shut off from the democratic world and its developing multilateral institutions for 40 years. That requires an alliance less dependent on American dynamism, an EU less preoccupied with the detail of economic and social integration and more willing to grapple with broader political issues.

What is needed is political leadership within Western Europe to convey to the public the scale of the changes needed and the long-term advantages to be won. That is the only way that resistance from entrenched interests will be overcome and established patterns of bureaucratic politics altered. The only Western leader who was willing to talk in strategic, even visionary, terms about the reshaping of Europe in the first nine months of 1997 was President Clinton, setting out the case for NATO enlargement in Madrid. West European publics will have to shoulder much of the burden of both NATO and EU enlargement as they move ahead; but it is also these who stand to gain most from their successful achievement. The challenge their governments face is to capture public imagination in support of an enterprise which is, after all, about the future security and prosperity of Europe as a whole. ☆

EU ENLARGEMENT:
COSTS & OPPORTUNITIES

BY DR HEATHER GRABBE AND DR KIRSTY HUGHES,
ROYAL INSTITUTE OF INTERNATIONAL AFFAIRS

Eastward enlargement is expected to bring a range of economic, political and security benefits to the European Union and to the Central and Eastern European (CEE) countries that have applied to join. A successful EU enlargement would be a major contribution to extending much further eastwards the zone of stability and security created in Western Europe since the Second World War, helping to heal divisions and making some amends for the post-War partition of Europe into spheres of influence. By providing a pan-European framework to encourage integration between East and West, the EU is already providing a central support for consolidating democracy and market reforms in the ten countries which have applied to join: Bulgaria, the Czech Republic, Estonia, Hungary, Latvia, Lithuania, Poland, Romania, Slovakia and Slovenia.

> *"Enlargement to encompass as many as 26 or more member states will entail fundamental changes to the nature and functioning of the EU"*

Joining the EU requires applicants to adapt their policies and institutions to take on the body of EU legislation (the *acquis communautaire*) and other requirements of membership. These are major challenges for countries undergoing simultaneous economic and political transition. In some areas transitional periods may be needed before they can meet EU standards, and there are concerns among member states that such arrangements should not distort the Single Market.

At the same time, enlargement to encompass as many as 26 or more member states will entail fundamental changes to the nature and functioning of the EU. The immediate impact of the first accessions will be felt primarily through their effect on policies and institutions. These two broad areas are increasingly a focus of debate within the current EU-15, and enlargement has the potential to exacerbate many of the tensions already present in the Union. Budgetary reform is particularly controversial, and a relatively swift solution to the challenges posed by new accessions is needed if fiscal concerns are not to cause a deliberate slowing of the enlargement process.

Negotiations with some and possibly all of the CEE applicants should start in early 1998 under the British Presidency of the Union. Predictions about when the first new members will join depend not only on the details of negotiations but also on other developments within and beyond the EU. Member states' attitudes to EU enlargement vary over how fast and how far enlargement should go. There are some key national preferences here: Denmark and Sweden are pressing hard for early EU membership for the Baltic states, for example, and Greece might veto the whole process if a divided Cyprus were not allowed to join. In addition, any delay in the launch of the EU's key project at present – the single currency – would be likely to affect enlargement because of the political crisis it would provoke.

THE ENLARGEMENT AGENDA
The EU set out general political and economic conditions for accession in 1993; these cover progress in post-communist transition and taking on the *acquis communautaire*, but they also include the Union's own capacity to absorb new member states. The four conditions are:

- Stability of institutions guaranteeing democracy, the rule of law, human rights and respect for and protection of minorities;

- The existence of a functioning market economy as well as the capacity to cope with competitive pressures and market forces within the Union;

- The ability to take on the obligations of membership, including adherence to the aims of political, economic and monetary union;

- The Union's capacity to absorb new members, while maintaining the momentum of European integration (European Council, June 1993).

In a report on enlargement, *Agenda 2000*, published in July 1997, the European Commission recommended that negotiations be opened with the Czech Republic, Estonia, Hungary, Poland and Slovenia, along with Cyprus, but even these six would not necessarily join at the same time and they are likely to accede with significant transitional periods and derogations. How rapidly the various applicants join depends not only on how quickly they can meet EU conditions but also on whether internal EU reforms fully address the needs of a much larger and more diverse Union.

Current trends already give grounds for some predictions concerning the sequencing and timing of accessions. Negotiations are likely to be fairly lengthy, given the much bigger economic and legal adjustments that even the front-runners face compared with the EFTA applicants. If negotiations took between four and six years, with another year for ratification, the first CEE countries would join between 2003 and 2005, assuming no delays owing to other developments. Earlier accession dates look highly optimistic given the complex process involved and the controversial nature of many of the issues surrounding enlargement.

In a positive scenario, the other applicants might join within five years of the first group, but a negative one might see this process take ten years or more. The overall process of eastward enlargement could thus last until 2010 or even 2015, assuming no major obstacles were encountered. By 2010, pressure could also have built up for yet wider expansion, both east to Ukraine and south to the remaining former Yugoslav countries and Albania.

THE IMPACT OF ENLARGEMENT ON EU POLICIES

East-West integration is expected to bring a range of economic and political benefits to both sides, but enlargement will also entail costs. The CEE countries will have to adopt a more complex *acquis communautaire* much more quickly than previous applicants. On the EU side, aid and assistance will have to be stepped up to help new members reach Single Market and other standards, and EU policies will have to be reformed to cover poorer and more numerous member states.

On joining the EU, new members will become eligible for transfers from the two main EU policies – the Common Agricultural Policy (CAP) and the regional aid funds, which together account for around 80% of the Community budget. Extending the CAP and regional funds in their present form even just to the most advanced CEE countries would require a politically unacceptable increase in the size of the Community budget. In absorbing all eleven current candidates, the EU would add 28% to its population but only 4% (at current levels) to its GDP. Moreover, average per capita GDP in the ten CEE countries is only one-eighth of the average EU level and their economies are more agricultural than EU members', so they would qualify for major transfers under the current policies. Poland is the most problematic applicant in this respect, having a population of nearly 39 million and a large agricultural sector.

However, there is no appetite among member states at present for transfers to the CEE applicants on the scale provided to the Mediterranean countries when they joined. Given the pressures on national public finances, the large member states do not want to increase their contributions to the Community budget, and several member states are particularly keen to see reform of the CAP.

The key to finding an acceptable solution to the policy challenges raised by CEE accessions is an overall deal on the future of the budget which ensures the support of all EU member states for enlargement. After all, every member state will have a veto over the accession treaties and every legislature will have to ratify them, so there are numerous opportunities for budgetary lobbies to disrupt the process.

There are essentially three competing pressures on the process of budgetary reform:

- *Maintaining budget discipline*. In the climate of fiscal austerity created by the EMU convergence criteria, the main net contributors are determined to ensure that the budget remains within its current ceiling as a percentage of EU GNP; indeed, Germany and the Netherlands are also demanding a reduction in their current contributions, while the UK wants to retain its rebate.

- *Reassuring current beneficiaries*. The net recipients of the structural and cohesion funds, led by Spain, along with farmers across the EU, could try to block the accessions if major cuts in transfers are threatened. Even Ireland, which is widely expected to graduate out of the Cohesion Fund owing to its economic success, has argued that this should only be a gradual process.

- *Ensuring that the CEE countries are not made second-class members of the EU* by being excluded from its central policies. The principle of equal treatment between member states is a central feature of EU membership; imposing very long transitional conditions on the CEE countries would create a multi-tier EU lasting at least into the medium term.

The first requirement is related to the second because several of the large net contributors also face strong domestic lobbying to continue support to their farmers or to particular

"Under the Commission's growth assumptions, the ten CEE applicants would receive just over a tenth of the budget over the next financial perspective, which amounts to a thousandth of EU GDP. A thousandth of EU GDP seems a very small price to pay for stabilising the region on our Eastern border and turning a former threat into substantial market opportunities"

regions. The political pressures on Germany and Italy are particularly problematic in this respect; the Mezzogiorno receives significant transfers from the EU budget that Rome does not want to see reduced. Germany is in the even more paradoxical position of wanting to reduce its budget contribution but also to limit reforms because Bonn is under pressure from regional governments to resist cuts in payments to farmers and to maintain regional aids, especially to the eastern länder. Farming lobbies across the EU have much greater political clout than their importance in GDP and employment might seem to warrant. These cross-cutting issues complicate member states' negotiating positions on the budget.

HOW TO REFORM THE BUDGET?

The Commission aimed to square this circle by proposing that the budget to run from 2000-2006 should keep to the 1999 expenditure ceiling of 1.27% of EU GNP, but assuming that economic expansion would allow the absolute size of the budget to increase. Assuming economic growth of 2.5% for the EU and 4% for the CEE countries, the Commission calculates that by 2006 there will be slightly more than 20 billion ECU (at 1997 prices) in additional resources available. The Commission also assumes that the first round of accession will not occur before 2002, and then the new members will have transitional arrangements (especially for extending the CAP), so the increase in expenditure for them will be gradual.

This framework allows the Commission to pencil in an absolute increase in expenditure on the CAP and a small reduction in regional aid for the EU-15, as well as an allocation of around 75 billion ECU for the applicant countries. The current member states would thus see an overall increase in net receipts from the budget from 2000-2006, although expenditure on some policies would be reduced. Despite some accessions occurring during this period, net contributors would be able to keep the 1.27% ceiling sacrosanct. The Commission proposes maintaining the current system for financing the budget over the next financial perspective, with a fundamental reform of the arrangements if and when the EU required an increase in the overall ceiling.

POLICY OPTIONS FOR THE CAP AND REGIONAL FUNDS

The Commission proposes incremental but eventually fundamental policy reform. Recipients would be weaned off their transfers very slowly, with reform stretching beyond 2006 into the next financial perspective.

Historically a core policy, the CAP retains a political significance well beyond the role of agriculture in the EU economy and has survived successive attempts at reform. Extending the CAP in its present form to new members with larger and more inefficient agricultural sectors would have major financial implications, although estimates vary because of uncertainties about potential agricultural output in CEE. Poland and Romania have the largest agricultural sectors at present and would qualify for major transfers, and on average agriculture is considerably more important as a proportion of employment and GDP in CEE than the current EU.

The CAP is also under pressure as a result of concern about the effects of subsidising intensive agriculture and the likely demands of the next round of WTO multilateral negotiations on agricultural trade due in 1999. Moreover, the priorities of the CAP are not directed towards the needs of economies in transition, having been formulated for the current EU members. It is clear that investment in CEE agriculture is needed to make it more efficient and competitive, particularly in food-processing, but the CAP is not geared to meet these needs at present. In particular, the market distortions necessitated by the CAP regime run counter to the general thrust of liberalisation undertaken by post-communist countries trying to create market economies.

The Commission's approach to the CAP, as outlined in *Agenda 2000*, is to continue the general thrust of the 1992 MacSharry reforms by reducing guaranteed prices and export subsidies, while increasing direct aid to farmers and decoupling it from production volume. Aid would thus be focused on increasing farmers' incomes, but without encouraging them to produce more, and the market distortions created by price-fixing would be reduced. There would also be additional funds available for new rural development measures and fisheries. These proposals are already generating controversy between member states, with public criticism of them from Germany and broad support from the UK.

Regional aid comes from the structural funds, which apply to all 15 member states, and the cohesion fund, which covers the four poorest current members (Greece, Ireland, Portugal and Spain). Under the current rules, new CEE members would divert key funds from major recipients because they are much poorer. The regional aid funds are also due to be reformed regardless of enlargement; there is particular concern about their effectiveness (in reducing economic disparities across the EU) in addition to problems of account-ability and corruption.

The Commission proposes that the structural funds be reformed to focus on a smaller proportion of the EU's population (around 35% instead of the current 50%) and on a lesser number of objectives, but most of the money would still go to existing member states rather than new members. There would be a slight overall cut in expenditure for the EU-15 countries, although it is unclear as yet where exactly the axe would fall within the objectives of the structural funds. However, EU-15 regions would also get new rural development accompanying measures under the CAP budget. Moreover, eligibility for the Cohesion Fund would not be reviewed until 2003, with a total allocation of 20 billion ECU for the whole period. These proposals would prevent any current net recipient of regional aid from being cut off from the funds immediately. However, cuts in expenditure are strongly opposed by the recipients of the Cohesion Fund and they are controversial within other member states; in the UK, for example, moves towards greater devolution could rally regions against cuts in transfers from the EU budget.

Will the proposed compromise satisfy all the interests in the current EU? The outcome depends on several factors. The first is how the *distribution* of transfers changes; the next financial perspective will see the start of major reforms in the way the CAP and regional aid funds operate, some of which will be strongly opposed by current recipients. Secondly, there is the question of whether the Commission's assumptions will be realised, particularly those on economic growth and the effec-tive operation of new policy structures. If economic growth is slower than expected or additional expenditure needs arise, the margin for manoeuvre will be correspondingly reduced.

Finally, there is the question of what policy reforms can be agreed by all the member states. Net recipients and contributors are already arguing that the others should pay more for enlarge-ment: for example, Northern member states are likely to argue that the proportion of the budget taken by the structural funds is too high, while some of the Southern ones want an overall increase in the size of the budget as a proportion of EU GNP.

WHAT ABOUT THE CEE COUNTRIES?
Under the Commission's growth assumptions, the ten CEE applicants would receive just over a tenth of the budget over the next financial perspective, which amounts to a thousandth of EU GDP. Between 2002 and 2006, the CEE-10 would receive 75 billion ECU; of this total, those countries that become members will gain access to CAP and regional aid transfers on accession amounting to 54 billion ECU (three-quarters of the total). In the pre-accession phase, the five front-runners would get 2.4 billion ECU for 2000-2001, consisting of funds from Phare, the structural funds and agricultural support.

All structural funds transfers will be subject to a limit of 4% of GDP, with the perverse effect that the richer CEE countries will receive more than the poorer ones. In addition, the new members will gain additional structural funds only as their economies grow larger, resulting in transfers increasing as their needs are actually decreasing, rather than the other way around. This means that in 2006 the CEE members will be receiving about half the amount per head going to Greece and Portugal, even though they are much poorer.

Over the entire budgetary period, the five who would remain outside the EU would receive a quarter of the budget allocation to the CEE-10 in pre-accession aid. Although the Commission proposes transferring the extra pre-accession funds to the other five once the front-runners have become members, the five backmarkers will be receiving substantially less than the new member states, threatening to open up increasing divisions between the two groups. Some current EU member states are also likely to oppose giving the five back-markers these additional pre-accession funds. Even by 2006, the ten applicants together will only account for 16% of the EU budget and the five backmarkers will account for 2.6%, a fraction of the amount received by the current members.

CONCLUSION
The accession of eleven relatively poor countries, even in a series of smaller accessions with long transitional periods, will inevitably affect both Community finances and the way the Union works, although not necessarily all at once. The fact that enlargement might be spread over a period of ten to twenty years or more, starting at the earliest in 2002, means that reforms on the EU side are likely to occur in stages rather than in one major move. The Commission's proposals are sufficient to get the enlargement process going, but not enough to complete the reforms within the next financial perspective. The EU will have to return to the question of budgetary reform at least once (in 2006), and the whole process will take over a decade to complete. A major concern about this gradual process of adjustment is whether a proper strategic assessment of desirable changes will be made, and whether the outcomes for institutions and policies will be coherent and effective.

The potential for the enlargement process to be seriously disrupted by disagreements between member states over budgetary, policy and institutional reform is still high. The CEE applicants are highly unlikely to receive transfers on anything like the scale of those to the Mediterranean members and Ireland, although there could be a substantial increase in comparison with current levels of assistance. Reforms are likely to reduce transfers to current recipients only gradually, and the CEE applicants will see only a very slow increase in the funds they receive, despite their very different stage of economic development. A thousandth of EU GDP seems a very small price to pay for stabilising the region on our Eastern border and turning a former threat into substantial market opportunities. Even this allocation will be controversial, yet the conclusion has to be that the EU is attempting to achieve a major historical step with remarkably low expenditure. ☆

GE Capital Services
Our Business Is Helping Yours®

PARTNERSHIPS FOR THE MILLENNIUM

GE Capital Services is one of the most successful and fastest-growing financial services companies operating in Europe.

Over the past ten years, GE Capital has achieved an average growth in profits of more than 20% a year, contributing 38% of our parent, GE's $7.28 billion net income in 1996. Our assets total over $227 billion world-wide.

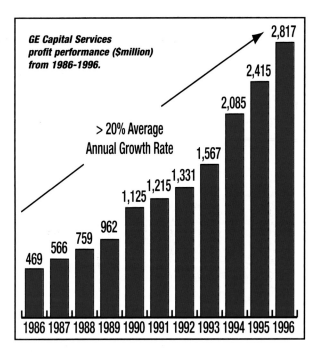

GE Capital Services profit performance ($million) from 1986-1996.

> 20% Average Annual Growth Rate

469, 566, 759, 962, 1,125, 1,215, 1,331, 1,567, 2,085, 2,415, 2,817

1986 1987 1988 1989 1990 1991 1992 1993 1994 1995 1996

With our financial strength, our recognised expertise in specialised financial services and our absolute commitment to integrity, GE Capital is fast becoming the first choice for European companies for whom success depends on working with a reliable and innovative partner.

COMPREHENSIVE SOLUTIONS TO BUILD OUR CUSTOMERS' COMPETITIVE EDGE

We set out to deliver creative solutions to your financing, leasing and servicing needs. We help you increase your productivity and efficiency by increasing your financing and operating flexibility.

GE Capital has 20 businesses operating in Europe.

CONSUMER SERVICES
• Auto Financing
• Consumer Savings & Insurance Group
• Global Consumer Finance

EQUIPMENT MANAGEMENT
• Commercial Air Leasing
• Computer Services
• Container Leasing
• Fleet Leasing
• Modular Structure Leasing
• Railcar Services
• Satellite Leasing
• Trailer Leasing

MID-MARKET FINANCING
• European Equipment Finance

SPECIALISED FINANCING
• Commercial Finance
• Commercial Real Estate
• Equity Group
• Structured Finance

SPECIALITY INSURANCE
• Credit Insurance
• Employers Reinsurance
• Mortgage Insurance
• Municipal Bond Insurance

COMPETITIVE EDGE

Since 1990, GE Capital has developed hundreds of long-term European partnerships in businesses ranging from consumer services and equipment management to insurance and commercial real estate.

We have given our partners a competitive edge by enabling them to provide their customers with greater value. For example, a major electrical goods retailer saw the frequency and value of repeat sales improve dramatically when we became their partner. We provided them with a credit product which uses an integrated point of sale platform for rapid credit authorisation. It also provides a multi-charge account feature to facilitate repeat transactions.

GE Capital Europe: flying the flags of opportunity.

> "
> **WE ARE HUGELY EXCITED ABOUT THE PROSPECTS FOR EUROPE. GE CAPITAL IS COMMITTED TO PROVIDING THE RESOURCES AND TECHNOLOGY NECESSARY TO SUPPORT OUR BUSINESS PARTNERS' GROWTH AND PROSPERITY.**
>
> **Christopher Mackenzie, President of GE Capital Europe.**
> "

LOOKING TO THE FUTURE

Deregulation and increasing liberalisation, coupled with a growing trend towards consolidation is presenting almost every business in Europe with new objectives and new challenges.

Through our already extensive European presence, our recognised financial strength and our comprehensive service offering, GE Capital is uniquely poised to help businesses take advantage of these extraordinary changes.

To find out how GE Capital could help your company, please call Christopher Mackenzie on + 44 (0) 171 302 6125.

LET'S LOOK AHEAD IN PARTNERSHIP

GE Capital Services
Our Business Is Helping Yours®

*"The Community was built to ensure
that never again would the countries of
Europe carry their differences to the
point where they inflicted such misery
on their own peoples and on the world"*

MAKING EUROPE SAFER:
FOREIGN POLICY & DEFENCE

BY THE RT. HON. LORD HURD OF WESTWELL, FORMER FOREIGN SECRETARY

The central purpose of the European Community, now the European Union, has always been political rather than economic. The impulse which led Jean Monnet and the other founding fathers through so many obstacles to found the Community was derived from the misery of two world wars started in Europe. The Community was built to ensure that never again would the countries of Europe carry their differences to the point where they inflicted such misery on their own peoples and on the world. But this passive or defensive purpose soon carried with it something more positive: the desire that eventually the members of the Community would speak with one voice in foreign affairs so that their united voice could carry more weight than the sum of their individual and divergent opinions. Allied to this, but more ambitious, was the aim of eventually including defence in the list of policies which were organised in common.

Progress has been slow but more substantial than is often supposed. The difficulties arise, in this as in other fields, not out of bloody-minded reluctance on the part of this nation or that, but from genuine differences of character and outlook among the member states. Britain and France, as former imperial powers, still have interests and anxieties across the world and a tradition of active foreign policy. They are both permanent members of the Security Council and neither has any intention of giving up that position or handing it over to a central European organisation. Until 1973 all members of the Community were also members of NATO. But in 1973 neutral Ireland was admitted and has now been joined by neutral Austria, Sweden and Finland. The neutrality of each of these countries has a different flavour, and they have all been active members of the UN and pioneers of international peace-keeping. But their approach to foreign policy has inevitably been at the other end of the spectrum from Britain and France. Germany has held a special position because of her own recent history – emotionally involved in international affairs, but until recently feeling reticent about anything like a forward foreign policy possibly involving the commitment of armed forces.

These historical differences are slowly becoming less important, with the result that it is steadily becoming easier and more normal for the Europe of 15 countries to agree on particular foreign policy positions. The next round of enlargement of the Union will bring in yet another foreign policy flavour, derived from the historical anxieties of (at least) Poland, Hungary and the Czechs. The new entrants will once again expect their anxieties and sympathies to be taken into account, but there need be nothing here to prevent the gradual growth of the habit of co-operation in Europe on foreign affairs. Co-operation is still the relevant word. This process was indeed called "political co-operation" when I first became familiar with it in the early Eighties, before Maastricht. The Treaty of Maastricht, which came into being after much travail at the beginning of 1993, put the process of consultation and agreement on foreign policy onto a legal basis.

But this part of the Treaty was not particularly controversial. The process remained inter-governmental – that is it depended on agreement between governments. The Commission is present at these discussions, as is entirely sensible, because the Commission under the Treaties speaks on behalf of us all in matters of trade. Trade and diplomacy are closely intertwined. It is the Commission, for example, which has to carry out on behalf of us all any decision to implement sanctions against a third country. But in matters of foreign policy the Commission does not have, as it does on economic matters, the sole right to make proposals, the so-called monopoly of initiative. Nor in foreign policy matters does the European Court have any jurisdiction, and the role of the European Parliament is strictly limited. The negotiators at Maastricht drew this line between on the one hand intergovernmental co-operation in foreign policy with each country essentially having a veto, and on the other hand integration on the economic matters covered by the Treaty of Rome, with wider use of majority voting, the Commission's monopoly initiative, the jurisdiction of the European Court and greater powers for the European Parliament. We made this distinction at Maastricht precisely because we, and in particular Britain and France, were not willing to yield to Community institutions our ultimate power of deciding our own policies.

Maastricht put the process on a statutory basis but did not, in my experience, greatly alter what happened. There is a genuine effort at meetings of European foreign ministers to reach agreement on common positions in foreign policy. Usually this effort is successful. The world tends to notice the disagreements and neglect the agreements. It would have been inconceivable twenty years ago to imagine the fifteen countries of the Union agreeing and carrying through, as we have, a policy towards Iran, or a policy towards human rights abuses in Myanmar (formerly Burma), or achieving the co-ordination and harmonised voting among European countries which is now the rule rather than the exception at the United Nations.

Nevertheless this slow progress has been greeted with impatience and dismay. The example chosen by the critics is almost always the former Yugoslavia, and in particular Bosnia. Here, on the edge of Europe, war broke out first in Croatia then in Bosnia, and terrible atrocities were committed. It took four years and in the end vigorous American leadership before the fighting could be ended. It is widely argued that divisions within the EU prevented Europe from effective intervention to bring about peace with justice in the former Yugoslavia. The story is encrusted with many myths, of which this is one.

The problem was not essentially one of division among the member states of the EU. We discussed Bosnia endlessly. There was one celebrated argument in December 1991 over the recognition of Croatia and Slovenia, but this was a difference of opinion about timing and procedure, not principle. For the rest, at meeting after meeting, we were not divided, but united in frustration. We had allowed the test of our own success to become our ability to settle a dispute outside our frontiers. It is not normally regarded as reasonable to test the success of a marriage by the ability of the partners to settle a dispute in the house next door. It was foolish at the outset for some European ministers to describe the Yugoslav crisis as an opportunity for Europe to show its mettle. We were not masters of events in the former Yugoslavia, nor could we have mastered events without a degree of intervention which nobody in Europe or the United States contemplated. We were none of us prepared to march into Bosnia, take it over and compel Bosnian Serbs, Bosnian Croats and Bosnian Muslims to live together under rules which we had devised. Failing that semi-imperial approach, European intervention was limited. It included substantial aid, a considerable peace-keeping intervention under the UN, sanctions against the government in Belgrade and ceaseless efforts to bring the parties to the negotiating table. We were none of us satisfied with the results of these efforts or with the fact that the fighting only stopped in 1995

after the parties were exhausted and the Americans had decided to take the lead in bringing the parties to the negotiating table.

The mis-reading of the Bosnian experience has, in my view, led the argument about a Common Foreign & Security Policy astray. Too much time is spent on matters of procedure. It is argued, particularly in Germany, that a greater degree of majority voting in these matters might have saved Bosnia. I believe that this emphasis on procedure has postponed the tackling of the real problem. From my experience I see no magic in majority voting. The two other successful international organisations which most closely influence the countries of Europe are NATO and the new World Trade Organisation. Both function successfully with unanimous voting. Noone suggests there that majority voting is needed. In the EU I cannot recall any substantial proposal by a member state in the Bosnian crisis which was blocked by a minority in the Council of Ministers.

There was, however, one side issue which is relevant to this argument. Most of us thought that the Greeks behaved unreasonably to their new neighbour, the Republic of Macedonia, formerly part of Yugoslavia. They persistently prevented the EU from giving effective help to the new country because of arguments between Greece and Macedonia over the name of Macedonia, the flag and a host of other matters. Had majority rule been in place we could have outvoted the Greeks on these matters long before they were in fact resolved. Would that have helped? The test is not a vote in the Council of Ministers but the effectiveness of the policy. The Greek stance had at the time the support of the overwhelming majority of Greeks, regardless of party. If we had outvoted the Greeks, they would not have complied. No Greek government at that time could have accepted our verdict and survived. We would have added a Greek problem to the Macedonian problem. Eventually the Greeks realised that they were on the wrong track and relaxed their stance.

The outcome of the Treaty of Amsterdam in 1997 shows that this particular procedural debate has not been carried much further. The rules have become more complicated. There is a somewhat greater provision for majority voting when policies which have been unanimously agreed come to be implemented. But, in the words of the House of Commons research paper on the Treaty, "It could be said that the Amsterdam Treaty is unlikely to promote the greater use of qualified majority voting in any controversial circumstances. The most it may do is to force governments which wish to block EU action in a particular area to state their reasons more openly and to be prepared to argue their case at the Summit level".

But the Treaty of Amsterdam does mark an advance in remedying another defect of the present system. Foreign policy decisions in member states depend on adequate intelligence and staff work to present ministers with an adequate analysis of the options. The European process has, by contrast, been somewhat shallow. Discussion has quite often been fleeting and ill-prepared. Nor when decisions have been agreed have there been adequate means for carrying them out. The Presidency of the Council of Ministers rotates every six months. The country which holds the Presidency is helped under the so-called Troika arrangement by its immediate predecessor and its successor, so that three foreign ministers can be available to attend wider international meetings and express the European view. This has often been an unimpressive arrangement. The Treaty of Amsterdam, following proposals made separately some time ago by both Britain and France, would set up a new policy planning and early warning unit, which would prepare policy options for Council meetings. More important, there would henceforward be a "high representative", a permanent official who would help the Presidency to formulate, prepare and carry out policy decisions. Despite this title this high representative will not be a giant "Mr Europe" overriding the views of democratically elected ministers. But he should provide a continuous strength which would give member states and our friends outside Europe, particularly the Americans, greater confidence in this European process.

What is needed now is less pecking away at procedure and more concentration on substance. The member states will not be able to agree on every foreign policy subject, but that is no reason for failing to work together effectively where agreement can be reached on almost all the main challenges to European security which one can foresee in coming decades. As regards Russia, I can see no argument against a European policy much more emphatically concerted and proclaimed than hitherto. The companies of Europe will compete fiercely in the Russian market, but that is a different question. There is no sense in trying to differentiate the diplomatic position of France, Britain or Germany towards Russia. None of us is going to make headway in Moscow with a policy of which the others disapprove. If we want to carry weight in the relationship with Russia we need to decide, speak and act as Europeans.

This is particularly important in our dealings with the United States. There was a time when Europeans were attracted by the Gaullist view of a Europe set up over and against the United States as a rival centre of power. That concept makes no sense today. Our danger is not that the Americans will turn imperialist or exercise overweening power. Our danger is that they will fluctuate, lose interest from time to time in difficult subjects, become weary of the burden of world leadership. It is overwhelmingly in the interest of all Europeans that the United States should not become weary. We need to establish ourselves as a valid partner, neither rival nor satellite, but an effective friend to whom they should listen and on whom they can rely.

If on foreign policy the doctrinal differences have been acute, on defence they have desperately frustrating. Most members of the EU belong to NATO, and NATO is a success story. That success depends in part on the huge investment which NATO has made in infrastructure, communications and the organisation of commands. Even the most resolute Gaullist now realises that it would be out of the question for Europe to try to duplicate this investment simply in order to provide Europe with a distinctive defence pedestal. On the other hand there has throughout been a strong feeling on the Continent that the European voice inside NATO should be more coherent and that Europe should be able to act outside the NATO context, should it find this necessary. In the Treaty of Maastricht we negotiated a somewhat untidy compromise based on the organisation of the Western European Union. This was originally founded at British initiative to fill the gap created by the collapse of the project for a European Defence when the French refused to ratify that Treaty in 1954.

The WEU is a separate organisation from the EU but the Treaty of Maastricht tied them together with untidy pieces of string. The proposal that the EU and the WEU should merge was resisted by both the Conservative and Labour British governments, supported in this instance by the neutral states. The Treaty of Amsterdam represents a further compromise. The possibility of eventual merger between the EU and WEU is mentioned, but also for the first time the importance of NATO is underlined in a purely European Treaty. I hope that this doctrinal argument has just about run its course. Fortunately inside NATO an arrangement has been negotiated which should supply what Europe needs. This is the so-called Combined Joint Task Force arrangement by which the WEU, acting at the request of the EU at Summit level, would be able to borrow NATO assets for specifically European tasks. Such tasks will probably fall within the scope already agreed in the WEU Petersberg Declaration, described in the Treaty of Amsterdam as "humanitarian and rescue tasks, peace-keeping tasks and tasks of forces in crisis management including peace- keeping". This clumsy compromise language clearly reflects a continuing difference of opinion. But the essential point is clear: there might from time to time be efforts, certainly on a limited scale, which the Europeans might wish to undertake as Europeans but in which the Americans and Canadians might not want to join. There is now provision for the Europeans to use assets which they have pledged to NATO for these purposes. In practice this would involve American acquiescence, though not American participation. It is somewhat cold-blooded to suggest that what is now needed is a not too serious crisis in which this agreement can be tested in practice. But at least we should have come towards the end of a prolonged and sometimes bitter theological dispute.

The arguments set out above may seem dry as dust and the progress imperceptible. Certainly the ratio between talk and action in these matters has been too high. There is a danger that the multitude of meetings and communiqués conceals the real progress which has been made. On all important external matters the interests of European countries are similar, on many of them identical. We should not spend too much time fussing about points which divide us, or trying evidently to refine our procedures. We should focus on substance so that Europe can make a worthy contribution to the continuing search for peace. ☆

"... *for many people who have never had dealings with
the Commission, the immediate response is an undefined
suspicion about an 'interfering bureaucracy', fed over the years
by a largely Eurosceptic media. This used to be characterised
by the flood of 'Euromyths' – such as the 'banning' of the bent
banana or the double-decker bus – which owed more to journalists' imagination than to their research skills"*

THE EUROPEAN COMMISSION: WHY WE NEED IT

BY GEOFFREY MARTIN, HEAD OF THE EUROPEAN COMMISSION REPRESENTATION IN THE UNITED KINGDOM

The European Union now touches the lives of people in the United Kingdom in many ways. Businessmen trade with their European partners, farmers work within an EU-wide marketplace, students and researchers travel throughout Europe to study side by side with their colleagues in other member states. But despite this everyday familiarity, the EU – and especially its institutions – remains much misunderstood within the UK.

This is particularly true of the European Commission, which for years has been demonised by much of the press as the bogeyman of Europe. It has been portrayed as a remote, foreign, faceless body churning out thousands of unwanted rules and regulations. For many people, that image – rules about square strawberries and bent bananas – has been their only experience of the Commission. Some have imagined it to be the engine behind the creation of some Euro-superstate, harmonising everything in its path and smothering national characteristics.

Despite the apparent doubts of some Eurosceptics, the Commission not only has a legitimate role in the UK, it has responsibilities and commitments which mean it would be failing in its duty if it stood aside.

THE ROLE OF THE COMMISSION
The Commission has three key roles in the EU: first, as "guardian of the Treaties", making sure that the Treaties and laws governing the EU are properly applied; second, proposing legislation to be put forward to the EU member states and the European Parliament; and third, as the administration implementing many EU policies. In all three cases, the Commission inevitably has a role in the UK. With the spotlight firmly on the EU, the UK Presidency of the EU will provide an excellent opportunity for more people to become aware of the role of the Commission and of the daily reality of its work in the UK.

The Commission as honest broker
The reality of international co-operation is that, however good the intentions of participants, some mechanism is needed to ensure "fair play". In the EU, the Commission is the catalyst of that mechanism, with the responsibility to blow the whistle when member states appear not to be applying laws properly. The headlines tend to be dominated by the occasions when the Commission believes that the UK is not keeping to the rules. But these occasions are far outweighed by the times when the Commission has championed the cause of British interests wanting to exercise their rights in other member states. British luxury cars in Italy, British airline companies in Portugal, British soft drinks in Greece, even British ski instructors in France have all been helped by the Commission to reap the benefits of the Single Market when member states have not been applying rules properly. Some may sniff that these are only small examples, but they are also practical examples, helping people in their everyday lives.

The job of the Commission is not to frustrate member states or to interfere unnecessarily, but to ensure the fair application of the rules. Only 4% of the possible infringements identified by the Commission in 1996 concerned the UK; conversely, much of the Commission's work as the EU's policeman is in the UK's favour. This does not mean Commission officials flooding into the UK with clipboards and rule books to make sure the rules are being kept: it is national civil servants who

We're into breaking barriers!

Thrust SSC uses composites and structural adhesives from Cytec Fiberite.

CYTEC

www.cytec.com

"The Commission's push to open up public works contracts, break down cartels and cap state aids in the Single Market clearly brings the greatest benefits to those prepared to look for economic opportunities beyond national boundaries"

administer most EU policies. British officials from the Ministry of Agriculture, Fisheries and Food run the Common Agricultural Policy in the UK and British customs officials collect customs dues on behalf of the EU. The relatively rare exceptions are cases where it has been agreed that direct intervention by Commission officials is the best way to demonstrate fairness – such as in the application of competition rules – or where they sometimes come to Britain to work side by side with UK officials, such as police or customs tackling suspected cases of fraud.

Opening markets in Europe and abroad
There are many areas where the UK in particular has benefited from Commission policy. The Commission has made no secret in recent years that free market principles are the bedrock of much of its work. The Commission's push to open up public works contracts, break down cartels and cap state aids in the Single Market clearly brings the greatest benefits to those prepared to look for economic opportunities beyond national boundaries – and UK companies have always been in the front line of those looking to profit. Some of the Commission's work in pushing towards a fully-functioning Single Market in areas such as telecoms have clearly drawn on the successful experience of liberalisation in the UK.

Beyond the EU, as well, the Commission has a special responsibility. It is the voice of the EU in international trade negotiations, and in recent years has put particular weight on its role in prising open overseas markets to the benefit of EU exporters. The Commission's ability to use the EU's economic weight to open markets worldwide has brought particular benefits to economic operators in the UK – when the Commission led the way in brokering a deal on financial services in the World Trade Organisation, it was the financial services companies of the City of London which stood most obviously to gain. These are the "big" examples of the way the Commission works – achievements which could rarely be brought about by countries acting on their own.

This role for the Commission may not grab the headlines as easily as stories of "Britain versus Brussels", but its influence on the UK in terms of jobs and prosperity has been and will continue to be profound.

MYTHS AND REALITIES

Perceptions of the European Commission in the UK vary widely. Many of those who have had close contact recognise the essential role the Commission can play. Some will pay public tribute to the Commission's work: industries which

have reaped the benefits, such as the Scotch whisky industry, now able to compete fairly in East Asian markets; or local authorities from Plymouth to Inverness, from Belfast to Newcastle, who have seen the part played by the Commission in ensuring that EU regional and social funds have a real impact on local regeneration.

But, for many people who have never had dealings with the Commission, the immediate response is an undefined suspicion about an "interfering bureaucracy", fed over the years by a largely Eurosceptic media. This used to be characterised by the flood of "Euromyths" – such as the "banning" of the bent banana or the double-decker bus – which owed more to journalists' imagination than to their research skills. Partly as a result of a prolonged campaign by Commission staff of pressing papers to justify their stories, such myths now appear relatively rarely. But many news stories are still distorted by an editorial slant inspired by Euroscepticism.

A Nationwide Information Network
The Commission works hard to provide information about its work, about the EU and its policies, and about its importance for the UK. This task was the job of the European Commission's Representation in the UK, based in London, with supporting Representations in Belfast, Cardiff and Edinburgh, but two important factors led to a fresh approach: first, the sheer weight of interest in European issues from the media, business, universities, local authorities, trade unions and the public at large; and second, a recognition that EU issues have become so enmeshed in the daily life of the member states that ring-fencing them from domestic matters no longer made sense. As a result, the Commission is increasingly looking to a partnership with UK government departments in providing information. It should not be the sole responsibility of the EC to keep the public informed about what is going on in the EU and about the benefits which flow from membership.

Additionally, and very importantly, there is now a devolved system for providing information across the whole country via a nationwide network of European relays. These include:

✦ 45 European Documentation Centres in university libraries across the UK, with up-to-date documents and databases;

✦ 21 European Information Centres for the business community, providing business intelligence on areas including European law and tender opportunities;

✦ Six rural "carrefours", or information points, with a focus on providing information for the rural community;

✦ 164 Public Information Relays in major public libraries.

This means a network of some 300 points in the UK regularly receiving EU information, both printed documents and on-line. In addition, more than 3,000 public libraries are now in

"Some will give public tribute to the Commission's work: industries which have reaped the benefits, such as the Scotch whisky industry, now able to compete fairly in East Asian markets; or local authorities from Plymouth to Inverness, from Belfast to Newcastle, who have seen the part played by the Commission in ensuring that EU regional and social funds have a real impact on local regeneration"

a position to meet some of the huge demand for information. The UK is the pioneer of this approach, and it is now planned that similar networks should be established in every EU member state.

A specific demand which has multiplied in recent years has been the call from schools and colleges for information about the EU as an essential part of the curriculum. To meet this demand, ten regional centres have been established to provide teachers and their pupils with information.

This effort is not just a response to curiosity about the EU; it is also a mechanism to help people in the UK have a real input into European policy-making. Increasingly, the Commission has been moving to a system of pre-legislative White and Green Papers on key policy areas, so that particular interests can be heard and taken into account at an early stage in the process. Of course, the Council of Ministers, the European Parliament and the other institutions remain the primary forum for interests from the member states to be articulated; but signalling particular issues "upstream" in the legislative process can be of great help to the Commission in drafting proposals in the first place. The network of European relays gives members of the public a chance to gain access to these documents and to make comments.

IMPROVING COMMUNICATION WITH BRUSSELS

It is not only the information role of the Commission

which has changed in recent years. To do its work properly, the Commission in Brussels needs to be aware of what is happening in the member states. Therefore the Representations in member states have gradually taken on a political role similar to that of a national embassy. This enables policy makers in Brussels to understand more about the interests of the member states, and member states' concerns or interests can be relayed to Brussels more effectively. Equally, the Representations are increasingly on hand to explain or clarify thinking in Brussels to government in the UK. The UK Presidency will be a good opportunity to illustrate the value of maximising the opportunities to make sure that the UK and Brussels are kept properly in touch. It can only be in the interests of good governance in the EU to have an effective channel of communication working in this way.

As a result, the Representation in London maintains close links with Parliament, political parties, government departments, business organisations, trade unions, local authorities, embassies of other member states, the media – in short, the body of opinion formers and policymakers in the UK. The Representations in Belfast, Cardiff and Edinburgh do the same job in Northern Ireland, Scotland and Wales.

The reality of UK politics over recent years has meant that this role has developed gradually and sensitively. The job of the Representation is not to act as proselytisers for European integration – that is properly the work of outside pressure groups. But as the Commission is often drawn into the political arguments about Europe in the UK, it has a responsibility to explain the case where necessary. It would be doing no favours to the debate about Europe in the UK for the Commission to stand aside. The Commission will continue to pursue its responsibility to develop an active role within the UK as in all member states, playing to the full its part in the public life of the United Kingdom. ☆

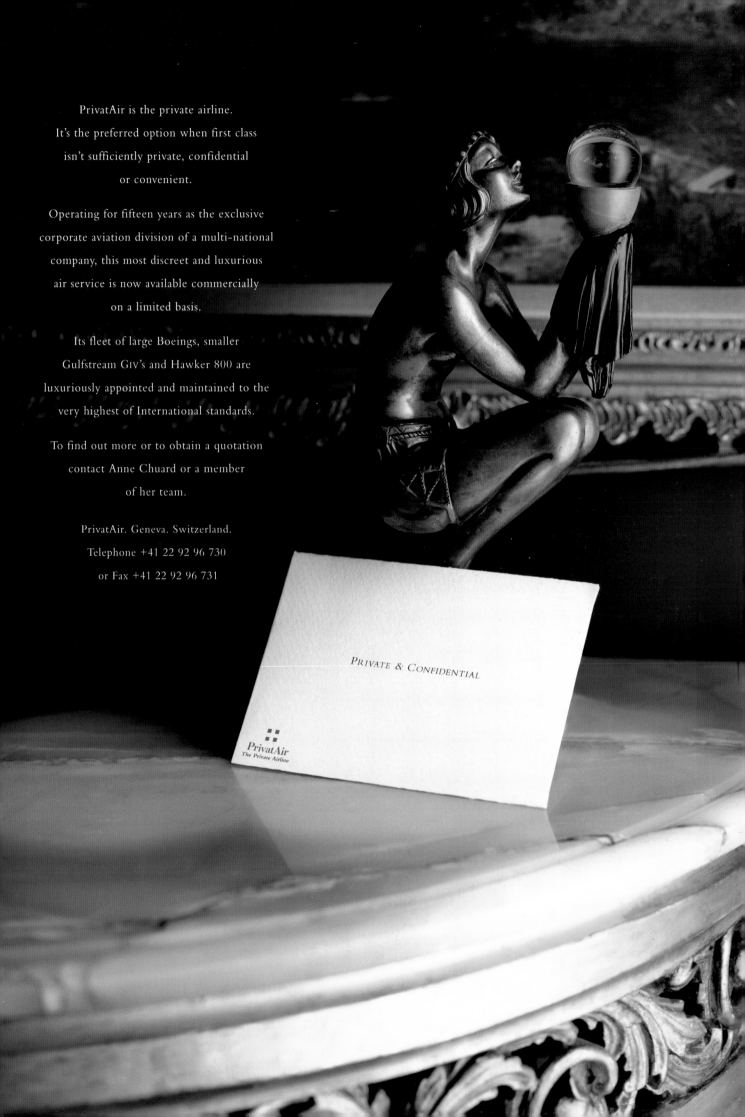

PrivatAir is the private airline.
It's the preferred option when first class
isn't sufficiently private, confidential
or convenient.

Operating for fifteen years as the exclusive
corporate aviation division of a multi-national
company, this most discreet and luxurious
air service is now available commercially
on a limited basis.

Its fleet of large Boeings, smaller
Gulfstream GIV's and Hawker 800 are
luxuriously appointed and maintained to the
very highest of International standards.

To find out more or to obtain a quotation
contact Anne Chuard or a member
of her team.

PrivatAir. Geneva. Switzerland.
Telephone +41 22 92 96 730
or Fax +41 22 92 96 731

PRIVATE & CONFIDENTIAL

PrivatAir
The Private Airline

"In the Union of the next century, with membership in the twenties, the input of the European Parliament will be vital, bringing together political interests at Continental level to balance the national interests in the Council"

THE EUROPEAN PARLIAMENT: WHAT IT DOES

BY MARTYN BOND, HEAD OF THE EUROPEAN PARLIAMENT OFFICE IN THE UK

Britain's relationship with the European Union is a very large and often controversial subject. Britain's relationship to the European Parliament is only one part of that, but it is a considerably more straight-forward one than many other aspects. The facts are simple and bear repeating.

The UK electorate sends 87 MEPs to the European Parliament. Elections take place every five years, the next in June 1999. The Parliament meets in Strasbourg each month for its plenary sessions and in Brussels for some additional plenary sessions as well as for its committee meetings. It has some 20 specialist committees, ranging from agriculture to women's rights. The Parliament has 626 members and the largest political group is the Party of European Socialists, numbering over 200 and led by North London MEP Pauline Green. The 62 UK Labour MEPs are led by Wayne David (South Wales Central) and the eighteen Conservatives by Edward McMillan-Scott (North Yorkshire). In addition there are two Liberal Democrats, two Scottish Nationalists, one Democratic Unionist, one Official Unionist and one SDLP MEP from Northern Ireland. The turnout in the UK at the last elections (June 1994) was 36%. When they are not in Strasbourg or Brussels at plenary sessions, in committees or meeting to caucus in their political groups, UK MEPs are usually in their constituencies holding surgeries, addressing meetings, replying to voters' enquiries and writing in the local press.

The European Parliament is a newcomer on the political scene. It changed from an appointed assembly to an elected chamber only in 1979. As an Assembly without any clear political majority and without a European government to maintain or to topple, it initially enjoyed minimal powers and operated essentially as a forum for political opinion across the member states (then only nine) and as a sounding board for a limited range of legislative proposals at European level. However, changes to the Treaties, particularly during the 1980s and the early 1990s, considerably increased its powers, both in the budgetary and the legislative fields, so that today it is a major player alongside the Commission and the Council of Ministers in shaping the future of the Union. Milestones along this road are a series of judgements by the Court of Justice and the major treaty revisions of the Single European Act (1987), the Maastricht Treaty (1992) and the Treaty of Amsterdam (1997). In the Union of today with 15 member states – and even more so in the Union of the next century with a membership in the twenties – the input of the European Parliament will be vital, bringing together political interests at Continental level to balance the national interests in the Council. It does not operate in a conflictual manner as at Westminster, but seeks consensus in order to maximise parliamentary influence in the legislative process. The political groups build alliances to ensure their viewpoints win through, even at the cost of some compromise.

The number of MEPs representing each party in the UK has changed considerably over the Parliament's brief life and looks set to change again at the next elections. In 1979 the Conservatives won 60 seats to Labour's 17; in 1994 Labour reversed the proportions, gaining 62 seats to the Conservatives' 18. The European debate – in particular the UK political parties' stance on issues of sovereignty – has left major fault lines through the national body politic in the past generation. Large constituencies each representing between six and eight Westminster constituencies – and the first past the post electoral system – have accentuated relatively minor swings of voter preference, and hence the UK's influence within the main political groups in the European Parliament.

"This public disinclination to take the European Parliament seriously may well be misguided, because it is already being overtaken by the facts. The Parliament's powers have increased dramatically since the first elections"

At the next elections the system will be changed to proportional representation based in all probability on regional lists, allowing a closer correlation between actual votes cast and the numbers of MEPs elected from each party. This is expected to lead to an increase in the representation of the minor parties and a rebalancing of the numbers between the two main parties; but as with all predictions, they can be upset by the actions of voters on election day. At this stage the only safe prediction is that the political parties will pay a lot of attention to the order of candidates' names on each regional list and that the selection procedures will be extremely important in determining who eventually goes to Strasbourg and Brussels as the representatives of the people of the UK.

Political parties are of course the vital link between the electorate and Parliaments. Not only do they select candidates but they issue manifestos and drive forward public debate on

matters of concern. They compete for votes and it has been to their shared disappointment that they have seen the UK turnout for successive European elections obstinately stuck in the mid-thirties: in 1979 it was 32.2%; in 1984 it was 32.6%; in 1989 it was 36.2%; in 1994 it was 36.4% – a gently rising trend but from a very low base. For the sake of comparison, the most recent election attracted 60% of the electorate in Germany, 52% in France and 59% in Spain. The average across the Union was 56.4%. There can be little doubt that the electorate in the UK regards European elections still as "second order" elections, more akin to a local than a general election, even though the British turnout does not compare unfavourably to the votes cast in an American presidential election.

This public disinclination to take the European Parliament seriously may well be misguided, because it is already being overtaken by the facts. In the changing balance of power among the main institutions – Council, Commission, Parliament and Court – it is the Parliament which has consistently gained in authority. The Parliament's powers have increased dramatically since the first elections. It can now amend legislation – indeed in some cases it is able to force the Council to compromises which the member states alone would not have contemplated. In addition, the Parliament also has a major say over the spending priorities of an annual budget for the Union of over £70 billion and has a decisive say on which countries may or may not join the Union. Not only does enlargement depend on the approval of the Council and of each member state after successful negotiations with the applicants, but the European Parliament will also give or withhold its assent on each case, expressing the views of the European electorate as a whole.

Repeated Treaty revisions have tried to ensure greater efficiency in the complicated process of legislating at European level (despite the growing number of states involved in the Council). Information now flows more freely between the European Parliament and national parliaments so that MPs and MEPs are better informed about each other's work. Recent efforts to ensure greater transparency and openness in the process are recognition of the need for the Institutions, including the European Parliament, to improve their acceptability in the eyes of the public. The European Parliament certainly understands the need to be more efficient and – like national parliaments – to enjoy the trust of the electorate.

Asked in a recent Eurobarometer opinion poll how acceptable or reliable it considers parliaments to be, the UK electorate is considerably more sceptical than most other countries about both their national parliament (Westminster 37%) and the European Parliament (Strasbourg 29%). In other countries figures typically range up to the mid-sixties and average about forty. Edmund Burke once remarked, during the debate about the French Revolution, that in English society the "cake of custom had not yet crumbled". In relation to European affairs there has hardly been time for the cake of custom to have set, let alone crumbled, and it is not altogether surprising that the European Parliament has not yet had time to establish a central position in voters' minds. But it is sad to see that Westminster, redolent with history and benefiting from the ceaseless attention of the media, has "crumbled" – in Burke's evocative phrase – and fallen so low in public esteem. Large numbers of people are dissatisfied with the workings of parliamentary democracy. They outnumber those who still feel the system is satisfactory: 45% to 43%. The mountain to climb in the UK has twin peaks: to ensure acceptability for the European Parliament and also to restore the trust in Westminster that has been severely eroded over the years.

One powerful argument often deployed for the loss of popular support for the institutions of parliamentary democracy in the UK is the absence of any training in citizenship in our schools. Where it is common for children in secondary school on the Continent and in America to learn about their constitution and the structure of society, the curriculum of British schools has seldom gone beyond the history and geography of the British Isles, and in many cases has not even ensured that children leave school with adequate knowledge of public affairs in the modern world. A European dimension has been almost completely lacking, and citizenship, in schools, has been seen as a novel and in some ways disturbing idea. All that may change shortly as reforms in the curriculum are introduced, but it goes some way to explain why the populace, exposed only to the sound bite and slogan reporting of the tabloids, has little understanding of or sympathy for the institutions of parliamentary democracy either at national or at European level.

But alongside ignorance and prejudice there is a great thirst for knowledge about Europe. Opinion poll after opinion poll reveals that the British public feels badly informed about the greatest issue of our generation: more than seven out of ten adults feel they are insufficiently informed; and nearly four out of ten would like the European Parliament to play a more important role in the life of the European Union than it does at present, easily outnumbering the two out of ten who want it to play a less important part. But in any straight choice between Westminster and Strasbourg (which, for instance, should have a bigger say on the subject of European policy?) a clear majority (55%) favours the national parliament while only a minority (29%) favours the European Parliament.

If the signals are mixed, they reflect confusion in the public mind. The UK Presidency of the Council, led by a government with a large Commons majority, and in sympathy with the broad mainstream of opinion in the European Parliament, can set out to clear away this confusion. From a leading position in Europe, it can encourage a well-informed and open debate in the UK on European issues in advance of the European Elections in June 1999. ☆

"If we are really serious about building a wider Europe, integrating our economies and increasing competitiveness, the dislocations that come from inadequate infrastructure and fragmented administration must be overcome"

EUROPE ON THE MOVE: THE TRANSPORT AGENDA

BY THE RT. HON. NEIL KINNOCK, MEMBER OF THE EUROPEAN COMMISSION

The logic for a European transport policy grew out of the Single Market: an efficient, competitive, safe and environmentally responsible transport system is vital if the Treaty obligation to free movement is to mean anything in practice. Just as in the last century the creation of national single markets required compatible transport systems and common rules, so in our generation the growth of the European and international markets needs much the same.

This is the basis of the case for the TransEuropean Transport Networks, known as TENs. If we are really serious about building a wider Europe, integrating our economies and increasing competitiveness, the dislocations that come from inadequate infrastructure and fragmented administration must be overcome. Part of the answer must come, of course, from co-operation and Community legislation that is effectively enforced; part from the use of compatible technology and common gauges – whether in the improvement of air traffic management or in the integration of rail systems – and part of the answer must come from investment in new infrastructure for land, water and air transport.

The European member states, with the approval of the European Parliament, have defined 14 priority projects and other transport links for improvement and upgrading. These links are not only between the countries of the Union but extend to the East to ensure that the transport system we are building now in the European Union is integrated with that of our Eastern neighbours, including those that have applied for EU membership. The idea is to turn the patchwork of existing links into a proper transport network. This may be a case of enlarging a motorway or electrifying a rail line or upgrading an airport, as well as projects involving state-of-the-art engineering such as the Öresund fixed link joining Denmark and Sweden. The role of the European Commission is to facilitate the completion of these projects. It only has a tiny budget to do so – the 1.8 billion Ecu available until the end of the century is to lever further funding by financing the initial feasibility studies, so the lion's share of the money will have to come from the private sector. The Commission is making huge efforts to foster partnerships between the public and private sector to find new ways of harnessing private capital and enterprise. TENs will not only help reduce transport times and costs: the investment involved will create new business as well as stimulating research and innovation in new technologies, and the creation and operation of some infrastructures will also provide the basis for permanent new enterprises and, most importantly, new jobs.

TACKLING ROAD CONGESTION
The completion of the TENs network is one of the keys to relieving the major transport problem facing Europe: congestion. Congestion is already epidemic, especially in the urban and industrialised areas, and jams are spreading along the main arteries. On present trends traffic volumes will double in the next 15 to 20 years. In these conditions, failure to get on with the task of strengthening and updating Europe's transport networks now means extra cost burdens, late delivery, more dangerous travel and greater environmental damage.

"The extraordinary growth in road traffic is due in part to the fact that alternative modes of transport are not sufficiently competitive, in part because the 'hidden costs' . . . are not currently covered by road users and, in part, to the fact that alternative modes of transport are not sufficiently competitive"

sustainable transport systems and fair and efficient pricing is clear: as a general rule people and businesses will only make full use of the transport system once it is they – rather than others or society as a whole – who bear the cost of not doing so. In any walk of life prices obviously have a major influence on people's behaviour. But in transport the taxes and charges most transport users pay on vehicles and fuels are "flat rate". As a result, it usually costs little more to drive heavily polluting cars and lorries than to drive clean vehicles, and the cost of driving on a clear rural road is not lower than the cost of using a busy road at peak time. Clearly, the system as it exists does not deter congestion and it offers no real inducement to move to uncongested times and routes.

The objective of a fair and efficient pricing policy is to correct that imbalance and to ensure that the prices charged for transport reflect more accurately the degree to which each individual journey causes congestion or environmental damage – in other words, you pay for what you use. The aim is to promote clarity in the connection between real transport costs and real transport prices and, crucially, to differentiate between efficient and inefficient transport behaviour. The policy is not about raising extra revenues; indeed, if it is to be workable and perceived as fair it is important it is not used as an excuse merely to make motoring more expensive. It is about reducing the pressures on the infrastructure and encouraging a shift away from the road to other modes of transport such as sea, rail or inward waterway.

The solution to congestion lies in a wide range of policies. We have, for instance, published a Green Paper – a consultative document – called *The Citizens' Network* in which we used illustrations of existing best practice to show both why we need public transport and how to make better use of it. Of course, major initiatives in this area are the responsibility of national, regional and local administrations, but the Commission can perform a valuable role in linking up these organisations so they can pool their experience.

Improved public transport is however only part of the story. Our aim of sustainable mobility will only be reached when we manage to make better use of the transport system as a whole. The extraordinary growth in road traffic is due in part to the fact that alternative modes of transport are not sufficiently competitive, in part because the "hidden costs" – of environmental and infrastructure damage, of increased accident costs, of medical treatment, e.g. for pollution-induced asthma – are not currently covered by road users and, in part, to the fact that alternative modes of transport are not sufficiently competitive.

Making more efficient use of the transport systems which we already have is basic to the thinking behind the Commission Green Paper *Towards Fair and Efficient Pricing in Transport*, published in December 1995. The link between creating

Fair and efficient pricing cannot change behaviour unless there are safe, competitive alternatives to road use, which is why so much of the Commission's future work will concentrate on ensuring other modes are modernised, revitalised and developed according to the needs of users rather than operators.

MOVING BY WATER
A series of policy documents, notably legislative proposals in the maritime sector, have already tackled the challenge of how to develop Europe's coastline better and enhance the potential of short sea shipping and the performance and commercial attractiveness of maritime transport. In order to encourage Community-registered ships, we have streamlined and updated the rules under which they operate. The future focus will be on the quality of the fleet to ensure the highest possible standards. This is not only for obvious reasons of safety but because Europe's seafaring know-how and the jobs it generates both at sea and in associate industries (e.g. marine insurance) onshore is fact being dissipated.

We have updated old working practices on Europe's canals so that the inland waterway system can better realise its potential as the most environmentally-friendly transport mode of all. In a system of interconnecting links, Europe's canals form a vital transport corridor linking the sea in the north to the interior in the South, West and, importantly,

"In 1970, 32% of all freight travelled by rail; by 1996 it was down to 15%. The share of freight travelling by road rose from 49% to 70% over the same period. There are different reasons for the decline, but the essential one is general customer dissatisfaction with rail service, convenience, reliability, flexibility and price in both the passenger and the freight sectors"

the same period. There are different reasons for the decline, but the essential one is general customer dissatisfaction with rail service, convenience, reliability, flexibility and price in both the passenger and the freight sectors.

The Commission last year published a strategy paper outlining legislation to revitalise Europe's railways in three principal areas: the improvement of public services, the introduction of market forces and the international integration of national rail systems. The proposals, now being discussed by EU transport ministers, are for several technical and policy changes and stress the need for a new mentality in railway management, from increased commercial operation, and for a stronger detachment from the State – regardless of ownership – as part of what we called a "Railway Renaissance".

As a first step we proposed that, as an urgent means of fostering the revitalisation of at least part of the sector, international Rail Freight Freeways should be developed. Rail Freight Freeways are international train pathways that can be developed to increase the attractiveness of rail freight by opening access for all operators and by facilitating and simplifying the use of rail infrastructure. The establishment under this policy of "one-stop shops" to organise the timetabling, provide clear and dependable information on charging systems, remove border delays and enhance the priority given to rail freight journeys is an exciting new development that should better respond to the needs of shippers. The first freeways will be operational at the beginning of 1998 and will link major ports in northern and southern Europe. The detailed studies and simulation undertaken by the Community of European Railways show that 17 additional freight train paths will be available on just one of the three North-South routes at commercially attractive average speeds of 60kph – a huge advance on the current average freight train speed on comparable journeys of just 16kph. If fully utilised on just one identified route between the Benelux countries and Italy, a Freeway could result in shifting about 400,000 truck journeys a year off the road and onto rail.

East. The modern European transport system of the future will be increasingly "intermodal", with loads carried to their destination by a combination of tram, truck, ship and barge. In autumn 1997 the Commission will publish the first strategy for Europe's ports, designed to ensure they are all properly linked to the hinterland and equipped to deal with ever-increasing volumes of trade.

MOVING BY RAIL

The greatest challenge of the coming months will be securing a shift to rail transport. The rail sector in Europe is close to extinction; drastic action is is needed. In 1970, 32% of all freight travelled by rail; by 1996 it was down to 15%. The share of freight travelling by road rose from 49% to 70% over

In all of our publications and initiatives in transport we are constantly emphasising the need to mobilise market forces in all modes in order to increase efficiency and commercial operations which, rather than contradicting essential public service obligations, can often strengthen the standards of service. That view comes from the recognition that there has

*The Falcon 900EX whisks you
non-stop from Frankfurt to Chicago
in under 11 hours.*

"For a plane to fly well, it must be beautiful."

—*Marcel Dassault*

Engineered with passion.

We've built over 6000 fighters and Falcons since our founder
uttered these simple, yet resonant, words.

Today, only Dassault makes both advanced fighter aircraft
and business jets. Falcons are known as the best designed,
best built, *best flying* business jets at the top of the market.
They have an inner beauty too—with large, functional cabins.

For information about the four Falcon models,
contact John Rosanvallon in the U.S. at (201) 541-4600 or
Jean-Claude Bouxin in Paris at 33 1 40 83 93 08.

to be reasonable balance in the changes which are essential in the general context of liberalisation in the Single Market.

MOVING BY AIR

The legal liberalisation of the civil aviation sector is now complete. Any airline established within the European Union will be able to offer services – scheduled or unscheduled – at the fares they choose, between any number of airports in the Union, subject to a common set of rules on licensing, financial solvency and competition.

The result has been new market entrants and lower fares as a result of increased competition. Between 1993 and 1996, the number of routes flown has grown from 490 to 520, and 30% of those are now operated by at least two carriers; some 70% of all flying passengers are now paying reduced fares. Since 50% of all air travel is on charter flights, between 90 and 95% of all passengers are now travelling at fares significantly lower than in 1993. That leaves some people still paying unacceptably high prices and the Commission is pledged to root out and punish unfair practice and anti-competitive behaviour.

We must also ensure that our European carriers are not unfairly disadvantaged in global markets – which is why we are negotiating an "open skies" agreement with the US and with the countries of Central and Eastern Europe which would lay down a framework for future joint ventures and alliances. The aim is to maximise the competitive advantages for European carriers and minimise the impediments to success that are being put and will be put in their way by major air transport powers in other parts of the world.

BETTER SAFETY

The Commission can only *propose* policy; the law is made by the Member States, but we intend to use our power of initiative to set a transport policy agenda that delivers to all transport users. Our aim is a more efficient, competitive system, but that must never be at the expense of safety. In the air sector we have spent and will spend further time on trying to create a European air safety agency: in land and sea transport we have taken measures to ensure the safe transport of dangerous goods; we have insisted on passenger registers and safer ferry design; and we have enhanced the ability of port officials to detain sub-standard shipping.

More than 45,000 people lose their lives every year on Europe's roads and 1.6 million are injured, so road safety must be a high priority. The pain and anguish caused by these accidents are obviously beyond measurement but there is a huge economic price paid too. The costs arising from medical expenses, emergency services, damage to property and lost economic output amount to about 45 billion Ecu a year. The Commission's plans to reduce this terrible toll and help to accelerate improvements in road safety are set out in a new *Strategy for Road Safety 1997-2001*. It takes as its starting point the huge social and economic benefits that better road safety performance could bring and, to provide a basis of action, suggests a "One Million Ecu test": any measure that can avoid a death at a cost of up to 1 million Ecu should, we

"In order to encourage Community-registered ships, we have streamlined and updated the rules under which they operate. The future focus will be on the quality of the fleet to ensure the highest possible standards"

believe, be given serious consideration for development. Beyond this we also stress the need to improve the gathering of information and the dissemination of best practice at Community level by strengthening accident avoidance measures, including great efforts to curb alcohol and drug use by drivers, reducing accidents caused by fatigue and developing better means of reducing the consequences of accidents, such as through the co-ordination and support of Safety Rating Programmes for new cars.

This is an ambitious programme but now, as never before, we have the technology that will make possible some of the changes (e.g. electronic road pricing systems) that in turn could influence the way people use the transport system. The Commission has a significant research and development budget and is using it to target market-orientated products and to ensure that the developments of the future contribute to our long-term goal of sustainable mobility. An efficiently functioning, safe, competitive transport system across Europe will ease movement, improve the quality of life and open new travel possibilities for the individual; for business it means improved trade, greater economic wealth and, on the back of that, jobs. It is a system we all have an interest in creating. ☆

We mean business

For over twenty years, Nissan has been Europe's best-selling Japanese automotive brand.

It is also a major European manufacturer. Employing over 9,500 people in plants in England

and Spain, Nissan has the capacity to produce 400,000 units annually. Two thirds of all

Nissan European sales are produced by these plants. Investment in the UK facility, which is

widely regarded as Europe's most efficient and productive car manufacturing plant, now

exceeds £1.25 billion. Nissan's European Technology Centres are based in the UK,

Belgium and Spain and represent an R&D investment of over £56 million. They are

complimented by a dedicated design unit, Nissan Design Europe, established in Germany

in 1992, to assimilate European tastes and styles into future Nissan models. Along with

Nissan's European headquarters, Parts Logistics Centre and Distribution Service, based in

the Netherlands, Nissan in Europe directly employs around 15,000 people. This doesn't

take into account the personnel in the 4,300 Nissan dealerships spread across 31

countries. Committed to building strong, mutually beneficial relationships within Europe,

Nissan's purchases of parts and components from its 380 European-based suppliers

is valued at around £1 billion annually. And with plans to increase the number of

European-built models, our investment in people and the economy is guaranteed to grow.

Committed to quality. **Committed to Europe.**

Nissan Europe NV, Corporate Affairs, PO Box 90295, 1006 BG Amsterdam, The Netherlands
e-mail corp.affairs@nissan-europe.com   http://www.nissan-europe.com

*"Governments across the continent are experimenting
with reforms – with changes in the structure of social
benefits, in tax regimes and in regulation. There is
also a search for new boundaries between state and
private provision . . . All governments admit that
reforms have much further to go"*

A COMPETITIVE EUROPE

BY FRANK VIBERT, DIRECTOR OF THE EUROPEAN POLICY FORUM

INTRODUCTION

When the advantages of membership of the European Union are being described, commentators focus on the economic benefits of being part of the Single Market and the political gains in joining together with other member states in common actions in foreign policy, in international trade talks or against cross border crime. There is, however, another type of advantage of no less importance that is not so often referred to: the advantage of being able to compare public policies over the whole range of what modern states try to do. The Union encourages such comparisons because, from across almost the entire range of government work, it brings ministers and senior civil servants together in regular contacts and because Community bodies such as the Commission and Eurostat focus much of their time on making such comparisons. Comparative thinking becomes a habit of mind. Such comparative thinking is not confined to just to the central governments of member states but increasingly affects local and regional government.

THE JOBS AND COMPETITIVENESS DEBATE

An illustration of the importance of making policy comparisons is provided by the current debates on how to generate more jobs in Europe and how to ensure that European manufacturers and providers of services remain internationally competitive. Because of the concern about the high level of unemployment in most member states, the draft Amsterdam treaty contains a new title on employment which requires each member state to make an annual report on its employment situation and policies and for these to be examined by all member states in the Council of Ministers. This type of technique, pioneered in other international organisations, is known as a system of "peer review".

What this means is that the policies of those countries that have been successful in reducing unemployment, such as those of the United Kingdom, the Netherlands, Ireland and, to a lesser extent, Denmark, can be compared with the policies of those countries that have not. What is informative about such comparisons is that they may suggest a range of *different* policy approaches. For example, the emphasis in the United Kingdom has been on flexible labour markets, the emphasis in Holland has been on negotiated agreements between the "social partners", and the emphasis in Ireland has been on trying to attract inward investment in high technology enterprises. Other member states can look at these examples and see if there is anything in these different approaches which might suit their own economic and social circumstances. Such comparisons will always be a two-way street. Britain has been more successful than Germany in creating jobs in recent years but nevertheless is seen as having much to learn from Germany in how to create a well-skilled labour force.

The debate about "competitiveness" is more complicated but is no less important. Some economists dislike the term "competitiveness" because it is a label for a number of different concerns which in turn call for different policy responses. These various concerns range from viewing the unemployment problem as a symptom of a manufacturing and services sector which is not sufficiently adaptable to changing markets, to concerns about the inefficiency of the public sector. In addition there are concerns about state-owned industries; crowding out by the state of private service providers in growth areas such as health and pensions; and the failure of European industry to capture a growing share of world trade in markets outside the internal market. There is concern that the structure of European industry has not changed quickly enough to take advantage of the more rapidly growing markets in services or in high technology; and that Europe is failing to reshape its defence industries after the end of the Cold War. Furthermore, research and development expenditure in Europe has not yielded the pay-offs anticipated, and there are fears that the workforce may not have the right skills and training. General opinion is that governments have swollen the cost basis of businesses by requiring them to accept too large a burden of social costs such as contributions to health or pension schemes.

BANK HANDLOWY W WARSZAWIE SA

ESTABLISHED 1870

LEADER OF THE POLISH MARKET

Bank Handlowy w Warszawie SA was established in 1870. Throughout the period of its operations, despite the changing political and economic conditions and despite the devastation done by wars, the Bank continued with its original functions. Since the change of political system and the introduction of market economy in 1989, BANK HANDLOWY W WARSZAWIE SA has played a key role in the Polish economy as a leading commercial bank.

The Bank's offer is constantly being enriched. New types of deposits and credits are introduced, as well as sophisticated banking services, which are a novelty on the Polish market (private banking, financial advisory, custody services, factoring). The Bank offers a wide range of products for big multinationals and Polish corporations. Almost 12,000 companies have chosen Handlowy as their banking partner. The list includes top names like KGHM Polska Miedź, Telekomunikacja Polska, Nestle Polska, Unilever Polska, Fiat Auto Poland and Daewoo-FSO Motors.

Bank Handlowy is Poland's best known bank abroad, primarily because for much of its history it focused on the country's foreign trade financing. Since 1989, when the country started its path towards liberalization, its market share of that business has fallen to about 30%. But to make up for it the bank has aggressively moved into other areas such as corporate and investment banking. This strategy has paid off so much so that in 1996 Handlowy outperformed every other major bank in the country with a 26% increase in net profits.

Although Handlowy is not the country's largest bank (it ranks third by assets and 15th by branch network), its standing in the international markets is incomparable with other Polish banks. It holds a rating of Baa3 - the same as given to Poland's sovereign obligations by Moody's. Its international name's recognition has also allowed the bank to place its securities on the Eurobond market in 1996, including USD 200 million in Eurobonds issued in April 1997 on the best terms that any borrower in the region has

yet been able to achieve. Both these successes demonstrate that Bank Handlowy enjoys a well-established reputation among foreign investors.

Time and again, the bank has been voted as the leading financial institution in Poland by prestigious publications. According to *The Banker* magazine, it was number five among the top 100 Central European banks in 1996 and the only Polish commercial bank to make the world's top 500. Last year *Central European* readers voted Handlowy the **best local bank in Poland**. *Euromoney* has also bestowed a number of awards on the bank in the past few years, most recently as **best bank in Poland**.

Handlowy's successful privatisation in June this year is a proof of the global confidence in the bank. Not only was the retail portion three and-a-half times oversubscribed, but the institutional demand was 17,4 times greater than the available shares with heavy demand from the US and UK-based global pension funds - funds which are keen to invest only in quality names. But perhaps the biggest testimony of faith in the future of the bank was the core share blocks purchased in the privatization by three well-known names - all leaders in their respective business lines: the Swiss-based, but globally acquisitive Zurich Insurance; the premier US investment bank JP Morgan; and the well-respected Swedish retail bank Swedbank. The three core investors, who jointly own 24% of Handlowy, will spearhead the bank's push into insurance, investment banking and retail products.

The Bank will be pursuing its strategy in the face of strong domestic competition and - as the integration with the European Union proceeds - mounting foreign competition alike. The privatisation of Bank Handlowy, in contributing to higher operating efficiency, should help gain a competitive advantage in the markets considered to be of fundamental importance, and should also promote the attainment of financial targets set out in the Bank's development strategy, prime among these being a return on equity that will satisfy the Bank's shareholders.

BANK HANDLOWY W WARSZAWIE SA

8 Chałubińskiego St., 00-950 Warszawa, P.O. Box 129
Telephone: (22) 690 10 00, Telefax: (22) 830 01 13
Telex 814811, SWIFT: BHWA PL PW
http://www.bh.com.pl

When there is no common diagnosis of what is exactly the nature of the "problem" there can be no agreement on any common "solution". When there is a range of possible weaknesses to address there is no single common policy which could provide an answer to all the problems. It is in these circumstances that comparisons are so important. Different approaches can be assessed, and then best practice identified and possibly assimilated elsewhere. The European Commission has recognised the importance of making comparisons which shed light on the many different aspects of the debate on competitiveness in its 1996 initiative on "benchmarking". Under this initiative, the Commission is aiming to encourage benchmarking as a technique for making comparisons about best practice, not only at the level of individual companies but also at the sector level, and in respect of the "framework conditions" which may determine whether Europe provides an attractive environment for world class businesses.

The debates in Europe about jobs and competitiveness are sensitive for the member states because they pose further questions about some of the most fundamental assumptions underlying the role of governments in post-War Europe. Have state-run education systems failed citizens in the most basic way by not equipping them with the means to earn their own living? Has the prevailing concept in Europe of the "social market", where the state steps in to modify the workings of the market, ended up by undermining the job and wealth-creating potential of the market? Has the idea of "social partnership", providing a form of corporate governance midway between unbridled "Anglo-Saxon" capitalism and now discredited socialism, and where workers and employers reach collective agreement on employment policy, now shown itself to be too inflexible to operate in the modern business world? These are the underlying questions which will become increasingly important in Europe. Britain stands to gain both as an exporter of public policies which have worked well in the United Kingdom and as an importer of public policy approaches which have worked well elsewhere.

OPENING UP EDUCATION SYSTEMS

The importance of education is signalled in the new employment provisions of the draft Amsterdam treaty by a reference to the need to promote "a skilled, trained and adaptable workforce". The significance of education has long been recognised in Europe because it was appreciated in the earliest days of market economics that education conferred benefits not only on the individual who received it but also on society as a whole, which benefited through having a literate and numerate population. Unfortunately, in recent decades what has passed as education policy in Europe has sometimes been no more than meeting the demand of the school and university-age population for a free good – with content defined by civil servants, teacher unions and educational specialists. All European countries face the challenge of opening up state-provided education to a wider range of signals as to what is needed. End-users such as business need to be able to send signals as to what their requirements are; parents need to have a legitimate voice; and students themselves also need to be able to match their own abilities with what is

being sought by end users. There is therefore a growing debate in a number of European countries about the content and quality of education and how to open up education systems to a wider range of external influences and user choice. Changes will affect all stages of the educational process but they may be particularly dramatic at the level of higher education where pricing is starting to be introduced as a signalling system – and pricing principles have much further to go.

When Adam Smith referred to the social benefits of an educated population he was not just referring to wealth creation but also to the general social benefits of a population with a better understanding of law and morality. This broader context of education remains relevant. Is it not possible that part of the competitiveness problem in Europe stems from educational establishments in a number of European countries that have purveyed an ethos that is anti-market and anti-enterprise and that have not viewed entrepreneurship as a positive social value?

RETHINKING THE SOCIAL MARKET

The new employment title of the Amsterdam Treaty also refers to the wider setting of economic policy, including the objective of "social cohesion". In one sense this reference simply recognises that unemployment itself is extremely divisive socially and the source of a number of other social ills. In another sense it suggests a more fundamental worry about the prevailing post-War concept in Europe of the social market under which governments throughout Europe have intervened in markets and regulated business in the name of promoting social cohesion. If the end result of such interventions has been to make business so expensive that jobs can no longer be created then the outcome has been the *reverse* of the intention to combat social exclusion.

The original concept of the social market (associated with Ludwig Erhard, the architect of Germany's post-War recovery) was that the institutions of the market could be more firmly anchored if it was accepted that governments would compensate those who, for reasons outside their control (such as sickness or old age), could not benefit from participation in the market. Many economists still agree that the original concept of compensation through income support funded by taxation is a viable approach to dealing with situations where markets do not work. But the original Erhard concept of a limited contract with the state has long been undermined. The point of betrayal in Germany, according to some economists, was when Christian Democrat Chancellor Adenauer switched Germany's pension system from a funded scheme to a "pay as you go" scheme (for electoral reasons). In any event it has been the experience across Europe that political interventions and regulations in the name of social objectives have gone far beyond income compensation to affect freedom of contract in most areas of business. Moreover, if taxation levels go too far beyond what people would willingly pay for social objectives, then the behaviour of those who are taxed begins to change. For example, employees may demand higher wages or reduced working hours to try to offset the tax bite taken by the state, or employers may relocate their businesses to elsewhere in the world. Thus the taxing activities of the state as well as the regulatory activities of the state can end up by making it less attractive for businesses to employ people. What is emerging in Europe is therefore a growing debate about levels of taxation and how to fund those social programs such as pensions, health and other forms of social insurance that have been met out of general taxation in post-War Europe.

As with the education debate, governments know that there are no ready-made answers as to how to reform the way in which social objectives are funded and delivered. Instead there is a healthy diversity of views about how and where to reduce levels of regulation and levels of taxation and how at the same time to help people provide against the risks they face during their lifetimes through unemployment, sickness or old age. At the moment in Europe, governments across the Continent are experimenting with reforms – with changes in the structure of social benefits, in tax regimes and in regulation. There is also a search for new boundaries between state and private provision as it is realised that private insurers can play a larger role under a suitable regulatory framework. One of the great strengths of private capital markets is their ability to shape products to meet particular client risks instead of the "one size fits all" of state provision, and people may increasingly wish to take advantage of this strength. Europe as a whole benefits from these experiments because a wide range of experience will become available for all countries to draw on. Britain has pioneered pension reform; Holland has been a leader in health sector reforms. All governments admit that reforms have much further to go.

Social Partnership and Corporate Governance
At Amsterdam, governments also decided to incorporate an agreement on social policy into the Treaty and the United Kingdom agreed to be part of it – thus ending its earlier "opt out". One provision of the articles on social policy which seem particularly relevant to Europe's employment and competitiveness problems is that which refers to the need to "take account of the diverse forms of national practices, in particular in the field of contractual relations". Diversity in contractual relations is important in part because the role of organised labour is changing as trade union membership declines in a number of countries; because the historical industrial bases of unions may now be less important; and because it is increasingly realised that those in jobs cannot credibly speak on behalf of the unemployed. Moreover, beneficial changes in the conditions affecting labour markets are not always represented by employee or employer organisations. Mass car ownership may have done more to affect employment possibilities than unionisation; it may not be coincidental that unionisation has declined as car ownership has increased. Some foresee a similar revolution in job possibilities arising from the personal computer. In addition, changing social patterns affecting working practices or participation in the workforce (such as single parent family formation or healthier old age) are also influencing attitudes to employment contracts. In

addition to those changes in the labour market, employers face strong pressures to adapt their businesses to meet competition both in the single market and in world markets. It will therefore make better sense for Europe to allow for diversity in contractual relations rather than to try to prescribe particular forms of relationship either in the labour market or in the structure of corporate governance.

A Framework for Comparisons
The debate about competitiveness and jobs highlights the importance of a comparative approach to key areas of public policy rather than common policies. This in turn raises the question of what kind of Europe will most easily promote such comparisons.

Clearly Europe must not be inward-looking. Comparisons outside the area are also going to be important. What lessons can be learnt from the formidable job creation record of the United States and from the resurgence of its high tech services industries? It was not accidental that Britain provided the environment where the industrial revolution took place. Equally it is not accidental that the United States has provided the environment for phenomena such as Silicon Valley. It would be equally unwise to ignore what can be learned from the public sector reforms of Australia or New Zealand or the pension reforms of Chile.

Equally clearly, Europe must not become too centralised. Centralisation means that the advantages of comparisons are lost as the centre tries to do everything and impose a common policy. The sharing of responsibilities between the centre and member states also has to be approached with caution because the sharing of responsibilities can be done in ways which discourage policy innovation.

Conclusion
When Britain emerged from the Second World War it did itself no favours by thinking that Lord Keynes had all the answers to questions about how to create a full employment economy, and by ignoring the more profound inquiry that had been conducted into the institutions of the market by Germany's social market theorists who laid the basis for the German economic "miracle". It was a double misfortune that when Britain did look outside for useful comparisons it looked no further than its immediate neighbour and copied the false lead of French indicative planning. Membership of the Common Market provided a much more comprehensive wake-up call to what might otherwise have become a very hermetic Britain, and membership of the European Union is a guarantee that Britain will not be insular in outlook. The wider framework for comparative thinking that the Union provides is one of its greatest benefits. As the debate about competitiveness continues and extends into the areas of education, the welfare state and corporate and labour market organisation, it will become increasingly clear that a culture of comparison is one of the most important advantages of membership and that a decentralised framework for public policy is the key to a successful European Union. ☆

"Whilst funding is vital, it does not guarantee success and rejuvenation. The necessary reclamation and infrastructure work should always follow the private investment"

PARTNERS IN URBAN REGENERATION:

A PERSONAL REFLECTION

BY DUNCAN HALL, CHIEF EXECUTIVE, TEESSIDE DEVELOPMENT CORPORATION

As we come to the end of the century we can see how the character of urban regeneration has fundamentally altered.

Initially, regeneration ranged from the creation of New Towns to meeting the demands of newly emerging industries such as steel and chemicals. However, over the last two decades, conversion or urban regeneration may be seen as a more generic phase applied to the demands of declining areas, ranging from inner city deprivation to the most recent effect of "the peace dividend", whereby large-scale facilities used exclusively for military purposes either closed or were severely reduced in size leading to substantial unemployment and distress for those communities which were over-reliant on a single industry.

The unfortunate consequences of the decline of a single industry can be seen particularly in steel-making, coalmining and shipbuilding. The radical changes in the European steel industry have brought job losses – with all their social and economic consequences. Inevitably, the spread of new technology in a worldwide industry will lead to future job losses. Europe's role is of vital importance given the winding up of the European Coal and Steel Community (ECSC) by 2002 and the progressive development of the EU's Structural Funds.

For more than twenty years I have been involved in very practical terms in the rejuvenation of areas which have been affected by dramatic economic decline. I believe that there are certain basic principles which need to be applied for urban regeneration to be successful.

The challenge of urban regeneration has in my view been fully captured by Mrs Monika Wulf-Mathies's statement in the Commission's publication *Europe's Cities*:

"As we approach the end of the twentieth century our towns and cities are becoming the focus of a host of pressing social, economic and environmental problems. Social exclusion threatens the very basis of our society founded as it is on a partial redistribution of wealth generated by the economy. This means that today's cities must bear a large part of the burden of reconciling economic competitiveness with social cohesion and sustainable development."

To meet this challenge there must be a better balance between public expenditure and private investment. As the World Bank stated in its Annual Report (1995): "Perhaps nothing has changed more rapidly in the 1990s than the financing structure for development." Ever increasing investment, it points out, is "due entirely to the growth in private flows".

However, as the Commission pointed out in a recent publication *Regional Policy and Cohesion*: "Experience suggests that the free play of economic forces is not enough by itself to ensure balanced development. The scale of the effort required to stimulate economic activity in the least advanced areas means that public funds must be used in conjunction with private investment."

Recognising the need for both public and private investment to secure urban regeneration is just one part of the story. We also need to ensure an *even* and *efficient* distribution of such growth because, all too often, the efforts of conversion result in empty buildings and not the hoped-for jobs and prosperity. An article in the *Financial Times* on the development and future of business parks in the UK underlined the disparity between aspirations and reality: "The classic image of business parks which captured the imagination in the late 1980s: all fountains, flower beds and tinted glass. But a vast underclass of sites scattered around the country is still waiting for business to make a move."

So what lessons can be learned which have a direct practical relevance to future conversion initiatives? The conclusions which I have reached are based on my experience at Corby in the East Midlands, where I became Chief Executive of the District Council in September 1979 (in the full knowledge of the impending closure of the largest integrated steel plant in Europe, announced on 1st November

New Kværner Technology Centre

The partnership between Kvaerner Process and Durham University at Stockton, working with Teesside Development Corporation, will be strengthened with the opening in mid-1998 of Kværner's new Technology Centre and new academic and residential buildings for University College, Stockton doubling its present capacity. Both these developments are on Teesside Development Corporation's Teesdale site.

Education and Commerce; Teesside's Perfect Partnership

The collaboration effectively combines the world class research skills of the University with the commercial and technology expertise of Kvaerner Process, resulting in a unique partnership.

University College Stockton

 University of Durham

KVÆRNER™

 TEES SIDE

DEVELOPMENT CORPORATION

University College Stockton, University Boulevard, Thornaby, Stockton-on-Tees TS17 6BH Tel: 01642 335321   Fax: 01642 618345
Kvaerner Process Technology Ltd, 20 Eastbourne Terrace, London W2 6LE Tel: 0171 957 3002   Fax: 0171 957 3922
Teesside Development Corporation, Dunedin House, Riverside Quay Stockton-on-Tees TS17 6BJ Tel: 01642 677123 Fax: 01642 676123

1979); and as Chief Executive of the country's largest Urban Development Corporation from September 1987.

CORBY

The beginning of the 1980s witnessed the rationalisation of the large-scale traditional industries. The problems in Corby were particularly acute. Unemployment stood at nearly 30%: the second highest in the UK. In simple terms the town's almost total dependence on the steel industry for so many years meant that when the closure arrived the town had nothing to fall back on and Corby's industrial and economic base had to be virtually created from scratch.

By mid-1989 there were over 700 firms in the area, more than 500 of them established or relocated in Corby since the beginning of 1980. Unemployment, which had stood at 30% in 1981 was down to around 6%, in line with the national average.

The growth of new industrial and commercial activity continued, providing job opportunities for the majority of school leavers, encouraging mothers to return to work and providing jobs for workers from other towns. The further scale and diversity of the economic growth has ensured that the town will never again find itself in a position where the collapse of a single industry can produce such traumatic results.

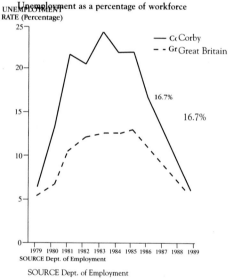

UNEMPLOYMENT as a percentage of workforce
RATE (Percentage)

SOURCE Dept. of Employment

SOURCE Dept. of Employment

THE CHART shows how Corby suffered compared with the rest of Britain and how spectacular was the scale of its recovery. Although unemployment in the town itself peaked at 30 per cent, the figures shown here are lower because they cover the wider Corby travel to work area.

TEESSIDE

When the Teesside Development Corporation was established in 1987 as the largest in the UK (and one of ultimately thirteen to be created) its remit was embodied in Section 136 of the Local Government Planning and Land Act 1980:

"To bring land and buildings into effective use, encouraging the development of existing and new industry and commerce, producing an attractive environment, ensuring that housing and social facilities are available to encourage people to live and work in the area and levering private sector investment into the area."

In a nutshell, the role of the Corporation was to create employment and improve the quality of life of the people.

Wasteland in Corby, 1980

Corby's industrial and economic base had to be created virtually from scratch

Teesside had, for more than a decade, suffered massive structural decline with the complete loss of its shipbuilding industries (indeed, in a peculiar parallel to my experience of final closure in Corby, I saw the last of the shipyards on The Tees close in November 1987); a massive decline in employment in the chemical and heavy engineering industries; and the direct effects of the restructuring of the British Steel Corporation. The decline was reflected in the unemployment figures, which rose to over 20%.

Teesside does not possess a capital city but is an amorphous group of four towns, each being directly affected by the decline of the differing traditional industries. The impact was, however, greater in terms of scale, as each of the towns was much larger than Corby.

As the Development Corporation reaches the end of its remit, we see that no fewer than 26,000 jobs have been created or protected. Private investment into the area now exceeds £1 billion and the Corporation has generated more than £100 million of capital receipts, meaning that more than 20% of its annual expenditure has been funded by the resources which it has generated itself.

LESSONS LEARNED

Both the local authority and the directly established Development Corporation achieved a remarkable economic renaissance in their respective areas. Their experience provides a fascinating perspective upon the approach to urban regeneration within the UK.

Corby was a New Town established specifically to serve the workforce with housing, leisure facilities and commercial development to enable it to expand readily. The Development Corporation, on the other hand, was a creation of government, which both owned and controlled it. Its uniqueness was that whilst it was responsible for 12,000 acres of land throughout the heart of Teesside, fewer than 1,000 people lived within its boundaries – such was the lega-

Derelict dockland at Hartlepool, 1990

Hartlepool Marina today

cy of the declining industries it inherited.

Funding. It seems an obvious comment, but appropriate funding to achieve the necessary reclamation, and infrastructure provision to meet the requirements of new industry, are prerequisites of economic diversification.

In Corby, the local authority received support from the Commission for New Towns. (Ironically, the New Town Development Corporation had been wound up in 1978 prior to the closure of the steelworks.) But it is the role of the European Commission which cannot be overstated, as the granting of assisted area status to Corby paved the way for the town to apply for European Community aid. In eight years it received some £130 million from the Community's regional, social and energy funds, which, I understand, is a record for any British town.

(The Development Corporation itself was directly funded by central government and during its 10-year lifetime received some £380 million of public funds.)

The absolute key, however, and the lesson to be learned is that whilst funding is vital, it does not guarantee success and rejuvenation. The necessary reclamation and infrastructure work should always *follow* the private investment. In other words, neither in Corby nor on Teesside has reclamation work been undertaken without the certainty of new investment. There is a temptation to layout the new industrial estates or business parks and wait for the investment to arrive – it may never come.

Land. All legislation in the UK since 1945 governing urban regeneration has provided development authorities with powers of compulsory purchase for land. Local authorities possess compulsory purchase powers and Development Corporations were given expedited powers of acquisition. In neither Corby nor Teesside were these powers applied: land acquisition took place by agreement. In Corby, the main acquisition was the agreement to purchase the former steelworks, amounting to 270 hectares; similarly, on Teesside the Development Corporation's

massive acquisition programme was all undertaken by agreement. Compulsion is in my view detrimental to sucessful regeneration and is usually unnecessary. Acquiring land by agreement has numerous benefits, the most important being the increase in investor confidence achieved by this approach.

The key lesson is not however the acquisition of land but the *control* of land resources. The whole development programme was based upon the purchase of the steelworks in Corby; on Teesside a variety of differing methods, from joint venture to equity sharing and share subscription, formed the basis of major development. Control of the land and, as mentioned before, the need to ensure that the investment arrives *before* work begins are intrinsic requirements of successful regeneration and conversion. It is crucial to avoid any costly large-scale land acquisition which does not carry with it investment commitment.

Strategy. In all the areas in which I have been involved directly or indirectly there has been something of a predilection for creating highly detailed master plans. Once a master plan exists, it becomes a fixed idea and its inflexibility can lead to a rejection of private sector investors. Inevitably the lead in the rejuvenation of a declining economic area is undertaken by a public authority: either by central government or local government, or most likely a combination of the two. However, the actual development will only take place if private investment is attracted. Plainly, therefore, whilst a strategic framework for development is desirable, the detail should be filled in by – and synchronized with – the investment decisions of the private sector.

Efficient Business Approach. Having established a workable strategy and the control of the land, public sector funding must respond to private sector investment. To achieve the necessary timescales to satisfy the private sector, there must be a clear and efficient decision-making process within the organisation as to land, infrastructure and reclamation programmes, along with a clear understanding of the needs of the private sector. The great benefit of a clear, businesslike approach to decision-taking and timescales is the level of confidence the organisation generates with its investing partners.

Marketing. I am constantly surprised at the low priority marketing receives and the subsequent lack of expenditure when dealing with urban regeneration initiatives. It is a fact of life that the decisions we take about, for example, what we eat, drink, wear or drive can be affected by the quality of marketing of the product. Yet with a much more precious commodity, *people* (who are, after all, the *raison d'être* of urban regeneration) we find all too often a total lack of thought-through marketing strategies for stimulating investment and rewarding success.

CONCLUSION

The two areas of Corby and Teesside represent remarkable achievements in conversion and urban regeneration – even if their responsible authorities were very different in conception and approach. Yet I believe that there is common ground in their strategies which yield the basic principles of successful urban regeneration. These principles, when properly applied, will, in my experience bring success to any initiative in urban regeneration or conversion. ☆

Tees Barrage

TEES*h*SIDE

Europe's largest Single Urban Regeneration Project

£1.3 billion of Private Sector Investment.

£113 million capital receipts generated.

12,000 square acres of land revitalised.

Support and assistance to over 400 companies.

Over 26,000 jobs created and protected.

New homes, offices, factories and first class retail facilities.

Unrivalled work, leisure and education opportunties.

Continuing inward investment from home and abroad.

The Teesside Success Story continues...

CREATED BY

TEES*h*SIDE
DEVELOPMENT CORPORATION

Dunedin House, Riverside Quay, Stockton-on-Tees TS17 6BJ Tel: (01642) 677123 Fax: (01642) 676123
E mail: Duncan.Hall@TEESSIDE.btinternet.com   Web Site: http://www.teesside-tdc.co.uk

Hartlepool Marina

Taylor Woodrow Construction

Teamwork *World Class* *Worldwide*

Approximately 6,000 ships, including vessels over 190,000 dwt, berth at Teesport and Hartlepool on the North-East coast of England each year. The two ports handle over 45mt of cargo per annum, ranking both in the UK top five. Each offers deep-water, lock-free facilities.

The Ports are at the heart of an area that is strongly associated with petrochemicals, engineering and manufacturing. Companies operating major facilities on an eleven-mile stretch of the River Tees include Amoco, BASF, British Steel, ICI, Kvaerner Oil & Gas, and Phillips Petroleum.

Two major North Sea pipelines come ashore on Teesside, and liquid bulk accounts for almost two-thirds of Teesport's total traffic volumes. The 28mt annual liquid bulk throughput is set to rise significantly in 1998 when both Phillips Petroleum and Amoco increase capacity.

A number of private wharves and jetties on the Tees offer handling and storage primarily for liquid and dry bulks. Other companies on the River are involved in specialist support services to the oil and gas sector. Several are located at Tees Offshore Base: a major UK facility for offshore support established by the Tees and Hartlepool Port Authority Ltd (THPAL).

Tees and Hartlepool Port Authority Ltd

THPAL is the statutory harbour authority for Teessides's two ports. The Powell Duffryn-owned company also operates major cargo-handling facilities at Tees Dock and Hartlepool, is a substantial landowner, and has subsidiary companies involved in warehousing and distribution. The Company employs over 450 people and is ISO 9002 accredited.

Cargo-handling at Tees Dock is dominated by large volumes of steel, project, general break bulk and unitised traffic. Hartlepool – the smaller facility – is geared more towards particular niche trades, including: vehicle handling, forest products, dry bulks, grain, perishable products and steel.

Both Tees Dock and Hartlepool offer deep-water, open access to the sea, and excellent road and rail links.

Investment and Development

Tees Dock is part of the Teesport estate – currently the focus of an ongoing, multi-million pound investment programme by THPAL. The first phase of the project commenced in summer 1997. So far, the Port's internal rail and road links have been redirected in order to improve access to individual terminals and release more land specifically for the development of the Ferry Terminal. The second phase of THPAL'S plans will include further expansion of facilities for unitised traffic but full details are yet to be finalised. In the meantime, the project has already generated a great deal of interest and is attracting new business.

A rail-freight connection was launched by English Welsh & Scottish Railway just one week after work finished on Teesport's improved rail link. Overnight trains now operate daily, transporting containers between Teesport and Scotland. The port also handles steel and bulk products by rail. THPAL sees rail expansion as an integral part of future development and growth, particularly in the unitised sector.

Unitised cargo traffic at Teesport has increased by 50% in the last five years, and currently accounts for 8% of Tees and Hartlepool's 45mt thorughput. This includes container traffic, which is now just under 300,000 teu per annum.

Unitised traffic is currently served by daily, direct connections to the Continent, and several sailings each week to Scandinavia and the Baltic region. Services operate from both the Ferry Terminal and Teesport Container Terminal. Additional sailings for short-sea unitised traffic are expected to come on stream in 1998.

Regular deep-sea liner services for general cargo also operate from Tees Dock, including sailings to West Africa, Ethopia, India, Greece, Israel and the Far East. ✳

A world class company

does not accept change

it anticipates it

In business,

things will never be the same again. Markets are more competitive than ever with a growing emphasis on quality and value for money.

Increasingly, there are new opportunities to work with clients in both the private and public sectors, to find better ways of providing the infrastructure, products or services they need.

We recognise the need to become more responsive to customer needs, more innovative and ready to adapt to changing and increasing demands from diverse customers in different markets. It is only through this process that we can maintain the uniqueness that is critical to our continued success.

The issue is not whether a company will undergo change, but how successfully it can both anticipate and maximise the opportunities it presents.

Tarmac

WORKING *TOGETHER*

Tarmac plc, Hilton Hall, Essington, Wolverhampton WV11 2BQ. Tel: +44 (0) 1902 307407. www.tarmac.co.uk

©TMC

Think of number one.

As Scotland's number one dealmakers*, we make a habit of bringing unexpected solutions to the table. Call us for original advice on everything from MBO's to project finance.

*Source: Scottish Business Insider, May 1997.

 **RMD** Corporate Finance

EDINBURGH 25 Melville Street EH3 7PE Telephone: 0131 225 4727. **GLASGOW** 17 Blythswood Square G2 4AD Telephone: 0141 248 5532.
ABERDEEN 2 Queens Terrace AB10 1XL Telephone: 01224 625888. **LONDON** 63 Queen Victoria Street EC4M 4UA Telephone: 0171 653 6300.

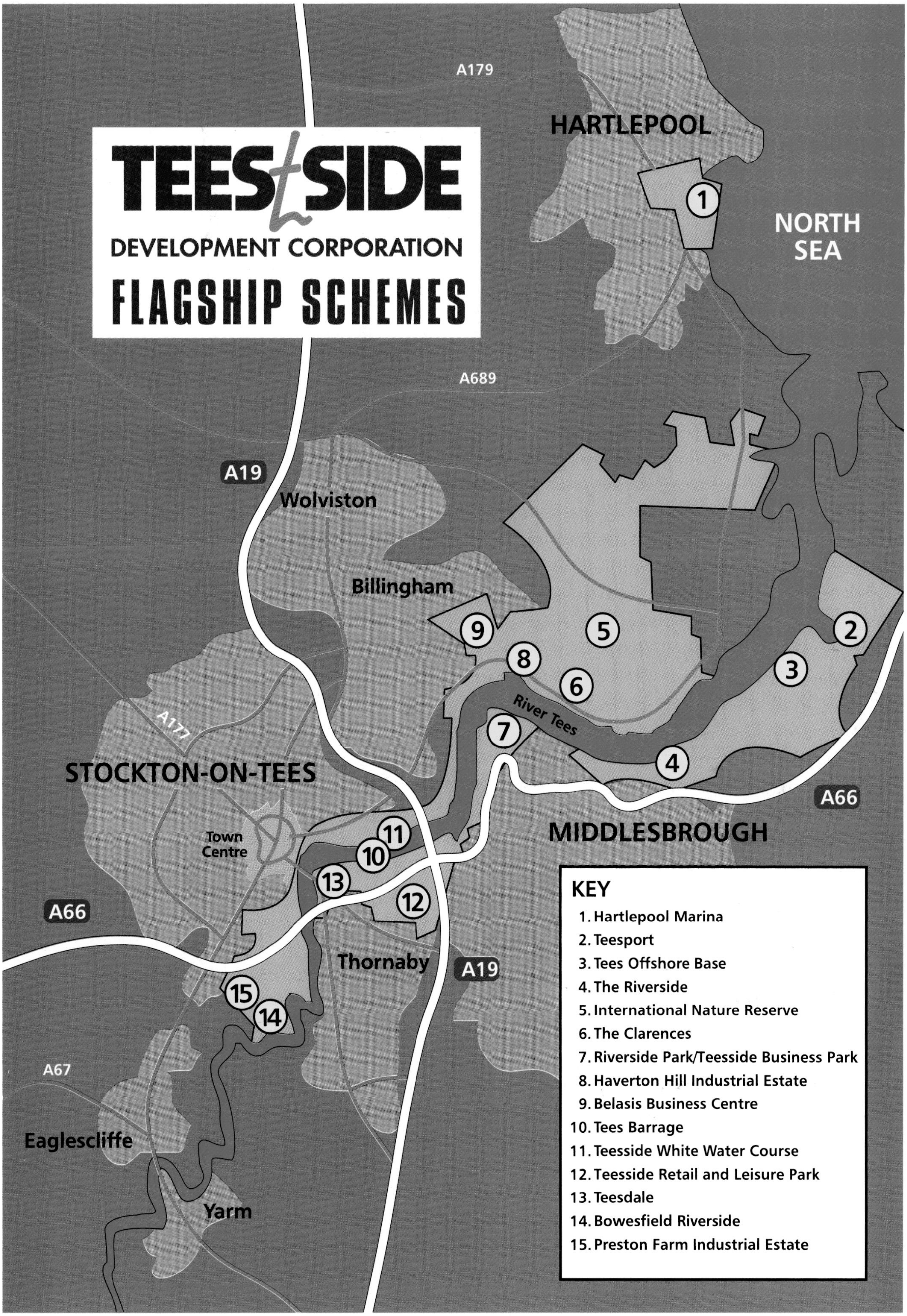

TEES SIDE
DEVELOPMENT CORPORATION
FLAGSHIP SCHEMES

A179

HARTLEPOOL

NORTH SEA

A689

A19

Wolviston

Billingham

River Tees

STOCKTON-ON-TEES

A177

A66

MIDDLESBROUGH

A19

Town Centre

Thornaby

A66

A67

Eaglescliffe

Yarm

KEY
1. Hartlepool Marina
2. Teesport
3. Tees Offshore Base
4. The Riverside
5. International Nature Reserve
6. The Clarences
7. Riverside Park/Teesside Business Park
8. Haverton Hill Industrial Estate
9. Belasis Business Centre
10. Tees Barrage
11. Teesside White Water Course
12. Teesside Retail and Leisure Park
13. Teesdale
14. Bowesfield Riverside
15. Preston Farm Industrial Estate

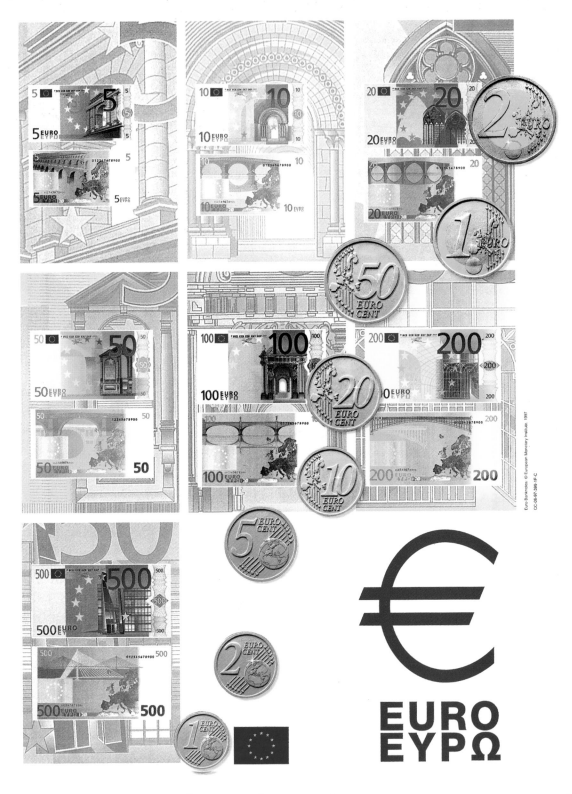

Euro-Banknotes. © European Monetary Institute 1997

CC-06-97-399-1F-C

"Although EMU involves risks, with a pragmatic approach to making it work well, the balance of argument is in its favour. That is why European governments are committed and the project is proceeding. The challenge now for the members of the European Union is to make the euro work well"

Economic & Monetary Union: Prospects, Problems and Opportunities

BY LORD CURRIE OF MARYLEBONE,
PROFESSOR OF ECONOMICS AT THE LONDON BUSINESS SCHOOL

Economic and Monetary Union (EMU) is very likely to happen on time, with a wide participation – surprising though it may seem to some commentators, particularly British, who have argued that it could never happen. This will be a remarkable historical venture: the formation of a major currency area between a group of advanced industrial countries that have traditionally guarded their independence jealously and within living memory by force of arms. This venture is not without risk, and if it works badly the economic, social and political costs to Europe and the rest of the world could be appreciable.

Given the risks, is it sensible to proceed with EMU, or should the whole project be abandoned or postponed, as its critics suggest? Inevitably a project as far-ranging and complex as EMU has both benefits and costs, and these have to be weighed.[1]

The benefits of EMU are several. At the simplest, a single currency in Europe will eliminate the transaction costs of having to switch from one currency to another: these include not just the financial cost of changing money, but also the complications in an increasingly integrated European Single Market of having to undergo complicated conversions to compare prices. More importantly, a single currency removes exchange rate risk from cross-border investments. It is true that such currency risk can be hedged in the modern-day sophisticated international financial markets, but only at a cost in terms of time and money that can be a deterrent, particularly for the smaller firm. Moreover, for major long-term location decisions (putting a factory in Scotland or Spain), it does not make sense to hedge the full currency risk over the lifetime of the project, because that increases exposure to other risks, such as that of domestic inflation. Removing separate currencies therefore eliminates an important obstacle to cross-border direct investment.

There are also benefits in terms of macroeconomic performance. The European Central Bank will clearly operate like the Bundesbank to maintain low and stable inflation. For those European countries, including the UK, that have suffered poor inflation records in the past, this is an important gain. The single currency will discipline national governments to pursue sensible fiscal policies: the striking transformation of the fiscal position of a number of countries in Europe, notably Italy, in the convergence process in the lead-up to EMU attests to this. EMU will also eliminate the possibility of destabilising and disruptive speculative movements of European currencies, also contributing to a more stable macroeconomic environment.

More broadly, by making it easier through price transparency to trade across borders in the Single Market, EMU will promote more intense competition. This may result in rationalisation and redundancies in the shorter term, but in the longer run the result will be greater efficiency in the Single Market as a whole, resulting in lower prices to consumers and enhanced competitiveness of European firms against the global competition. Thus EMU is an important complement to the Single Market programme.

These are important benefits. But a balanced discussion of EMU must recognise that it is not without costs. For critics of European federalism, the additional centralisation of the powers of monetary policy implied by EMU may be objection enough to the whole project. Those of a less doctrinal bent will identify other costs. Some of these are transitional: thus the adoption of a single currency does impose high costs of converting, ranging from the cost of converting machines to getting used to prices quoted in euros, not national currencies. Other costs are continuing. Thus the ceding of monetary sovereignty does eliminate the possibility of using domestic monetary policy at a national level to stabilise the national economy when it is out of step with other economies in the EMU zone. While monetary policy has not always been used to best effect in a number of countries, including the UK, in the past, the inability to use monetary policy to help stabilise country-specific cycles is an undoubted cost. This needs to be balanced against the macroeconomic benefits discussed above.

---

1. For a detailed assessment of these, see the author's *The Pros and Cons of EMU*, Economist Intelligence Unit, 1997. See also his forthcoming report *Will the Euro Work? The Ins and Outs of EMU*, Economist Intelligence Unit, January1998.

Associated with this is the loss of exchange rate flexibility, which reduces the scope under EMU for countries to adjust to loss of international competitiveness. Since devaluations have been misused by many European countries in the past, the cost of this may not be as high as it appears. But the loss of exchange rate flexibility does highlight the need for other mechanisms, notably in the labour market, to effect adjustment. Critics of EMU observe with force that labour markets in Europe adjust much less effectively than the much more flexible and dynamic US economy.

There are also concerns about the absence of accountability of the new European Central Bank. This could well be an advantage, taking monetary policy out of politics, but not if it results in a lack of legitimacy and tensions between national governments and electorates and the European Central Bank. Similar concerns are expressed over the constraining effects of the Growth and Stability Pact, which aims to limit the size of fiscal deficits that national governments can run.

Others place at the door of EMU the slowness with which the European Union has dealt with the enlargement issue, especially the strategically crucial widening to the East. Europe has always found it difficult to address simultaneously its widening and deepening agendas: the argument is that pursuing the deepening agenda through EMU was the wrong choice at this crucial time.

Any assessment of EMU must weigh these benefits and costs. In so doing, it is important to recognise that the balance of costs and benefits will alter over time. Some of the costs are transitional, while the resulting efficiency gains are long-term. The lack of flexibility under EMU that concerns many critics is something that may well change over time, as national policymakers recognise the need to adjust labour market policies in a more flexible direction to tackle problems of European unemployment. Institutional issues of accountability and possible tensions between the European Central Bank and national governments can be tackled and resolved pragmatically over time. And even if widening to Eastern Europe has, in fact, been held back by the focus on EMU, it is now a successful EMU that is most likely to generate the confidence to tackle the enlargement issue with vigour.

So although EMU involves risks, with a pragmatic approach to making it work well, the balance of argument is in its favour. That is why European governments are committed and the project is proceeding. The challenge now for the members of the European Union is to make the euro work well.

This involves two main responses from European policymakers. The first is to ensure that appropriate demand side policies are in place to ensure that the euro works well. The second is to ensure the right supply side policies. We discuss each in turn.

One of the risks under EMU is that the euro will prove volatile against other currencies, notably the dollar and yen. This would be damaging for the European economy, adding to macroeconomic fluctuations and unemployment. This could arise through conflicts between monetary and fiscal policy. Thus if national finance ministers relax fiscal discipline once under the wire of the Maastricht convergence criteria, then fiscal deficits might grow again. If that happened, the European Central Bank would rightly respond with higher interest rates, to head off inflationary pressures. The resulting combination of tight monetary/loose fiscal policy would be reminiscent of the policy stance in the US in the early 1980s. It could easily result in a volatile and over-valued debut for the euro.

To avoid this danger does not require additional mechanisms to co-ordinate fiscal and monetary policy. What it requires is continued fiscal discipline at a national level. This highlights the need to ensure that the Growth and Stability Pact works. National governments should not be satisfied with reaching the 3% Maastricht ceiling on fiscal deficit: they should aim lower, to 0-1% on average. This will then allow automatic fiscal stabilisers to operate within the constraints of the Growth and Stability Pact to help stabilise economic cycles at the national level. Continued fiscal restraint allows a more relaxed monetary stance without risking inflation. This is the most benign policy combination, with or without EMU, but it will contribute to the smooth operation of the euro.

On the supply side, European policymakers need to recognise the need for greater flexibility of labour and product markets to make up for the loss of scope for exchange rate adjustment. The inflexibility in a number of European economies will otherwise mean continuing high unemployment in Europe, and an inauspicious launch of EMU. Greater dynamism and flexibility will allow Europe to respond better, without increased unemployment, to the increased competition and restructuring that the euro will bring, as well as to competition from the rest of the world.

This is a crucial policy agenda for Europe to pursue, both during and beyond the British Presidency. It will be necessary to recognise that flexibility can take different forms: the contrast between the UK's deregulation route to flexibility and the Netherlands' co-ordinated centralised approach illustrates the range of possibilities. This is an issue on which subsidiarity should prevail: provided it pursues the flexibility agenda with vigour, each country can choose the policies that suit it best. That is not to say that anything goes: the 35 hour week in France represents a move in precisely the wrong direction, that will increase, not ease, adjustment problems in Europe.

These are key issues for the UK Presidency. But the UK will also have to address the question of its own membership. The Government is committed to membership in principle, and to joining when appropriate conditions are met. Ruling out membership in the first wave was absolutely right, because of the different state of the UK cycle and the high level of the pound. But standing aside in the longer term could well impose high costs, as European industry restructures in response to the euro. The continuing challenge for the British Government beyond its Presidency will be to ensure that the UK is able to join early, soon after the turn of the century, and that entry is not delayed until the middle of the next decade. ☆

Now we're even more

OPEN

for

BUSINESS

THE NEW ELECTRONIC ORDER BOOK

Our new electronic order book provides · a more efficient and open way of trading. It is transforming the way brokers deal on the London Stock Exchange, creating a more attractive environment in which to buy and sell shares.

FTSE 100 company stocks can now be traded at the touch of a button on our fully-automated system – reducing costs and improving prices.

The order book is making our market even more competitive and transparent, helping keep London at the heart of international finance.

London **STOCK EXCHANGE**

For further information contact our information service on +44 171 797 1372, Fax +44 171 410 6861, www.londonstockex.co.uk. or write to London Stock Exchange, Old Broad Street, London EC2N 1HP, United Kingdom.

"The advent of the euro will encourage the development of broader, deeper and more liquid markets in financial instruments of all kinds to replace markets that are currently fragmented because they are denominated in the various individual national currencies"

PREPARING THE CITY FOR THE EURO

BY EDDIE GEORGE, GOVERNOR OF THE BANK OF ENGLAND

There is no doubt that the introduction of the Single European Currency will have important implications for this country, whatever decision the UK eventually takes on membership. And it is essential, as the Chancellor has said, that the UK Government and UK businesses prepare intensively so that we will be in a position to take the decision to join the single currency, should we wish to do so, in the next Parliament. But the City of London in particular has to prepare on a shorter timescale because, notwithstanding the Government's decision not to seek membership of the single currency on 1 January 1999, the wholesale financial markets must be ready to trade the euro and euro-denominated financial instruments from the start of Monetary Union.

The advent of the euro will encourage the development of broader, deeper and more liquid markets in financial instruments of all kinds to replace markets that are currently fragmented because they are denominated in the various individual national currencies. The euro therefore represents an opportunity for the City of London, not least because, as the history of the euromarkets demonstrates, the location of financial activity does not depend on the local currency. Financial markets do business wherever it can most conveniently, efficiently and profitably be carried on. The reality of this is underlined by the fact that foreign-owned institutions – from Europe and around the world – continue to build their presence in London, notwithstanding the UK's position on joining the single currency. Moreover, competition between financial centres is not a matter of beggar my neighbour. International or intra-regional trade and investment activity is not, at the macroeconomic level, a zero-sum game. It is very much a *positive* sum game; and this is true of financial, just as much as of any other kind of economic activity. Thus all European financial centres have the same basic interest: to make the euro a success.

But if London is to take advantage of the opportunities created by the euro, it must be well-prepared technically. In fact, there is encouraging evidence that UK institutions and markets are taking the steps necessary to ensure that they are ready for the introduction of the euro. The Bank of England has been, and will continue to be, heavily engaged in encouraging and assisting the City of London to be ready. Our role is focused on three main tasks. First, we are seeking to ensure that the necessary infrastructure is developed in the UK to allow anyone who wishes to do so to use the euro in wholesale payments, and in the London financial markets, from 1 January 1999. Second, we have sought to promote discussion between the European Monetary Institute (EMI), national central banks and market participants across Europe about practical issues on which the market is seeking a degree of co-ordination. And, third, we have provided information so that all the people involved in the preparations are as well informed as possible: we have done this, for example, through our quarterly publication *Practical Issues Arising from the Introduction of the Euro*[1], which has been produced since September 1996 and which is now distributed to 32,000 recipients across the City and beyond – including 4,000 who are overseas.

---

1. Available from Public Enquiries at the Bank of England on 0171 601 4012

"... there is encouraging evidence that UK institutions and markets are taking the steps necessary to ensure that they are ready for the introduction of the euro. The Bank of England has been, and will continue to be, heavily engaged in encouraging and assisting the City of London to be ready"

The Bank has been working primarily through the many professional market associations which are active in London. For instance, payments experts are working to develop the euro payments system framework, lawyers are contributing to the development of the euro legal framework, accountants on the accounting and tax implications and so on. This enables the best use of the depth and breadth of expertise available in London. Two areas of preparation are particularly important, and have required extensive collaboration across a range of practitioners, namely the payments infrastructure for the euro, and the market framework for the use of the euro.

We are constructing payments arrangements in euro in London which we intend to be at least as efficient and cheap as anywhere else in Europe, even while the UK is not a member of EMU. Within the UK, the real-time gross settlement system (RTGS) which came into operation in the spring of last year is being developed so that it will be able to operate in euro. When the UK joins, the UK sterling system will effectively become a euro system. And, while the UK is "out", a parallel euro system will sit alongside the sterling system: it will enable the members of CHAPS to process euro payments as a foreign currency within the UK and across borders within the EU, through its link to the pan-European RTGS system – TARGET – which is being developed.

The idea behind TARGET is to link together the national RTGS systems of EU Member States so that large value payments can be made or received *between* Member States throughout the EU area, with finality and in real time, in exactly the same way as they can at present be made and received *within* Member States with national RTGS systems denominated in their own national currencies. One of the main purposes of TARGET is to support closer European economic and financial integration by reducing the risks in pan-European payments – just as national RTGS systems reduce the risks in national payment systems. The other

main purpose of TARGET is to integrate the euro money market so as to ensure that the same short term euro interest rate – determined by the single monetary policy of the European Central Bank – prevails throughout the euro area. TARGET is a project which we strongly support.

The second important aspect of preparation is the development of a comprehensive market framework for the use of the euro in London. The euro Regulations help to provide the legal part of the framework. But to make sure that the euro market in London, as elsewhere in Europe, is as deep and liquid as possible, we also need to harmonise market conventions on new issues of securities in the euro money and bond markets, conventions in the foreign exchange markets, etc. Market associations have now agreed the basis on which conventions in these markets should be harmonised, and the Bank has encouraged their initiative. The problem has been to see how EU-wide decisions will be taken. Harmonised practices may develop spontaneously in the markets, but there is no guarantee of this. So it is very helpful that the EMI Council decided with our encouragement in September to "welcome and support" harmonised market conventions on the basis proposed by the market associations. There remains however a good deal to be done everywhere – in co-ordinating price sources, for example, as methods of redenomination. But in all of these respects London is well up with the game.

There is, therefore, a tremendous amount of work being undertaken in the City in preparation for Monetary Union. And so there needs to be! The City is currently a uniquely international – not national nor regional – financial centre which contributes enormously to the UK economy and the well-being of the UK population. But the City does not hold this pre-eminent position as of right – rather, it *earns* it. Clearly, going forward we need to continue to work to earn this position. And, in terms of working to be ready for the euro, I am confident that the City will be! ☆

ADVANTAGE
WORLDWIDE

We've been helping our clients achieve dramatic performance improvement for more than 70 years. From A. T. Kearney offices in 61 cities, our people travel the globe to work for clients in 90 countries.

Our European offices are assisting clients to address and plan the opportunities of a seamless Europe and secure the benefits of the forthcoming EMU age.

ATKEARNEY

Management Consultants

An EDS company

For more information
A.T. Kearney Limited, Lansdowne House, Berkeley Square, London W1X 5DH
Tel +44 (0)171 468 8000 Fax +44 (0)171 468 8001
http://www.atkearney.com

Alexandria Amsterdam Atlanta Baltimore Beijing Berlin Boston Brussels Buenos Aires Cambridge Caracas Chicago Cleveland Copenhagen Coraopolis Costa Mesa Dallas Denver Düsseldorf Helsinki Hong Kong Houston Kuala Lumpur Lisbon London Los Angeles Madrid Melbourne Mexico City Miami Milan Minneapolis Moscow Munich New York Oslo Ottawa Paris Phoenix Pittsburgh Plano Prague Redwood City Richland Rome Rosslyn San Diego San Francisco Santa Clara São Paolo Seoul Singapore Southfield Stamford Stockholm Stuttgart Sydney Tokyo Toronto Warsaw Wellington Zurich and other cities.

EUROPEAN INTEGRATION
THE ROLE OF THE EUROPEAN INVESTMENT BANK

by
Sir Brian Unwin
EIB President and Chairman of the Board

Introduction

The European Union is on the verge of taking some of the most radical and far-reaching steps forward in its history: its enlargement by welcoming new member states into the Union from Central and Eastern Europe, and the move to Economic and Monetary Union and with it the introduction of the new single currency, the Euro. The European Investment Bank (EIB), with its historic role of promoting social and economic integration, will play a particularly crucial part in the coming decade in helping to steer the Union through theses radical changes.

The role of the EIB

The EIB, the EU's long-term lending arm, was set up in 1958 under the Treaty of Rome with the basic mission to promote the Union's balanced development. It does this by raising funds on the capital markets (at fine rates with its AAA credit rating) for onlending long-term, with a small margin, for sound economic projects that further EU policies.

The Bank's main priority is to support development in the less-favoured regions - accounting for over two-thirds of its lending. Another core aim is to finance communications and energy transfer infrastructure that will bind

Sir Brian Unwin

Europe more closely together, in particular improvement of the strategically vital Trans-European Networks (TENs), the crucial arteries for the freedom of movement within the single market and with its neighbours.

Investment in European industry to strengthen its competitiveness in world markets is another objective, with a special focus on high-tech projects, or investment integrating industry activities at a European level, as well as the activities of small and medium-sized enterprises. Equally the Bank finances schemes to protect the environment and ensure secure energy supplies.

In the United Kingdom, the Bank's lending is now running at an annual rate of some £2 billion, with an increasing emphasis on projects combin-ing public and private sector investment. Recent examples include the Second Severn Crossing, the Heathrow-London Express rail link, construction of the undersea gasline between the UK and Belgium, development and manufacture of the new Jaguar engine, and numerous projects by the UK water companies.

Over the past 40 years, in terms of financing the Bank has grown into the largest of the world's multilateral borrowers and lenders. In 1997, the Bank expects to lend up to ECU 24 billion and to raise the same amount on capital markets in over 20 currencies. This lending contributes to the annual creation of aggregate new investment of some ECU 60 billion, representing about 5% of gross capital investment averaged across the European Union.

Outside the Union

While 90% of the Bank's lending is in its Member States, the Bank also supports investment in over 100 non-member countries in the support of the Union's external aid and co-operation policies. The EIB thus operates in the Mediterranean region, in the African, Caribbean and Pacific group of countries, in South Africa, Latin America and Asia, as well as in Central and Eastern Europe.

Amsterdam, growth and employment

The Amsterdam European Council in June 1997 highlighted the important contribution the EIB is already making to creating employment opportunities in Europe and requested the Bank to intensify these activities. Since then the EIB has rapidly developed its Amsterdam Special Action Programme (ASAP) which will run up to the year 2000.

Under ASAP the Bank has launched a "special window" to support technology related and high growth SMEs by widening their access to venture capital, and to develop other facilities providing risk-sharing or subordinated financing. The Bank will back this activity by calling on up to ECU 1 billion from its annual surpluses over the next three years. As the first "special window" operation, the EIB has set up through the intermediary of the European Investment Fund (EIF), the ECU 125 million European Technology Facility for investment, through specialist venture capital funds, in technology and high growth SMEs. Similar schemes are being established with partner banks in different EU countries.

The two other pillars of ASAP are the extension of the Bank's area of activity into the important labour-intensive areas of health, education and urban renovation, and the intensification of lending for TENs.

Economic and Monetary Union and the Euro

The Bank is therefore already making a major contribution to preparing the ground for the introduction of EMU through financing investment to strengthen sustained economic development in the EU. After EMU, the pattern and volume of EIB lending will become particularly relevant, especially in assisted areas, where persistent regional differences could become increasingly important.

At the same time, as the largest multinational borrower, the EIB is also providing positive support for the future single currency, the Euro. Early in 1997, it issued its first 1 billion Euro bond and has launched a series of benchmark "Euro-tributary bonds" in EU currencies, which will be fungible with the EIB's Euro issues. These will strengthen market liquidity in the Euro from 1999 onwards. With outstanding debt of over ECU 100 billion, of which more than half is denominated in EU currencies and in the ECU to be redeemed after 1 January 1999, and with a yearly borrowing programme of over ECU 20 billion, the Bank will have a large role in preparing the way for a deep and liquid Euro market and to help EU capital markets adjust to EMU.

Enlargement

The EIB is already playing a significant role in the EU's enlargement by financing investment to bring the economies of Central and Eastern Europe up to the levels required for membership, helping to improve their infrastructure, industry and environment. Since 1990, the Bank has channelled over ECU 5 billion into the region, and during 1997 received a fresh mandate to lend a further ECU 3.5 billion up to end-1999. In addition the EIB is establishing a new "pre-accession lending facility" for the region which will give it even greater flexibility and scope to reinforce enlargement efforts, particularly in the fields of infrastructure and investment linking the region's economies more closely with that of the EU. ■

THE TREATY OF AMSTERDAM

BY DR TIMOTHY BAINBRIDGE, AUTHOR OF
THE PENGUIN COMPANION TO EUROPEAN UNION

> *"The Treaty of Amsterdam will be another stage in the gradual progress towards a wider, more flexible Union, which is better equipped, by means of more open and less cumbersome procedures, to respond to the needs and expectations of its citizens"*

Formally signed on 2 October 1997, the Treaty of Amsterdam was the outcome of the third major review of the Treaties upon which the European Union is founded. It now awaits ratification in each of the 15 signatory states, and it cannot enter into force until this process is complete. In order to understand the substance of the changes embodied in the Treaty of Amsterdam, we must first consider the mechanics of Treaty revision and the way in which this new Treaty fits into what has now become an almost continuous process.

The original Treaty of Rome (1957) allowed any member state to propose amendments to the Treaty. These amendments would then be considered by the other signatory states meeting in what has become known as an Intergovernmental Conference (IGC) and, if unanimously approved, would be submitted to each national parliament for ratification. The process was, and largely remains, one of negotiation between sovereign governments: the involvement of the Community institutions, according to the letter of the Treaty, was kept to a strict minimum.

In the event, the provisions of the Treaty of Rome remained unamended for nearly 30 years. Except for changes to the institutions made necessary by the enlargement of the Community to include Denmark, Ireland and the United Kingdom (1973), Greece (1981), and Portugal and Spain (1986), the first wide-ranging set of changes to the Treaty was the Single European Act (SEA) of 1986. In spite of its name, the SEA was in fact two quite separate documents. The first laid down new procedures to improve member states' co-operation in the field of foreign policy. The second specified changes to the voting system used in the Council of Ministers, in order primarily to speed up the passage of the legislation needed to complete the Single Market by the 1992 deadline. Basically, many areas in which progress could only be made on the basis of unanimity – increasingly difficult to achieve in a more diverse Community of twelve member states – now became subject to decisions taken by majority (known as "qualified majority voting", since each member state's vote in the Council is weighted roughly in proportion to its population). At the same time, the European Parliament was given more say in respect of certain categories of legislation under a new two-reading procedure.

The SEA entered into force in November 1987. Less than a year later, at a Summit meeting in Hanover in June 1988, the Twelve set up a committee under Jacques Delors, then President of the Commission, to report on how progress could be made towards Economic and Monetary Union (EMU). The Delors Report was discussed by the Heads of Government in Madrid in June 1989, and it was clear that the Report's recommendations were of such importance that they would entail a further round of revisions to the Treaty. Accordingly, the decision was taken to convene an IGC to discuss them.

In April 1990, President Mitterrand of France, Chancellor Kohl of Germany, and the Belgian Government put forward ambitious proposals for closer political integration. This increased the momentum towards a full-scale review of the Treaties, and it was decided to convene two IGCs in parallel: the first, conducted by finance ministers, on EMU; and the second, conducted by foreign ministers, on political union. Meanwhile, the political context was changing very rapidly. By the time the two IGCs began in December 1990, the former East Germany had been incorporated into the Community, three countries (Austria, Cyprus and Malta) had applied for membership, and the collapse of Communism in Central and Eastern Europe raised the prospect of several more applications being put forward in the near future.

The conclusions of these two IGCs were set out in a document formally known as the Treaty on European Union but more widely known as the Maastricht Treaty, after the Dutch city in which agreement was finally reached amongst the Heads of Government in December 1991. The Treaty was in seven parts. The first proclaimed the establishment of the European Union and set out the general principles upon which it was founded (such as "respect [for] the national identities of its Member States"). The second section contained amendments to the Treaty of Rome, including those with a bearing on EMU (from the final stage of which the United Kingdom secured an "opt out"). The third and fourth sections contained amendments to the European Coal and Steel Community and European Atomic Energy Community Treaties. The fifth and sixth sections set up the so-called "pillars", the Common Foreign and Security Policy (CFSP) and co-operation between member states in Justice and Home Affairs (JHA) matters. Although part of the European Union, these two areas of EU activity are reserved primarily for direct co-operation between governments: the involvement of EU institutions (the Commission, the European Parliament, the Court of Justice) is kept to a minimum. The seventh and final section contained general provisions, such as those on Treaty amendment and on the procedures to be followed in response to applications for membership.

Ambitious in scope, the Maastricht Treaty was inevitably a diffuse and confusing document. Much of it made sense only to those already familiar with existing Treaty provisions. The fact of its having been negotiated within a tightly-knit group of politicians, diplomats and civil servants was a further disadvantage. Many of its most controversial provisions – on EMU, on EU citizenship, on more powers for the European

Parliament – were couched in language which provided ample scope for misunderstanding. For these and for other reasons, the Treaty had a protracted and difficult passage through the ratification stage: referenda in Denmark, France and Ireland, a legal challenge in Germany and innumerable closely-fought debates in the House of Commons. In the event, ratification was not completed until October 1993. The Treaty came into effect the following month.

The misgivings to the effect that the Maastricht Treaty was too ambitious were matched on the other hand by disappointment that it did not go far enough. In the final round of negotiations, the German and Benelux Governments secured a commitment that the Treaty provisions would be reviewed before the end of 1996: in effect, that a further IGC would be convened within a few years. It was this Conference which resulted in the Treaty of Amsterdam.

The Member States recognised that because of a lack of public confidence in the outcome of the negotiations the Maastricht Treaty had been a near-disaster. Accordingly, by way of prelude to the main Conference, a so-called "Reflection Group" was set up, composed of representatives of the foreign ministers and of the Commission and two mem-

bers of the European Parliament. Their task was to consult as widely as possible, with a view to identifying the key issues and laying the groundwork for possible compromises. The Reflection Group started its work in June 1995 (that is, less than two years since the Maastricht Treaty had come into effect). The IGC began the following year, and the new Treaty was agreed at a Summit meeting in Amsterdam in June 1997.

Several themes ran through the negotiations. The first was to prepare and, if necessary, to modify the institutions and procedures of the Union with a view to its enlargement to 20 or more states within the decade. The second was to bring the Union "closer to the citizen", which meant a style of decision-making which was both simpler and more accessible. The third was to equip the Union with the means to meet new challenges, such as the fight against international crime, and to address intractable problems of long standing, such as the 18 million people who remain unemployed. The fourth was to strengthen the EU's voice in world affairs.

The Treaty of Amsterdam seeks to improve the efficiency of the EU institutions in several ways. At the level of the Council, more use is to be made of majority voting, although fundamental questions such as taxation, the EU budget and

> **"It is not the end of the road. Another IGC will be convened 'at least one year before the membership of the European Union exceeds twenty'. For the foreseeable future, IGCs and the controversies to which they give rise will be an inescapable part of the politics of the European Union"**

constitutional issues remain subject to unanimity. The position of the President of the Commission is strengthened by giving him or her more say in the appointment of the other Commissioners. The number of members of the European Parliament (currently 626) will be limited to 700, however large the Union becomes. And the overall flexibility of the Union is enhanced by the introduction of ground rules which will allow some member states to go faster than others in particular areas of policy. This was done in recognition of the greater diversity of a Union of 20 or more states.

In most areas of EU decision-making, "co-decision" between the Council of Ministers and the European Parliament will become the norm. At the same time, national parliaments are encouraged to take a closer interest in EU affairs. In future, there will be a minimum period of six weeks within which national parliaments may make their views known on a proposal before the Council. With few exceptions, individuals will enjoy a much greater right of access to EU documents, and the Council will no longer be able to legislate in secret. The fundamental rights of individuals *vis-à-vis* the EU institutions are fully safeguarded in the Treaty, and actions may be brought in the Court of Justice in the event of an alleged breach. For the first time, the European Council may bring sanctions to bear upon member states which flout basic human or civil rights or the rule of law.

Five years from the date when the Treaty of Amsterdam comes into effect, much of the work currently done within the Justice and Home Affairs "pillar" of the Maastricht Treaty is likely to be fully incorporated into normal EU decision-making. The effect of this is to make the free movement of people at the frontiers between member states (including questions of asylum and immigration) subject to EU rules. The right of Ireland and the United Kingdom to continue to apply frontier checks is, however, explicitly safeguarded. Police and judicial co-operation on criminal matters will remain exclusively in the domain of national governments, although new procedures and new legal instruments will be introduced to make it more effective.

The Treaty of Amsterdam contains a new chapter on employment. This marks the member states' determination to make the promotion of employment one of the central tasks of the Union. Although national governments will remain responsible for their own policies, a greater measure of co-ordination will be applied at EU level through annual reviews by the Heads of Government, guidelines laid down by the Council of Ministers, and a new Employment Committee. The employment chapter builds on the "Social Protocol" annexed to the Maastricht Treaty, from which John Major secured an "opt out". The Labour Government elected in May 1997 has reversed this policy and accepts the employment provisions of the new Treaty.

The Common Foreign and Security Policy (CFSP), introduced by the Maastricht Treaty, remains largely outside the ambit of the EU institutions. However, the coherence and effectiveness of the CFSP is to be enhanced by the creation of a new policy planning and early warning unit to speed up the Union's response to emergencies. Relations between the EU and the Western European Union (WEU) – the European arm of NATO – are clarified and strengthened. New provisions in the Treaty of Amsterdam underscore the Union's involvement, through the WEU, in the peace-keeping, humanitarian, and crisis management tasks which have become increasingly important since the end of the Cold War. In all CFSP matters, the President-in-Office of the Council of Ministers is given new responsibilities, assisted by a Secretary-General, to put across the Union's position in international fora and in the media.

The Treaty of Amsterdam, like its predecessors the SEA and the Maastricht Treaty, will be another stage in the gradual progress towards a wider, more flexible Union, which is better equipped, by means of more open and less cumbersome procedures, to respond to the needs and expectations of its citizens. But it is not the end of the road. In the course of the negotiations, the member states addressed, but could not resolve, a number of other important questions, such as adjustments to the system of weighted votes in the Council, which directly affects the balance between large and small states. This question was linked to that of the number of Commissioners. The only agreement which the member states could reach was to decide in a protocol that from the date of the next enlargement there shall be only one Commissioner per member state, as long as the voting system in the Council has been modified "in a manner acceptable to all member states". In order to discuss these modifications in the context of a "comprehensive review of the composition and functioning of the institutions", another IGC will be convened "at least one year before the membership of the European Union exceeds twenty". This year, membership negotiations will begin with six applicant states, and these will entail further adjustments to the institutions. Five more applicants are awaiting their turn. In 1999, the single currency will be established and a new financial framework agreed. So there can be little doubt that, for the foreseeable future, IGCs and the controversies to which they give rise will be an inescapable part of the politics of the European Union. ☆

Is your advertising agency small enough?
Or are they big enough not to care?

At Red, we believe that being small is a numerical fact, not a state of mind.
If you want a small agency that's big on ideas, talk to Red. 0181 533 3300

"... *criminal gangs now operate across national boundaries, so that the proceeds of crime committed in one country may be invested thousands of miles away from where the crime was committed; and other forms of crime, such as the drugs trade, rely upon networks of criminals working together across a series of countries*"

MAKING EUROPE SAFER FOR THE CITIZEN

BY MATTHEW SOWEMIMO, DIRECTOR OF RESEARCH, THE EUROPEAN MOVEMENT

MEETING THE CHALLENGE OF FIGHTING CRIME

Crime is increasingly an international and highly sophisticated activity. An offence taking place on a street corner in Britain may have its roots thousands of miles away; criminal gangs now operate across national boundaries, so that the proceeds of crime committed in one country may be invested thousands of miles away from where the crime was committed; and other forms of crime, such as the drugs trade, rely upon networks of criminals working together across a series of countries.

International crime has also expanded into wholly new areas of criminal activity, such as environmental crime. For example, the European countries committed themselves to a CFC ban ten years ago but have now become the target of criminal gangs which are smuggling CFC gases into Europe. In addition, old and well-established forms of crime, such as bribery and fraud, have taken on a whole new dimension. This is particularly true in the area of fraud against the European Union budget.

Cross-border crime demands a cross-border response. In this area the EU has a vital role to play in fighting international criminals, many of whom are key contributors to everyday crimes, such as drug pushing in British neighbourhoods. National action alone is inadequate as a solution to the scale and sophistication of modern crime. Separate and uncoordinated national action against crime would enable criminals to exploit the different legal systems within Europe. Drug smugglers would never be monitored and caught unless the police authorities throughout Europe were talking to one another in order to plan arrests. For example, a joint Anglo-Dutch police operation led to the capture of Curtis Warren, a major British drugs baron, in Rotterdam after he attempted to smuggle £75 million worth of cocaine into Britain.

The EU has responded to the challenge of international crime by setting up co-operation between its member states in justice and home affairs matters. In taking joint action against international crime the EU is also responding to the concerns of its citizens. Opinion surveys have shown clearly that European citizens want the EU to refocus its attention on fighting crime. The 1997 Opinion Research Business survey found that 57% of the British people surveyed believed that organised crime would be better tackled at a European level, with 72% of respondents favouring EU action over national action in the fight against terrorism.

The Maastricht Treaty gave the EU countries the authority to work together in key areas such as policing, criminal law, border controls and customs checks. The Treaty's rules ensured that co-operation in these areas leaves the Member States with the final say, rather than the European institutions.

National decision-making governs justice and home affairs because many EU member states, including Britain, believe that policy-making in this area relates to the core functions of a state. The Amsterdam Treaty, while maintaining the principle of national decision making in areas like policing, strengthened the effectiveness of the EU's anti-crime framework.

EUROPEAN POLICING

European police co-operation is the most important contribution to the fight against cross-border crime. The centrepiece of Europe's fight against organised crime is the European Police Office (Europol). Europol was established by EU justice ministers in 1993 and is based in the Hague under the leadership of Jurgen Storbeck. When Europol was first set up it was given the remit of exchanging and analysing intelligence on drug trafficking. By 1994, Europol's remit was extended to motor vehicle crime, money laundering and the trade in radioactive and nuclear materials. Europol receives intelligence on these matters from the national police forces of all the EU member states.

A LOST ART RETURNS TO LONDON

PRIVATE DINING AT THE LANESBOROUGH

In Britain, the National Criminal Intelligence Service (NCIS) acts as a contact point for Europol.

The benefits of pooling intelligence to fight cross-border crime can be illustrated by one example of Europol's activities: a German who escaped from prison in 1992 fled to South America and set up a network for smuggling cocaine to Europe. A second German organised the finance and arranged to import the drugs via Portugal. In September 1996, 50kg of cocaine arrived in a yacht sailed by two Italians. A consignment was smuggled by a Spaniard to Germany via Paris. The load was seized on arrival in Germany and the courier and two German organisers were arrested. So too, were five other members of the network in Germany. The head of the organisation was captured by the Madrid police on arrival in Spain from Brazil. The two Italian smugglers were caught and more stashes of cocaine were seized when police raided a house in Portugal.

This successful operation yielded such comprehensive results because the initial investigation by the Heilbronn police in south-west Germany was transformed into a European-wide operation as a result of Europol's involvement. In 1996 Europol dealt with no fewer than 2,400 cases.

Europol will be able to take an enhanced role in the fight against international crime after the parliaments of the EU member states have passed the Europol Convention. The Convention, signed by European justice ministers in 1995, allows Europol to widen the scope of its activities and gives new resources to the organisation. The Convention will allow Europol to set up its own database, whereas at the moment Europol can only analyse data provided by the EU member states. The Convention will also allow Europol to liaise with international agencies outside Europe, like the FBI, in order to fight crime. International liaison is crucial to Europol's task as, in areas like the drug trade routes, chains thread through all parts of the globe. Europol also holds regular meetings with Interpol to prevent duplication in the activities of the two organisations.

British police officers have always liaised with their opposite numbers in other European countries but Europol will ensure that this becomes much more sophisticated and proactive. Unlike Interpol, Europol can undertake a central analysis of crime. Europol will also have access to some types of intelligence material which would be denied to Interpol. EU countries which have generally been reluctant to hand over intelligence are more willing to assist Europol because the data protection rules in the convention were agreed by all EU states.

Europol also has the advantage of having officers from all the European countries based in one place. This degree of pooled intelligence and expertise allows for far more effective targeting of key criminals than bilateral police contacts. A bilateral investigation between the French and British police forces into a major drugs gang would not be able to identify all the links in the drugs supply chain as effectively as an organisation which can pull in intelligence from all the member states.

> *"British police officers have always liaised with their opposite numbers in other European countries but Europol will ensure that this becomes much more sophisticated and proactive. Unlike Interpol, Europol can undertake a central analysis of crime. Europol will also have access to some types of intelligence material which would be denied to Interpol"*

New challenges to European police co-operation are developing in Central and Eastern Europe. Organised criminal gangs are becoming increasingly active in Eastern Europe, especially in the context of the "trade" in illegal immigration. These concerns have prompted the EU's High Level Group on organised crime to recommend that the Central and Eastern European countries which have applied to join the EU should be obliged to incorporate aspects of the EU's anti-crime legislation as a condition of their acceptance into full membership of the Union.

A European FBI?
Ministers and heads of government in the EU states are currently engaged in debate and discussion about Europol's future role. The German Government has consistently declared its support for Europol taking on an operational role and becoming a "European FBI".

Operational powers for Europol relate principally to two issues – Europol officers taking a role on the ground and the widening of Europol's remit. An "on the ground" role would mean that Europol officers become involved in carrying out actual investigations on the sovereign territory of the member states. Europol officers would therefore be involved in operations down to the level of pursuing suspects and making arrests. The Amsterdam Treaty takes a step down this road by allowing Europol officers to act in a support capacity "on the ground" to national police units. Police forces in different parts of the Union would be able to call upon the expertise of Europol officers in areas like trade in counterfeit goods.

Those who advocate an operational role for Europol would also wish to see the organisation's remit extended beyond those areas covered by Article 2 of the Convention. The Convention itself foreshadows such an expansion of the organisation's remit in its annex. The annex lists 18 areas in which Europol could become active, subject to the agreement of justice ministers. These areas include: crimes against the person, such as racial crime; property crime, in areas like computers; and environmental crime, such as trade in endangered species. If Europol's remit were extended to some, if not all, of these areas then it would rival national police forces in its authority. The provision in the Amsterdam Treaty

"A bilateral investigation between the French and British police forces into a major drugs gang would not be able to identify all the links in the drugs supply chain as effectively as an organisation which can pull in intelligence from all the member states"

which allows for Europol support units to be sent in to work alongside national police forces blurs the line between intelligence gathering and operations. The British Government opposes the creation of a European FBI but is strongly supportive of the Europol's work under the terms of the Convention. Europol can only take a fully operational role with the agreement of all EU member states.

CRIMINAL LAW CO-OPERATION

Another area where EU joint action is crucial to fighting crime is criminal law. European member states have worked together since 1993 to ensure that they harmonise aspects of their criminal law in order to prevent criminals exploiting differences in the legal systems of member states. The two key areas where this has taken place are in anti-fraud policy and racism.

Fraud

The anti-fraud aspect of EU co-operation has centred on safeguards against those who have sought to defraud the EU budget. The bulk of the EU's budget is spent and administered in each of the member states, which means that unless tough controls are put in place in the member states, taxpayers across the Union will see their money wasted or channelled into criminal organisations. The EU programmes which have become the main targets of fraudsters are the Common Agricultural Policy and the structural funds. Other types of cross-frontier fraudulent activity, such as the smuggling of

cigarettes to avoid customs duties, hits national budgets as well as the EU budget.

The EU ministers have signed an anti-fraud convention – the Convention for the Protection of EU Financial Interests – which forms a key component of the Union's anti-crime strategy. The convention lays down a single definition of fraud which should be a criminal offence in all states and subject to penalties, including imprisonment. The Amsterdam Treaty extends majority voting into anti-fraud policy. This means that in future no single country will be in a position to block more stringent anti-fraud policies.

Racism and xenophobia

The European Parliament has, over the past ten years, drawn attention to the problem of racism in the EU member states. The Parliament has particularly focused on the threat of organised fascist and racist activity. European leaders have responded to the anxieties which members of the European Parliament (MEPs) have identified, by enacting anti-racist legislation.

In 1996 European ministers passed an anti-racist "joint action" within the criminal law co-operation area. The joint action commits member states to criminalise a range of racist behaviour, such as the dissemination of racist literature. In addition, the legislation commits judicial authorities in member states to exchange information amongst themselves to support prosecutions against racist groups which are based in one of the member states but which circulate racist material outside their own country. So, for example, this law would require that if the British police discovered that anti-semitic literature had been sent to Britain from another member state, they could refer this evidence to the authorities in that state, in order that the organisation which published the material could be prosecuted.

BORDERS AND FREE MOVEMENT

The Single Market has now been established for four years, based around free movement of capital, goods, services and people. Although free movement brings with it many economic and cultural opportunities, without proper safeguards it also offers a means for criminals to further their activities. The EU countries have sought to accompany free movement rights with such safeguards.

The commitment of European states to free movement of persons led to the creation of the Schengen agreement. Schengen was signed by Belgium, France, Germany, Luxembourg and the Netherlands in June 1990 and since then Italy, Spain and Portugal have joined. The Schengen Agreement was originally set up outside EU structures, but the Amsterdam Treaty incorporates its provisions into the EU. Schengen abolishes internal border controls between its members so, for example, a Portuguese person travelling to Spain would not be subject to systematic passport checks.

The removal of internal borders between the participating states obviously means that the criteria for determining who should be allowed across the external border of the Schengen countries are of crucial importance. This is because, within the Schengen area, if only one member state had a lax immigration policy or ineffective external controls, the other member states would have reason to fear that they would as a consequence see the entry of large numbers of illegal immigrants.

The Schengen countries have therefore committed themselves to abide by a common policy on the issue of visas. Other controls require that external borders should only be crossed at fixed hours and that conditions of entry for aliens visiting for short periods are adhered to. The Schengen countries have also set up the Schengen Information System (SIS). The SIS allows police and customs authorities to get access to reports on persons and objects so that they can refuse entry to them at internal frontiers. The SIS system is designed to provide intelligence support so that criminals are not able to capitalise on the removal of customs checks at internal borders.

Both Conservative and Labour Governments have consistently opposed giving up the UK's frontier controls on people. As a result the Government secured a series of legal guarantees in the Amsterdam Treaty which allow the UK to maintain frontier controls. UK frontier controls ensure that there are systematic customs checks on people entering the UK. The Foreign Secretary, Robin Cook, argued that Britain, as an island position, is in a very different situation

to countries which share land borders and which therefore have a greater interest in operating a common policy.

The Amsterdam Treaty not only upholds Britain's right to maintain border controls but also ensures that the UK will not be subject to any new common immigration and asylum policies decided by the 13 member states who participate in Schengen. However if Britain wishes to adopt aspects of EU border control legislation, then it can do so, subject to the approval of all the other member states.

HOW ARE DECISIONS MADE IN JUSTICE AND HOME AFFAIRS?

It is worth repeating that co-operation in justice and home affairs matters is decided by *national governments*. All matters concerning policing and criminal law co-operation are decided through the unanimous agreement of national governments.

Decisions about matters like Europol and criminal law co-operation are made by justice ministers from the fifteen member states. Both national governments and the European Commission have the power to propose new laws. The European Parliament has the right to be consulted about these laws.

All the EU states have the right to decide whether they wish their national courts to judge any legal challenges to the EU's activities in policing and criminal law co-operation, or whether they wish to refer cases to the European Court of Justice (ECJ). The large majority of other member states have chosen to refer cases related to matters like the Europol Convention to the ECJ for final judgement. The Prime Minister, Tony Blair, has made it clear that Britain will not refer such cases to the ECJ.

THE NEXT STEP

EU joint action in justice and home affairs has provided an indispensable line of defence against organised crime. Drug traffickers, fraudsters or extreme right-wing activists now find that European countries are sharing intelligence on their activities, denying them legal loopholes that allowed them to evade arrest or punishment. They can also expect that countries outside Europe are better briefed on their plans. Britain on its own could not put in place laws to prevent drugs money being laundered in Belgium. British police officers acting alone could not effectively monitor antique thieves based in Germany who plan to raid several British country houses and sell their acquisitions in Portugal.

It is because justice and home affairs touch upon each country's own conception of citizenship and state power that policy change can only realistically take place as a result of the agreement of all member states. However, some people argue that giving a greater role to Community institutions, like the ECJ and the Commission, would ensure clarity about Europol's remit and consistent application of the Europol Convention rules throughout the EU. In the future, European leaders will have to decide whether they can reconcile such a demand with the understanding of national soverignty. ☆

CITIZENSHIP OF THE EUROPEAN UNION

BY PROFESSOR ELIZABETH MEEHAN, THE QUEEN'S UNIVERSITY, BELFAST

"The general principles of the Union laid down in Maastricht have been amended to focus upon 'liberty, democracy, respect for human rights and fundamental freedoms, and the rule of law' "

Jacques Santer's commentary on the Treaty of Amsterdam, agreed on 17 June 1997, says:

"This Treaty is for you. It lays the foundations for the Europe we want to build in the twenty-first century. It sets out the rules of the game governments will have to observe and it establishes rights for all the citizens." (European Commission, 1997b, p. 2)

Citizenship of the Union came into being formally in Article 8 of the Maastricht Treaty. As a personal status, it was confirmed in the Amsterdam Treaty, which also consolidates and extends citizens' rights. Though it was not until Maastricht that some transnational political rights were introduced (nationally-based elections to the European Parliament were first held in 1979), elements of common citizenship were already arising from the 1957 Treaty of Rome; that is, if we accept the view of its best known exponent, T. H. Marshall, that citizenship is realised through a triad of civil, political and social rights. These elements of common citizenship can be seen in the European Community's (EC) regulation of legal and social rights. This chapter outlines developments from Rome to Maastricht and explains what was added at Amsterdam. Criticisms of EU citizenship are referred to but the conclusion here is that its provisions are dynamic and can continue to make the EU more meaningful for "ordinary" people.

From the Treaty of Rome to the Treaty of Maastricht

The goal of freedom of movement (Article 118 of the Treaty of Rome) is the foundation for some equivalents of traditional civil rights, since elucidated in the jurisprudence of the European Court of Justice (ECJ); for example, relating to residence, the administration of justice and ownership of immovable property – for economically active migrants within the Community. Almost from the outset, the ECJ established that the Treaty of Rome gave a common legal right to individual nationals, migrant or not. This was their right to expect, and duty to ensure, that states, including their own, complied with Community law (*van Gend en Loos v. Nederlandse Administratie der Belastigen*, Case No 26/62, [1962] ECR 1).

European social rights are not directly redistributive. Rather, the Community regulates entitlements (mainly for workers) in member states through legal principles, the most important of which is non-discrimination. The principle of freedom of movement gave rise to two Regulations outlawing nationality-based discrimination against migrant workers' access to insurance-based social benefits (revised as Regulation 1408/71), and against them and their families in other social assistance (revised as Regulation 1612/68). Sex-based discrimination was made unlawful in Article 119 of the Treaty of Rome which required equal pay for men and women doing the same work. Between 1975 and the mid-1980s, five Directives followed which widened the scope of equal pay, extended the right of equality into other conditions of employment, applied the principle to statutory and occupational social security schemes and gave comparable entitlements to self-employed women. Another Directive, passed in 1992, protects pregnant women workers and guarantees levels of maternity pay and leave.

Rights not based on the non-discrimination principle include: Directives in the 1980s on consultation over redundancy plans and protection of employment conditions when work is transferred to another undertaking; and other Directives, stemming from the Single European Act of 1987, requiring consultation and protection in situations of risk and hazard at work. The latter, and others relating to the young and elderly, were introduced through the 1989 Community Charter of Fundamental Social Rights of Workers.

The Treaty of Maastricht "constitutionalises" the notion of "Union Citizen". A citizen of the Union is anyone, worker or not, who is a national of a member state. The Treaty also goes further in recognising the universalistic justification for citizenship by referring to the relevance to the EU of the 1950 European Convention on Human Rights and Fundamental Freedoms (ECHR). (This Convention is a set of provisions agreed upon by the Council of Europe, founded in 1947 and comprising more countries than the EU.) The Maastricht Treaty incorporates rights to information and redress within the common institutions, and requires member states to agree upon certain transnational political rights. The last provision includes the right of a national of any member state to be pro-

tected by the diplomatic and consular services of another state when outside the Union and the rights to vote and stand for office in municipal and European elections (not general elections) wherever they reside within the Union. Though citizenship is often considered an individualistic concept, it is notable that the Maastricht Treaty "constitutionalises" a channel for people collectively to influence common policies through the Committee of the Regions.

From the Treaty of Maastricht to the Treaty of Amsterdam

Almost as soon as the Maastricht Treaty came into force, preparations began for the next stage – with lobbying and extensive deliberations in the Reflection Group, the Comité des Sages and the Inter-Governmental Conference. The Treaty that was agreed in June 1997 began as a text drafted by the Irish Presidency in the second half of 1996 and it retains the priorities of the Irish drafters, including provisions relating to citizenship (Institute of European Affairs, 24.6.97). The general principles of the Union laid down in Maastricht have been amended to focus upon "liberty, democracy, respect for human rights and fundamental freedoms, and the rule of law" (Amended Article F of Maastricht, European Commission, 1997a, p. 5). The amended Article affirms that rights specified in the European Convention will be respected as principles of Community law. A new paragraph in the Preamble adds confirmation of respect for the social rights of the 1961 European Social Charter (an addendum to the Convention) and the Community's own 1989 Charter (ibid). A new Article 6a amends the Treaty of Rome to enable the EU to take action, if it wishes, "to combat discrimination based on sex, racial or ethnic origin, religion or belief, disability, age or sexual orientation" (ibid p. 9).

In this connection, two changes in the United Kingdom are noteworthy. Soon after winning the 1997 General Election, the new Labour Government announced that it would end the "opt-out" from further EU social developments that the previous government had secured in the Maastricht Treaty, thus enabling social policy to be re-incorporated into the main body of the Amsterdam Treaty. Secondly, the Government has announced that it will reform the way in which the UK meets its obligations under the ECHR. Legislation will be introduced to reduce the time and difficulty for UK citizens in claiming ECHR rights by enabling them to appeal to the Convention's provisions directly in domestic courts instead of having to exhaust all potential domestic remedies before gaining access to the ECHR court at Strasbourg.

The concrete provisions designed to buttress these principles do not extend Maastricht's primary political rights to general elections. But the Amsterdam Treaty does introduce new legal and secondary political rights which could, depending on implementation, become significant. And, despite controversy prior to agreement over unemployment and poverty, it extends scope for action in the socio-economic sphere.

New legal and political protection includes: the entitlement

The Conrad N. Hilton Foundation invites nominations for the 1998 Hilton Humanitarian Prize.

Please help us identify the organization—anywhere in this world—that has made the most extraordinary contribution toward alleviating human suffering.

The prize is one million dollars (US$1,000,000) awarded to an established non-profit, charitable, or non-governmental organization that has shown extraordinary merit in combatting the effects of extreme human affliction, whatever the cause.

The prize is not a grant, based on future goals; it is an award for extraordinary accomplishment as determined by a distinguished, independent panel of jurors.

Previous honorees have been <u>Operation Smile</u> and the <u>International Rescue Committee</u>.

Nominators' packets are available now.

Deadline for nominations is January 30,1998. The prize will be awarded in September, 1998.

THE JURY WILL CONSIDER:

Historic achievement and recent performance

Innovative program design

Organizational capacity and administrative efficiency

Collaboration with others

Most importantly, long term impact

Nominations Manager, Conrad N. Hilton Humanitarian Prize
10100 Santa Monica Boulevard, Suite 740 Los Angeles, California, 90067-4011 USA

Telephone: (310) 556-8178 Facsimile: (310) 556-8130 e-mail: Prize@HiltonFoundation.org

of individuals to take EU institutions to the ECJ over any action which they think breaches their rights (European Commission, 1997b, p. 7); and new Articles Fa in the Maastricht Treaty and 236 in the Rome Treaty which enable the European Council to deal with a member state in "serious and persistent breach" of the general principles of rights, including by suspending its voting rights (ibid, pp. 6-7).

The ability of citizens to influence or participate in Union policy is covered in several Chapters. For example, a Protocol on subsidiarity (ibid, Chapter 9), while mostly about the respective responsibilities of states and common institutions, retains the aspiration "that decisions are taken as closely as possible to the citizens of the Union". Rights of access to the documents of the Commission, Council and Parliament are re-affirmed in a Chapter on transparency (ibid, p. 94) and the Council is obliged to make public the record of voting on legislation (European Commission, 1996b, p. 7). Communication with citizens should be in their own language (new Article 8d, Maastricht, European Commission, 1996a, p. 76). Individuals are protected against the misuse of personal data in a new Article 213b in the Treaty of Rome (ibid, p. 11).

The capacities of peoples' elected representatives to act on their behalf are to be improved through more efficient arrangements for scrutiny of EU proposals by national parliaments (ibid, Chapter 19) and by the extension, and simplification, of the European Parliament's co-decisionmaking powers *vis à vis* the Council of Ministers (ibid, Chapter 14). There are additional obligations on the European Parliament to consult the Economic and Social Committee and the Committee of the Regions (ibid, Chapter 18).

The civil right of freedom of movement is considerably consolidated in Chapter 2 (ibid, pp. 12-15) of the Amsterdam Treaty, which introduces a new Title into the Treaty of Rome to incorporate, over the next five years, the Schengen Convention (now including Norway and Iceland) and much of the Justice and Home Affairs pillar of the Maastricht Treaty. This will make provisions subject to Community processes of consultation and judicial review. Measures to be adopted cover: the free movement of EU citizens and "third country" nationals when crossing internal borders; consistent procedures at external borders and common visa rules; common minimum standards in the treatment of asylum seekers and refugees; common policies on legal and illegal immigration; and common conditions for "third country" nationals. There have been amendments to Title VI of the Maastricht Treaty in which Protocols allow derogations for Denmark and protect the Common Travel Area between Ireland and the United Kingdom. All three may participate in proposed initiatives if they are seen as consistent with their interests. But, while the UK and Ireland may apply controls at frontiers with other member states, travellers to the latter from either of the former may be subject to comparable checks.

Socio-economic provisions and rights are dealt with in two Chapters. Chapter 3 introduces into the Treaty of Rome a new Title on employment, not to extend citizens' rights but to co-ordinate national policies, under EU guidance and monitoring, so as to achieve "a high level of employment" and "a skilled, trained and adaptable workforce" (ibid, p. 57). Rights at work excluding pay and industrial disputes but including consultation over proposals with the "social partners" are part of the subject of Chapter 4 on Social Policy. This is now integral to the Treaties, the UK having "opted-in" to Maastricht's Protocol on the Social Agreement. The new Chapter promises further directives to improve consultation, to reduce exclusion from the labour market (and, therefore, one source of poverty) and to make sex equality more real. In response to an unfavourable ruling on positive action in the ECJ (*Kalanke v. Freie Hansestadt Bremen*, ECJ [1995] Case C-450/93), the Chapter explicitly authorises measures "to make it easier for the underrepresented sex to pursue a vocational activity or to prevent or compensate for disadvantages in professional careers" (ibid p. 67). Action is promised (though subject to unanimous voting and, hence, difficult to achieve) on social security; conditions when contracts are terminated; worker participation in company policy; employment conditions for third country nationals; and job creation.

Other conditions which affect the lives of citizens are also covered. Proposed actions include: harmonised and national measures to reduce environmental risks in general and at work, including impact assessments of all policies (ibid, Chapter 5); the overcoming of major health scourges and attention to the health implications of all other policies (ibid, Chapter 6); and consumer protection (ibid, Chapter 7).

ASSESSMENTS OF CITIZENSHIP FROM THE TREATY OF ROME TO THE TREATY OF AMSTERDAM

The only possible bases for rights in the Treaty of Rome – freedom of movement of goods, capital, labour and services – led to the criticism that European rights were restricted to the "citizen-as-worker" (making it particularly defective for women and all those not in regular, conventional employment) instead of reflecting the normative principle that people are citizens because they are human beings. Also, although ECJ jurisprudence tended to expand the scope of rights and to limit anomalies within and across states, at least until the 1980s, the legal instruments and enforcement procedures can make it difficult to realise rights that are, in practice, common across the Community. It is also argued that the evolution of European citizenship replicated in a larger arena the physical and social exclusion of people without the right nationality. (Third country migrants within the Community, however, do have some protection under the original Treaty of Rome if they are members of a migrant EU family or live in states which adhere to a non-binding Recommendation that they be treated the same as intra-Community migrants. They may also benefit from agreements between the Community and third countries.)

Concerns about the narrowness of rights began to be acknowledged in the mid-1970s, grew with the momentum of discussion of an "ever closer union" in the 1980s, and were reflected in the Maastricht Treaty. Though there are positive assessments of Maastricht and prior developments (see below), the 1991 Treaty has been criticised for not going far enough.

All critics note that the status of the EU citizen continues to rest upon nationality of a member state and that this remains a prerogative of member state governments. They also note the exclusion of general elections and potential derogations from provisions for municipal and European elections. These are possible where there are specific problems, especially questions of national identities, as in Luxembourg where the proportion of residents from other member states is larger than elsewhere (Closa,1995). O'Leary (1995) argues that: the pre-existing direct link (*van Gend en Loos* – see above) between individuals and the centre is slight, a view reinforced by a German ruling about the 1991 Treaty (*Manfred Brunner and others v. The European Union Treaty*, Cases 2 BvR 2134/92 and 2159/92 [1994] 1 CMLR 57; see also Harmsen, 1994). He goes on to argue that the new voting rights are little more than reciprocal arrangements which could exist, and sometimes do, irrespective of union; and that it will be difficult in practice to use the right to diplomatic and consular protection by other member states. Curtin and Meijers (1995) identify hypocrisy on the part of member state governments, except Denmark and the Netherlands, in their ostensible intention to enhance rights to information. Member states' restrictive applications of these measures to information about border policies reinforce at a European level the "closure" effects of citizenship on people from outside. In the social field, the Commission's capacity to expand a regulatory regime of rights is restricted to what it may opportunistically introduce in a context of a reluctant Council of Ministers (Mazey, 1966). Critics of Maastricht also stress the limitations of local partnership, regional subsidiarity and the status, powers and budget of the Committee of the Regions. Such criticisms would need to be met if the Amsterdam Treaty is, indeed, to live up to its promise outlined by Jacques Santer.

So far there has been a cautious welcome for the Amsterdam Treaty. Positive views (e.g., Oreja, 18.6.97; IEA, 24.6.97) have been expressed about the adoption of strong normative principles of rights; the new basis for combating all forms of discrimination; the procedures for dealing with infringements of rights; the inclusion of the Employment Chapter; the references to reducing exclusion; and the proposal to set standards for "third country" nationals at work and in free movement. The Treaty's references to national and Union representative bodies goes a little way towards Chryssochou's (1996) insistence that "democratic deficits" need to be addressed on both planes if the experience of citizenship is to be realised to its full. On the other hand, the Commission itself reflects some of the concerns of voluntary organisations by regretting the limitations of social policy (European Commission, 1997b, p. 6). It also notes that "the institutional system is not yet entirely equal to the challenges" and the opaqueness of the Treaty's text (Oreja, 18.6.97). Moreover, "under many . . . headings, . . . the provisions may be criticised as being general rather than specific and aspirational rather than tangible" (IEA, 24.6.97).

But, as a foil to criticisms of the limitations of Maastricht, there is an alternative assessment of EU developments which can be applied equally to Amsterdam. For example, Weiner (1995) argues that citizenship, including "access" and "belonging" as well as rights, has never been static or uniform. In her account, the regulation of social rights and relations between Community institutions and the social, local and regional "partners" (pre-dating Maastricht) are part of "access" and "belonging". The period of acceleration towards union is, in Weiner's account, a time of discernible movement in the paradigm of citizenship, containing the seeds of new practice in the triggering of rights. In particular, markets and migration make "place" – as well as nationality – the conceptual and practical precondition for activating legal, political and social rights. This could become significant not only for nationals of member states but also for lawfully resident "third country" migrants, as seems to be beginning in Amsterdam.

Even if early reactions to the Amsterdam Treaty are guarded, the movement reflected in it seems to vindicate O'Keefe's view that "the importance of the TEU [Maastricht] citizenship provisions lie not in their content but rather in the promise they hold out for the future. The concept is a dynamic one, capable of being added to or strengthened but not diminished" (cited in Chryssochou, p. 30). The same can be said in turn about Amsterdam. Moreover, the EU's ability to sustain its dual claim of being "for its citizens" (European Commission, 1997b) while also "respect[ing] the national identities of its Member States" (European Commission, 1997a, p. 5) depends upon such dynamism. ☆

Bibliography

Closa, Carlos, 1995, 'Citizenship of the Union and Nationality of Member States' *Common Market Law Review* 32. pp. 487-518.

Curun, Deirdre and Meijers, Herman, 1995, 'The Principle of Open Government in Schengen and the European Union: Democratic Retrogression', *Common Market Law Review* 32. pp. 391-442.

Chryssochou, Dimitris, 1996, 'Democratic Theory and European Integration: The Challenge to Conceptual Innovation' in Smith, Hazel (ed), new thinking in politics and international relations. *Kent Papers in Politics and International Relations*, Series 5, No. 52. Canterbury: University of Kent. pp. 20-33

European Commission, 1996a, *Draft Treaty of Amsterdam* (17.6.97), CONF/4001/97. Brussels, 19.6.97.

European Commission, 1996b, *A New Treaty for Europe. Citizens' Guide.* Luxembourg: Office for Official Publications of the European Communities.

Harmsen, Robert, 1994, 'Integration as Adaptation: National Courts and the Politics of Community Law'. Paper presented at Annual Conference of Political Studies Association of Ireland.

Institute of European Affairs, 1996-97, IGC UPDATEs, Nos 1-9, esp. No. 9 of 24.6.97. Dublin: Institute of European Affairs.

Mazey, Sonia, 1996, 'The Development of EU Policies: Bureaucratic Expansion on Behalf of Women?', *Public Administration* 73(4). pp. 591-609.

O'Leary, Siofra, 1995, 'The Relationship between Community Citizenship and the Fundamental Rights in Community Law', *Common Market Law Review* 32. pp. 519-544.

Oreja, Marcellino (European Commissioner), 1996-97, Series of Newsletters on IGC and progress of Treaty, especially that of 18.6.97.

Weiner, Antje, 1995, *Building Institutions: The Developing Practice of European Citizenship.* Ottawa: PhD Thesis, Department of Political Science, Carleton University.

Programme for the **UK Presidency**
1998

Britain is a constructive, thoughtful, innovative member of the European Union. The British Council programme during the first six months of 1998 is designed to support Britain's Presidency and to emphasise the British contribution to Europe. Highlights include:

JANUARY

38 European Young Lawyers arrive in London and Edinburgh
for the 1998 European Young Lawyers Scheme

FEBRUARY

The 1998 European Senior Civil Servants Seminar, Oxford

MARCH

Societies in Transition: Asia & Europe at a Moment of Change, London
a Young Leaders' Conference linked to the ASEM II Summit

Henry Moore Centenary Exhibition, Vienna

UK Pack Age Exhibition, Paris: *an exhibition of packaging, design and technology*

APRIL

The Prague Conference: At the Crossroads of Europe
a high level conference dealing with issues in European enlargement and change

MAY

Presidency Conference on European Partnerships in Education, Training and Youth, London

Making Enlargement Work, Athens/Corfu
a research conference for young social scientists organised in partnership with DGXII

JUNE

Future of Work and Employment Policy in Europe, Belfast
a seminar for senior policy advisers, academics and employement law specialists

The European Series 1998, Madrid/Brussels/London
*a three site seminar for young leaders from across the world, delivered
in partnership with the* Financial Times

More information on these and other events is available from
http://www.britcoun.org/

The British Council, registered in England as Charity No. 209131,
is the United Kingdom's international network for education, culture and development services

THE BRITISH COUNCIL: PROJECTING THE NEW BRITAIN

BY SIR MARTIN JACOMB, CHAIRMAN OF THE BRITISH COUNCIL

"During the British Presidency the key theme for the Council will be our work for the younger generation"

During the UK's Presidency of the European Union in the first half of 1998, the British Council will be sending messages throughout Europe to the rising generation – those who will shape and determine its future. The medium will vary – messages will be delivered by word, deed, Internet and, if necessary, in bottles delivered through classrooms, libraries, exchanges, tours and conferences. The Council is at the heart of what the Foreign Secretary has described as "People's Diplomacy": projecting directly to the people of Europe, of whatever age and from whatever corner of our continent, our culture and language in their broadest contexts.

During the British Presidency the key theme for the Council will be our work for the younger generation. The aim is the networking of youth in Europe. Effectively we want to put European youth into cyberspace. Through a series of schemes, competitions, conferences, exchanges, visits, tours and expeditions, we will put the youth of Europe in touch with itself – a project in which we have had much success already.

We in Britain and in the British Council, along with our media allies like the BBC World Service, are uniquely placed: Europe is the biggest producer of computer software outside the United States, and Britain produces roughly 60% of all Europe's software. Already – a single example – we have managed to put hundreds of thousands of young Europeans together through a sponsored e-mail scheme.

Not that electronic and cyber contact can ever be a substitute for the personal touch but, through a whole series of conferences for specialist professionals, students, young opinion formers and policymakers, we have already established a formidable network of those who will shape our continent's destiny for generations to come. In 1995 we initiated – in partnership with the *Financial Times* – the European Series, a flagship event which brings together 100 young opinion formers from across the globe to a travelling conference through Europe, looking at European issues through the eyes of Britain and one other member state. The speaking panel – at 120, usually larger than the participant

list – is a galaxy of very senior talent from across Europe, including Commissioners, ministers, politicians, industrialists and newspaper editors. In 1998 the European Series will open in Madrid, before moving to Brussels and London; in 1999 its European location will be Berlin.

The European Series itself is now the centrepiece of a programme of European conferences. Among its offspring, dedicated as always to building networks and brokering influential and stimulating discussion, is a special conference in April on European enlargement, which will take place in Prague and will be chaired by David Williamson, until very recently Secretary-General of the European Commission. Other Presidency events in this programme include a major conference in Greece for academic researchers on enlargement issues – again building networks within an expanding Europe – and another young leaders' conference which precedes the Asia-Europe Summit Meeting in London in April, and which will air some of the broader issues facing ASEM in a younger and unofficial forum. In September a similar programme will bring together young leaders from Latin America and Europe, itself a roadshow that will take a hundred participants from Madrid through Brussels to London. The more combustible fringe of southern Europe will be the focus of a special conference in Sicily next March on "Instability in the Balkans" – an offshoot of the highly successful Anglo-Italian Conference at Pontignano, now entering its fifth year.

This spring, across the board, most of our projects will be for young people at the threshold of their careers. Through the British Youth Council, a thousand students and young adults will visit this country from Europe, and the same number of young Britons will visit Europe for stays of up to a fortnight. This will be matched by two special youth conferences during the UK's EU Presidency and the regular schemes for young professionals, like the much acclaimed European Young Lawyers Scheme which has brought hundreds of young lawyers from an ever growing number of European countries to London and Edinburgh since 1963 – and which in 1998 should see a stablemate launched in the form of a scheme for young Russian lawyers.

In the perception of many Europeans this year the banner of Britain and its culture will be carried by the arts. Many countries see the state of the arts as the litmus test for the state of a nation, and Britain passes this test with flying colours. The prestige and accomplishment of our actors, painters, musicians, poets, essayists, designers, television and film producers and novelists have rarely stood so high. The plays and concerts will be there in abundance – celebrating a

> **"However many Europes there are, we aim to speak to them all through education and information, instruction and enlightenment, entertainment and sheer fun"**

new optimism about Britain's partnership in Europe. Flair and novelty will not be absent either, from the European tours of theatre companies like Trestle and DV8 Physical Theatre to the Pack Age exhibition, a celebration of packaging design, including the best of the great British cardboard box.

The British Council will be promoting a series of special performances, exhibitions and visits to underline the rejuvenation of Britain and a fresh start in Europe. The Presidency will be marked by a range of gilt-edged projections of British arts, from the exhibition of *Poems on the Underground* in Brussels to touring performances of the Royal Shakespeare Company's *Romeo and Juliet* and the National Youth Orchestra.

The Europe of the new democracies will have a special place in the promotion of exchanges and training in English. Before 1989, in the then communist countries of Eastern and Central Europe, the arts provided a glimpse of a freer world. In much the same way the English language played a vital role in keeping intellectual freedom alive and has a unique place in the story of their liberation.

English is seen by many of these countries as the language of diplomacy and intellectual debate. But it is much more than just that: it is the language of international youth, of pop culture and of the Internet. Britain takes its language for granted at its peril – and the British Council is tireless in its promotion.

The British Council believes it is uniquely placed to help East and Central European countries as they emerge from the mental as well as physical oppressions of the Cold War. It can be a ground-breaker, a facilitator, and friend, without fear of accusation of bias or narrow partisanship. Today it supports in some measure more than 40,000 teachers of English. With the DfEE in London it has sent 150 British schoolteachers specialising in the teaching of foreign languages, including Russian, into Eastern Europe. The Council has even been involved in a short course of *Peacekeeper's English* for members of the Belarus armed services volunteering for duties as UN military monitors.

The struggle for intellectual freedom in East and Central Europe has been long and hard; and many recognise the British Council's role in it – a role we will be building on this year. "When the Teachers' Resource Centre was opened in Panska

Street," a teacher wrote recently from Bratislava, "my thoughts travelled back to the late Forties. Every visit to the then British Institute in Stefanovika Street was impregnated with fear. Fear to be caught on leaving the Institute, detained, questioned, threatened. And yet we kept visiting it with love and anguish."

Across Southern and Eastern Europe newly empowered English teachers have echoed these sentiments. "While a student, between 1982 and 1986, English revealed itself through the books and cassettes of the British Library in Bucharest," wrote a teacher from Romania. "This was nothing but an oasis of peaceful and warm culture in our cold town." There has been, across the region, a dramatic and novel expansion of the British Council's library system, a network of learning and study centres where students can use the latest visual and audio aids, through cassettes and on-line network programmes, to learn, meet and mingle through the medium of English. Effectively the British Council is building a network of classrooms without walls. There are now 40 such major Resource Centres maintained by the Council across Europe, in addition to its famed library network, which lends more than 10 million volumes to individual readers each year.

Inside the EU the Council's promotion of English and British ideals and ideas has proved liberating, too, and there is much of this to celebrate in our EU Presidency term. The Council is revered still in Barcelona for keeping the study of English alive in the city in Franco's time, and at the same time supporting in Britain the study of Catalan, which had been suppressed. In 1940 the British Council School in Madrid was established, a singular and hugely successful experiment in bilingual Anglo-Spanish primary education. It offered the prospect of an outward-looking education at a time of claustrophobic inwardness. It was attractive particularly to those who dreamed of a better, freer Spain. It is small wonder then that its alumni register reads like a roll-call of those who have fashioned today's Spain.

Now the size of a small university and teaching all levels up to matriculation, the School is to be celebrated this Presidency year with the opening of a new British Council school on the same lines in Alicante, possibly with several others to follow in other regions of Spain. Overall in Spain we now see 40,000 students of English pass through our various centres each year, and employ almost a thousand teachers.

With the dramatic changes in the map of post-Cold War Europe, diplomats and politicians often ask how many Europes there now are. For the British Council the real question is not *how many* but *how to get at them?* However many Europes there are, we aim to speak to them all through education and information, instruction and enlightenment, entertainment and sheer fun. Our aim for the Presidency is to network for Britain, and for Europe to bring together the younger generation of our vibrant, evolving continent. By building on youth we are building for the future: the Europe of the new millennium is in the hands of those to whom we now speak through the special genius of our language and our culture. ☆

"The nation state is reorganising itself internally to give a greater voice to local needs and priorities. Where these institutions do not exist there is a growing demand to create them"

EUROPE
AND ITS REGIONS

BY DR ROBERT LEONARDI, JEAN MONNET FELLOW AT THE EUROPEAN INSTITUTE,
LONDON SCHOOL OF ECONOMICS

The outcome of the 1997 referenda in Scotland and Wales creating directly-elected regional governments has served to eliminate an anomaly within the European Union. Except for Britain, all of the other large member states (Italy, France and Spain) along with some of the smaller states (e.g. Belgium, Portugal and Greece) have, during the last two decades, restructured their national administrative systems and sub-national levels of government for the purpose of transferring decision-making powers in a number of socio-economic sectors from national to regional levels.

The Federal Republic of Germany and Austria were constituted in the post-War period as federal systems, but for a long time they represented the exception rather than the rule in Europe. The other nation states were characterised by highly-centralised decision-making and implementation structures. This was particularly true for the countries following a Napoleonic state model, such as France, Italy, Belgium, Spain, Portugal and others. In Germany the federal nature of the system was re-emphasised in 1989 by the reunification process. When the territories of the ex-DDR were incorporated within the Federal Republic, this came about not through the annexation of the former DDR as a whole but rather through the accession into the German Federal Republic of the five East German länder. In this manner, the DDR ceased to exist because its länder asked to join the Federal Republic.

The other large member states in the EU restructured their national political and administrative systems in the 1970s and 1980s through the introduction of autonomous governmental bodies at the regional level. Regional decentralisation served also to redefine the powers of local governments and their linkages with the regional and national levels. In the case of Italy, regional decentralisation was part of the full implementation of the 1947 Constitution and a response to the rising political demand for greater citizen input into policy-making affecting local and regional areas. The country had long suffered from the lack of responsiveness of central administrative elites to local concerns; the creation of the regions in 1970 was seen as a means of giving the voters an instrument for making the policy-making system more accountable.

Regionalisation in Spain is an integral part of the democratisation process introduced by the 1977 Constitution. In Spain the notions of democracy and representative government have historically been tied to the existence of powerful regional governments in the traditionally autonomous areas: Catalonia, the Basque Country and Galicia, though when the regional system was created it was extended throughout the national territory.

France had to wait until 1985 before introducing a nationwide regional system. The introduction of the regions was considered an indispensable reform in rationalising the national administrative structure and bringing decision-making powers closer to the people. France's regional system avoided making any exceptions or giving one region more power than any of the others in the formulation of policy.

The British response to demands for regionalisation has been closely linked to the protection of democratic procedures and the commitment to consult with the voters prior to the introduction of any regional reform. The current government has pledged to consult with the people through a referendum to decide whether to introduce directly-elected regional government bodies. The implications of the policy are that by the year 2000 Britain will have directly-elected regional bodies in Scotland and Wales, but in the English regions such developments will have to wait for the mobilisation of a clear demand from the grass roots. Within the UK, Northern Ireland represents a special case. Here, the reconstitution of a fully-functioning regional assembly (Stormont) depends on progress in the peace process and the ability to control sectarian violence. The Labour Government is committed, where regional governments are absent, to create regional chambers to co-ordinate policies in transport, territorial planning, economic development and the organisation of bids for European funding and participation in the EU's activities in Europe-wide land use planning. In contrast to regional governments, these chambers will not be independent from the national administration, nor will the members be directly elected by the citizens.

In Portugal and Greece the devolution of powers from the central to sub-national bodies has animated the national political debate for over a decade. In 1993 the Greek government transformed the prefecture councils into directly-elected bodies. At the present time, the Portuguese parliament is engaged in a debate on the nature and structure of regional governments and the boundaries that the regions should have on the mainland. The situation for the two Portuguese island groupings (the Azores and Madeira) is different. With the ratification of the new Portuguese Constitution in 1976, these two island communities were given autonomy in creating regional assemblies with decision-making powers.

Debates on the nature and content of devolutionary practice are also taking place in other political systems (e.g. Sweden, Finland, Ireland and Denmark) where the issue of how best to implement European and national policies has forced its way onto the national political agenda. The pervasive nature of the problem raises the question: why has regionalisation appeared on the political agenda in such a large number of nation states in Europe? Is the phenomenon due to the process of European integration or does it have more to do with the changing demands placed on decision-making and implementation within nation states and the demand for greater accountability by the citizens at large? Another plausible hypothesis is that regionalisation is a product of a change in the economic structure in post-industrial societies and the need to achieve greater competitiveness in European and world markets.

Finding more effective ways of administering policies at the sub-national level has acquired a new meaning and importance in the EU. The last two reforms of the Rome Treaty – Maastricht in 1992 and Amsterdam in 1997 – have significantly redefined the European integration process and granted a greater voice to individual citizens and organised groups oper-

> "*Finding more effective ways of administering policies at the sub-national level has acquired a new meaning and importance in the EU. The last two reforms of the Rome Treaty – Maastricht in 1992 and Amsterdam in 1997 – have significantly redefined the European integration process and granted a greater voice to individual citizens and organised groups operating at the sub-national level*"

ating at the sub-national level. A significant role has been allocated to sub-national actors in the implementation of Structural Funds policy as well as in the search for more effective means of administering social, urban and planning policies. Lobbying has become an important function in attracting funds from the European level, and without an adequate resource base and administrative structure it is difficult to be effective in influencing decisions in Brussels or even in the national capital. In addition, the last two revisions of the Rome Treaty have given a greater voice in European affairs to directly-elected representatives of regional, county and municipal governmental entities through the creation of the Committee of Regions (COR).

These innovations reflect a dual process of change underway in the EU. First of all, the nation state is reorganising itself internally to give a greater voice to local needs and priorities and to transfer the responsibility for implementing policies in a number of socio-economic sectors to existing or new sub-national representative bodies. Where these institutions do not exist there is a growing demand to create them, so that the regions will be placed on the same competitive level as other areas both within Europe and in one's own country, where there are functioning regional governments. Secondly, there is a growing demand from local political forces and voluntary groups to open up the EU's decision-making process to a greater amount of regional government input through the COR and through the permanent national representative bodies in Brussels. That input needs to be organised, and one of the logical ways this can be done is through the existence of strong regional governments able to argue their case in Brussels and in the national capital.

Today, regionalisation is a much broader phenomenon than it ever was in the past. Regionalism is no longer a topic of concern for ethnically or culturally distinct areas: it affects *all* regions in the EU. Europe is moving toward a reorganisation of its economic, social and political life to take into account the new needs generated by a single market and the greater capacity to interact on the part of sub-national institutions and voluntary groups at the European level. As a result of these changes, the EU is not becoming a centralised entity, as some critics maintain. The rise of regionalism is a sign that the institutional structure of the Union is moving in the *opposite* direction, towards diffused decision-making powers and the devolution of policy implementation down to the national and sub-national levels.

From the beginning of the 1980s, scholars analysing the growth and diffusion of small and medium sized enterprises (SMEs) and the consolidation of industrial districts have hypothesised that SMEs and the grouping of SMEs into industrial districts did not represent a temporary or passing phenomenon. Detailed analyses revealed that a fundamental restructuring had already taken place in European industry. European industry was moving the emphasis from the traditional industrial model based on Fordist modes of production and economies of scale to an alternative economic model (first theorised by Alfred Marshall in relation to nineteenth century Sheffield) which emphasised the role of small and medium sized enterprises linked together through sectoral networks and co-operating closely with local and regional government bodies.

The lack of size requires small and medium sized enterprises to organise on a horizontal scale. Attempts to grow and expand through the absorption of other firms is not a viable option if the SMEs are to maintain their internal flexibility, reduced management structure and responsiveness to market demands. Thus, the geographic place and the surrounding social milieu are of crucial importance in determining the success of interaction among local firms. The firms that are present within industrial districts are organised on the basis of networks – that is, they interact in a specified manner in terms of their positions in the production phase for individual products or services – and their competitiveness in national and international markets is in great part due to their flexibility and specialisation achieved in single phases of the production process.

Recent studies have verified that the ability of the net-worked, flexible specialisation model to evolve is significantly dependent on the existence of effective sub-national governments capable of providing crucial administrative and programmatic support for local industry. The lack of "internal" economies of scale make SMEs dependent on the "external" economies created by the industrial districts, and on the economic infrastructures and social services provided by regional and local governments. Where industrial districts have consolidated themselves as competitive sites in the global market, SMEs can take advantage of the physical infrastructure (e.g. roads, lighting, water and sewers) made available by local and regional governments, but they are also dependent upon the quality of social services (e.g. day-care centres, all-day programmes in elementary and secondary schools and aid for the elderly) and services to firms (e.g. marketing studies, organisation of fairs and conferences to promote individual products, access to credit and new technologies, and the training of skilled workers and managers).

The role of regional and local governments in servicing industrial districts through the provision of community services and infrastructure cannot be conceived as a distortion of competition within the EU. These governmental entities provide services to the citizens of a territory and not to individual firms. Nor can this support be conceived as a subsidy because, once again, it does not constitute a grant to one or a group of particular firms. On the contrary, given that the services provided are community-wide, anyone in the territory has the opportunity to take advantage of them. Without such support, the local firms would have to finance their own private infrastructure and provide their own private social services to workers and their families. Thus, effective governments with power and the ability to respond to the needs of the local economy are of primary importance in guaranteeing the success and well-being of an area as part of the sharing of responsibilities between the public and private sector in a modern, competitive economy.

The changing nature of the demand placed on sub-national governmental levels has led to a redefinition of the relationships between levels of government. In Europe this redefinition has assumed the name of *subsidiarity*. The concept of subsidiarity is fundamentally tied to a communitarian rather than individualistic definition of political community. In the modern use of the term, the concept has its roots in Catholic and Socialist thought rather than in Marxism. At its foundation is the assumption that the local community provides the first building block in the creation of a national political community. According to this conception, it is not the nation state that creates the local political community, even if it incorporates its boundaries and institutional structure. Rather, it is the local political community which precedes the nation state and, as a consequence, has an inalienable right to preserve its local autonomy and identity and be in a position to respond to the needs of its citizens where the nation state or higher institutional bodies are unable to do so.

According to the subsidiarity principle, states need to pay close attention to where powers and responsibilities are allocated. Certain functions may find their natural level where they enjoy economies of scale – such as, for example, defence, the administration of justice, foreign policy or monetary policy – and, therefore, need to be allocated to the highest level in the political system. Other policies dealing with the delivery of services to individual citizens need to be more customised to local needs and thus are more usefully administered at the regional and local levels.

What the notion of subsidiarity denies is that there can be only one level of government with the right to administer all policies and assume the responsibility for all decision making. Subsidiarity adopts the view that there are multiple levels of needs and, accordingly, policies need to be administered at different levels in order to maximise citizens' satisfaction. If this principle is not taken into account, then the problem of the efficiency of governments in responding to citizens' demands is compounded by the growing differentiation of needs across social class, age, sex, religious and territorial groups.

In the last analysis, it is important for all levels of government that administrative responsiveness be enhanced and citizens encouraged to participate in the determination of government priorities and decisions. Not only do the citizens benefit from such opportunities, but it could be argued that governments also stand to gain from such reforms. Regionalism and devolution of greater responsibilities to sub-national institutions provide an indication that national governments respect their people and believe that they can be trusted in managing local affairs – *and* contribute to the well-being of the entire nation. ☆

"During the 1980s, a number of serious environmental
incidents convinced Europe's governments that
the EC needed a proper legal framework in order to
tackle pollution on an international scale"

THE GREENING OF EUROPE

BY ED GALLAGHER, CHIEF EXECUTIVE OF THE ENVIRONMENT AGENCY

INTRODUCTION

Pollution respects no national boundaries. Co-operation and common action at both the European and international level is, therefore, crucial to environmental protection. The past twenty years have seen a significant growth in European and international agreements to protect the environment in response to the need for a co-operation framework.

The Environment Agency for England and Wales has a wide-ranging role relating to different aspects of environmental management and protection, including responsibility for the practical implementation of over thirty European Community environment directives covering water quality, waste, industrial emissions and conservation. The proper implementation and enforcement of EC environment legislation is, of course, crucial if we are to reap the benefits of European Union membership in terms of a cleaner environment. This article outlines the Environment Agency's view of the EU's environment policy on the basis of its experience as a regulator working at the "coalface" of the legislation to help ensure the UK meets its obligations.

So how did the EC Environment Policy develop?

At the founding of the EC during the 1950s, the environment was not perceived as being a problem – it was not even mentioned in the original 1957 Treaty of Rome. By the 1970s, however, post-war economic growth in Europe had begun to take its toll on the environment and in 1972 the EC adopted its first five year environment action programme to control pollution.

Since 1973, a further four action programmes have been agreed. The current Fifth Action Programme *Towards Sustainability* is based on the idea of shared responsibility for achieving sustainability among all sectors of society: government, citizens and industry.

During the 1980s, a number of serious environmental incidents convinced Europe's governments that the EC needed a proper legal framework in order to tackle pollution on an international scale. As a result, environmental policy formally became part of the EC Treaty in the Single European Act of 1986. The goals of this environment policy are:

✦   To preserve, protect and improve the quality of the environment;

✦   To contribute towards the protection of human health;

✦   To ensure a prudent and rational utilisation of natural resources.

Preventative action, dealing with environmental damage at source, and "the polluter pays" are the underlying principles on which this policy is based.

Today, over three hundred directives have been agreed to protect Europe's environment, covering water management, air quality, conservation and waste management. Much of the UK's environmental legislation now originates from the EU.

"Effective implementation and enforcement of legislation remains a big problem for the EU and in the area of environment policy it has a particularly poor record. The reason for this could be that some member states have been slow to ratify the EC directives in their countries and, even where legal implementation has taken place, practical compliance remains elusive or incomplete"

The pressure to meet the standards laid down in these EC environment directives has led to substantial environmental improvements in the UK over the last two decades. The UK can now boast of major improvements in the quality of its rivers, canals, lakes and coastal bathing waters, as well as a significant decline in the number of major water pollution incidents. The amount of hazardous contaminants being discharged into the sea has been reduced and measures are being taken to reduce pollution and improve waste disposal.

There is, of course, still a lot of room for progress in cleaning up the legacy of the industrial past and, in England and Wales, the Environment Agency is working closely with Government and other environmental organisations to improve the situation.

The UK's influence in the shaping of European environment policy is growing. Germany and the Netherlands are no longer the lone green champions in the EU. The UK, for example, initiated the EU regulation on eco-auditing for businesses and supported the introduction of the EC eco-label on "environment friendly" products to raise consumer awareness. The recently agreed directive on integrated pollution prevention and control is probably the most significant UK initiative, as it introduces the UK approach of controlling pollution from major industries to the rest of the EU.

The proper implementation and enforcement of EC legislation in the EU is an area of particular concern to the UK. The numerous directives designed to protect the environment are not worth the paper they are written on unless national governments take the necessary action back home.

It falls to the Environment Agency, which is responsible for environmental protection in England and Wales, to put many of the EU's environment laws into practice and to enforce the agreements struck by Environment Ministers in Brussels at the national, regional and local level.

The Environment Agency is one of the many hundreds of "competent authorities" responsible for the operation and enforcement of EC law on the ground. So how does the Environment Agency carry out this role?

The implementation of EC legislation is a complex process and the details will vary considerably from member state to member state and from directive to directive. However, the process can be broken down into four stages:

+ Transposing the directive into national legislation;
+ Practical implementation;
+ Assessing compliance with the directive;
+ Evaluating and reporting.

The Bathing Water Directive, one of the most well-known directives in the UK, provides a good example of how EC environment legislation is put into practice. Agreed in 1976, the Bathing Water Directive sets water quality standards to maintain and improve the quality of bathing waters.

To assess compliance with the directive, the Environment Agency carries out an extensive monitoring programme during the summer at designated beaches to check whether the standards are being met. The samples are tested in the Agency's laboratories and the resulting data, which are collected centrally, are sent to the Department of Environment, Transport and the Regions in London. The Department then files an annual report to the European Commission as it is the duty of the Commission to ensure that EC directives are properly implemented in all member states.

An annual report on the state of bathing waters in the EU provides information to the public on where to find the cleanest beaches. The report also provides a yardstick against which to measure implementation of the Bathing Water Directive in the different member states.

The Environment Agency also publishes its own annual report on the state of bathing beaches in England and Wales, which is also available on the Internet (www.environmentagency.gov.uk); district and local authorities display the data on bulletin boards at local beaches. These publications and displays, together with the European Blue Flag awarded to the cleanest beaches, mean that the benefits of EC bathing water standards are well-known throughout the UK.

Monitoring bathing waters is, however, only part of the story. The Environment Agency is also responsible for *enforcing* the directive and has the power to prosecute the polluters if they break the law. The pressure to meet the EC bathing water standards has led to improvements in sewage treatment schemes all around the British coast.

Effective implementation and enforcement of legislation remains a big problem for the EU and in the area of environment policy it has a particularly poor record. The reason for this could be that some member states have been slow to ratify the EC directives in their countries and, even where legal implementation has taken place, practical compliance remains elusive or incomplete.

According to the Annual Report on Monitoring the Application of Community Law there were 265 breaches of EC law in 1995. All member states are in the dock at some point or another for failing to honour their EC commitments. While the European Court of Justice can cause political embarrassment, it is public opinion and domestic political pressure which are more likely to encourage a government to fulfil its EC commitments.

The UK Government has been particularly keen to find a solution to this problem. A recent House of Lords Report, *Making Community Environmental Law Work*, recommends greater consultation prior to the adoption of EC legislation with more thought as to how the laws will operate in practice. The Environment Agency shares this view and has been active in providing scientific and technical advice both to government and the EU institutions to ensure that the adoption of laws is based on sound science and that laws are enforceable in practice.

To find solutions to common problems of implementation and enforcement, the Environment Agency has built up contacts with other EU countries. It also carries out collaborative research. The EU Network for the Implementation and Enforcement of Environmental Law (IMPEL) was set up in 1992 as a result of a UK initiative to provide a forum for Europe's environmental regulators. As well as developing guidelines on best practice, IMPEL also highlights potential operational problems with the legislation to national governments and the European Commission. IMPEL is beginning to play an important role in helping to ensure that environmental legislation is applied more effectively.

One of the major difficulties in assessing the relative performance of member states has been the lack of comparable data.

Methods of sampling and analysis may vary, technology may be lacking and data collection may be insufficient to give an accurate picture of the state of Europe's environment. Without the right information, Europe's environmental problems cannot be properly assessed, nor the appropriate action taken. To bridge this information gap, the UK supported the establishment of the European Environment Agency (EEA).

The EEA was set up in 1994 with the task of providing "objective, reliable and comparable information at the European level enabling [the member states] to take the requisite measures to protect the environment, to assess the results of such measures, to ensure that the public is properly informed about the state of the environment".

The EEA is well placed to help improve overall standards and consistency in monitoring methods and reporting arrangements, as well as making information available to the public. Bringing together information on the environment is a very complex issue and more work is needed in this area. This is why our own Environment Agency is hosting a major European conference during the UK Presidency in June, which will bring together leading experts and practitioners to discuss the environmental measurement framework that is needed to assess the state of Europe's environment.

With the majority of environmental legislation now originating from Europe, our own Environment Agency has an important role to play in ensuring that this legislation is both based on sound science and can be implemented successfully on the ground.

Environmental problems are not confined by national boundaries. Only by working in co-operation with other European countries will we, therefore, be able to achieve the significant environmental improvements that we all desire. ☆

BBC MPM:
MAKING A DIFFERENCE TO PEOPLE'S LIVES

by Joan Connolly, BBC MPM Ltd.

In June this year, during the Marshall Plan 50th anniversary commemorations in the Hague, the German Chancellor, Helmut Kohl, was moved to tears as he listened to President Clinton recount the German leader's own tale of receiving Marshall aid soup "that warmed hands and hearts" after the War.

The American-sponsored European Recovery Programme (Marshall Plan) distributed $13 billion worth of aid across 16 European nations in an attempt to create stable conditions in Europe after the Second World War and, in Marshall's own words, to "help Europeans help themselves". Its achievements in terms of the rebuilding of war-torn Europe and its legacies in the shape of NATO and the Organization for Economic Co-operation and Development (OECD) cannot be denied.

In 1991, in the wake of the Soviet Union's collapse, there was again a need to get Western aid up and running to ease the transition to democracy and market economies of our European neighbours. It was clear that soup was not the only aid needed by the ordinary people of the Soviet Union and Eastern Europe as they struggled to make sense of the enormous changes that threatened to throw their otherwise strictly-controlled lives into turmoil following the collapse of Communism. Many organisations quickly responded with imaginative and far-reaching programmes, such as the EU's Tacis programme and the British Government's Know How Fund.

The Marshall Plan was very much of its time. In 1991, with the aims of the Marshall Plan in mind, John Tusa, then managing director of the BBC World Service, advanced the idea of a modern day Plan. It was clear that most aid projects aimed at the former Soviet Union would only touch a tiny percentage of the population. But the vast mass of people needed to understand the changes, debate them, and – crucially – to feel included in the dramatic changes taking place. Though it could not match the original Plan in resources, Tusa's idea was that by using the power of the mass media, a sizeable impact could be made on huge numbers of the population. In this way, comparatively small amounts of aid would benefit millions.

So the BBC Marshall Plan of the Mind Trust (BBC MPM) was set up by the World Service to satisfy the need for

practical help and advice amongst the Russian population. For five years now BBC MPM has been promoting quality public education programmes, working in partnership with local broadcasters. Sustainability has been integral to BBC MPM's approach. We sought to encourage partnership not patronage, with skills as well as knowledge transfer at the core.

Eventually, if we do our job properly, the Russians, and now Ukrainians, Romanians, Mongols and Uzbeks, won't need us any longer. We will have made a lasting and sustainable impact, like *teaching* a man to fish instead of giving him fish. Already we are seeing the impact of our work through the experience of former trainees.

BBC MPM has now passed on its skills to over two hundred producers, and at least eleven independent radio stations, from Nizhny Novgorod to Novosibirsk, are producing BBC MPM-style programmes. One station, Radio Rostova, in Rostov-on-Don, is making no fewer than five different series, inspired by MPM, including a weekly 45-minute business magazine and a daily 45-minute programme on media and democracy. Our network of partner stations across Russia also continues to flourish, numbering some 150 at the last count.

Initially, the predominant theme of BBC MPM's radio and television programmes was business and market economics. Our longest running programmes, *How Business Works* and the daily radio soap opera *Dom Syem, Podjezd Chetirie* (House 7 Entrance 4), still concern themselves with business on various levels. HBW examines both macro and micro-economics, and *Dom Syem* continues to promote business education through its storylines. One recent example involved retired scientist Anatoly, whose new business idea hit problems from the word go.

As the need for information has increased, BBC MPM has responded with a much broader range of programmes. To date our series have covered subjects including democracy, civil society development, enterprise restructuring, agricultural reform, the law and individual rights, and the development of non-governmental organisations (NGOs). A major concern is the necessity to raise awareness of changes which seemed merely to make life more intolerable. If this fails, then people will no longer vote for

change. In Russia today increasing cynicism and apathy pervades society. The challenge is to stimulate and encourage people to believe that they can take more control of their lives, to help themselves. BBC MPM tackles this by portraying positive examples of initiatives to which others can aspire. It is currently a partner in a European Tacis enviroment project aimed at the NIS and Mongolia. The project's philosophy is that the power of the media cannot be underestimated and its brief is "to give people the feeling that they can make a difference".

BBC MPM continually responds to comments and feedback from our audiences. We received thousands of letters from all age groups and backgrounds. In telling us why they liked a particular programme, they often reveal details of their own situations: their worries and fears and also how BBC MPM's programmes have helped change their lives. A listener in the Ryazan region, Russia, recently wrote: "Thanks to your programmes I have become more assertive. In fact you gave me the confidence to go to court and fight for the rights of my child."

In October 1997, BBC MPM hit the headlines when the British Prime Minister, Tony Blair, took a starring role in our long-running educational soap *Dom Syem, Podjezd Chetirie*, promoting the importance of education. In the West the power of popular radio and television drama has long been recognised. The use of broadcast drama as a PR tool is on the increase in Britain, with issues-led organisations bombarding script writers to help get complex issues on the public agenda. BBC MPM's experience has been very different.

In Russia and Romania (where, in partnership with Radio Romania, we make the educational soap *Piata Rotunda* (Round Square)) BBC MPM, with its overtly educational brief, has pioneered partnerships with NGOs to help us frame our storylines. For example, in Romania, BBC MPM worked closely with UNFPA and UNICEF on story-lines about abortion and adoption.

Some of the knock-on effects of our broadcasts are frankly bizarre. One wonderful example comes from our Romania radio soap. As prizes in a recent listener competition, the production team decided to give out fridge magnets bearing the programme title: *Piata Rotunda*. A factory in Bucharest took the order and rang back a few days later saying: "Production is going well. But what are they? No one has ever asked us to make them before." We know that over the years we have made a positive difference to many people's lives, but stimulating the Romanian fridge magnet industry we certainly didn't expect.

Thanks to the great support BBC MPM has received from the British Government's Know How Fund and from the European Union, we have been able to make a difference to many lives. But as the reform process continues (and most experts now agree that it will take generations rather than decades), there will be more losers in the "transition" process. The imminent problem of half a million Russian army officers to be thrown on the scrap heap will mean that the form of life-long learning pioneered by BBC MPM will be more vital than ever. ✳

" Poverty elimination is achievable and affordable. It is both right and in our own interests to create a stable and secure world in which economic, political and cultural links flourish and in which all sections of the population in all parts of the world will have a role to play"

THE DEVELOPING WORLD:
IMPROVING THE EU's EFFECTIVENESS

BY THE RT. HON. CLARE SHORT MP,
SECRETARY OF STATE FOR INTERNATIONAL DEVELOPMENT

It is notable that the 25th anniversary of the UK's membership of the European Union falls at a time when the UK holds the EU Presidency. The responsibility that comes with the Presidency requires each Department to consider their priorities for EU action. As the Secretary of State for International Development, I am particularly concerned with the Community's policies towards people in the developing world and how they can contribute to the goal of eliminating world poverty.

1.3 billion people live on less than 65 pence a day. 1.5 billion people lack access to safe water. More than 1 billion people are illiterate and around 17 million people die each year from preventable diseases. More than one third of children are malnourished. From these figures it is clear that the world faces a tremendous challenge to eliminate poverty and bring sustainable improvements in opportunities and choices for poor people. We must all rise to that challenge. First, because it is *right* to do so: every generation has had a moral duty to reach out to the poor and needy and to try and create a more just world. And second, because we have a *common interest* in doing so: global warming, deforestation, polluted and over-fished oceans, shortage of fresh water, population pressures and insufficient land on which to grow food will otherwise endanger the lives of everyone – rich and poor, developed and developing.

The European Union is committed to the "campaign against poverty". Its wide-ranging aid programme is focused on sustainable economic and social development. It seeks to improve the conditions for developing countries to create enduring livelihoods for poor people. But development is not just about aid. Policies in other areas such as trade, the environment and agriculture can affect development objectives as well. In most of these areas the EC must do better. Our task now is to see that the Community's commitments turn intent into practice. Reform of the Common Agricultural Policy is particularly important if the lower income countries are to have a chance to develop. I want to see an effective, efficient and coherent Community development co-operation programme focused on the poorest. I also want the Community to sign up to international development targets which commit us to work towards the elimination of poverty and to measure its progress towards achieving this goal.

The Community's aid programme is substantial. It became the fifth largest in the world in the 1990s, providing about £4.5 billion. The UK's contribution to this, through its share of the EC Budget and its contribution to the European Development Fund, is about 30% of the UK's aid programme. Frequently commentators talk as though bilateral programmes are always preferable. But no country can work everywhere. This is why our multilateral work is also important. Channelling assistance through the EC also enables the UK to support development in countries where we do not have expertise in our existing bilateral programme, as well as providing a forum in which member states can share their experience and promote best practice. Our aim is to ensure that best practice is applied. We want programmes that make an efficient and effective contribution to the goal of eliminating poverty.

The Community's programmes extend widely. The Lomé Convention covers the EC's aid, trade and political dialogue with 71 Africa, Caribbean and Pacific (ACP) states. The current Convention expires in the year 2000, and we are now discussing what will follow. The EC also has programmes for Asia and Latin America, the Mediterranean and Central and Eastern Europe, and provides food aid, humanitarian assistance and support for non-governmental organisations. In all of these areas, the UK is working for continued improvements to enhance the position of the poorest and to improve effectiveness.

"*Development is not just about aid. Policies in other areas such as trade, the environment and agriculture can affect development objectives as well. In most of these areas the EC must do better*"

will seek to play an active and constructive role in the Development Council. We will work with the Commission, other member states, the European Parliament and other interested bodies.

Working with the EU involves co-operation, dialogue and a sharing of ideas on a number of different levels. At the strategic level there are co-operation frameworks such as the Lomé Convention and the geographical aid Regulations. At the project and policy levels we work through the Commission's management committees, expert groups and day-to-day contacts. In recipient countries, we have regular contact with EC delegations. Increasingly we hope to work together to develop comprehensive programmes of assistance for sectors such as education, health and transport. We will also continue to encourage the EC to co-ordinate its policy with other donors and to incorporate consideration of gender, poverty and the environment into all its operations.

Development assistance is an important part of the way in which we can help to tackle poverty. But it is not by any means the only aspect of our relationship with developing countries. Both nationally and internationally there is a complex web of political, trade, defence, environmental, agricultural and financial relations. To have real impact on poverty we must ensure that the EU, the international financial institutions and other donors consider the development effects of all these different policies. Too often in the past, trade or agricultural policy has undermined development, and development assistance has only partly made up for the damage done. The UK will work within the EU and the World Trade Organisation for increased multilateral liberalisation of trade in goods and services, and the continued dismantling of tariff and non-tariff barriers worldwide. We recognise that the dismantling of trade barriers takes time. But we will continue to work for the best possible access to EU markets for developing countries, in particular for those countries that need this most to compete in world markets.

The UK Presidency has just begun. It is an important time. The UK will be at the centre of EU business. We will be in the chair for the preparation of the Lomé negotiating mandate before negotiations with the ACP states get under way in September 1998. This is a priority area for the Presidency. There are other areas which we will want to take forward as part of our wider aims. We want to increase the poverty focus of Community aid, and improve the effectiveness of its programmes. The international development targets are designed to provide milestones against which progress towards the goal of poverty elimination can be measured. We want to secure EU commitment to these so that the whole international community works together to meet them. We will also focus on follow-up to past resolutions on poverty and gender and consider what more needs to be done to ensure they are fully and effectively implemented. There is no point in passing yet more sets of resolutions unless we can be sure that those we have already are being effectively implemented and followed up. To achieve these objectives, we

Poverty elimination is achievable and affordable. It is both right and in our own interests to create a stable and secure world in which economic, political and cultural links flourish and in which all sections of the population in all parts of the world will have a role to play. A world in which poverty is eliminated and there are sustainable improvements and choices for poor people. The EU has a major contribution to make to achieve this. But there needs to be an improvement in performance. I look forward to the next 25 years of partnership and hope that when we celebrate our 50th anniversary of membership we and our grandchildren will be able to take pride in the more decent and stable world the EU has helped to create. ☆

Are you looking for a bank that sees investors as individuals?

✔ Do you wish to receive personal advice and friendly service?

✔ Do you want the maximum benefit from your savings?

✔ Are you prepared to invest £ 10,000 or more?

If your answer is YES, you need Jyske Bank's private banking service. You will find that placing money abroad is simple and a good idea.

WELCOME

Private Banking the Friendly Way

Most good international banks offer security, quality and access to the full range of international investment products. But being a bank with Danish roots, we offer you something extra: personal advice in which attention to detail and friendly service are to the fore.

To receive further information call free on
0 800 378 415

or directly to our Copenhagen office, see below.

🌀 JYSKE BANK

Private Banking the Friendly Way

Jyske Bank, London Branch
FREEPOST LON5323 • 10/12 Alie Street • London E1 8BR
Tel. 0171 264 7700 • Fax 0171 264 7717

Jyske Bank, Private Banking (International)
Vesterbrogade 9 • 1780 Copenhagen V
Tel +45 33 78 78 01 • Fax +45 33 78 78 11

COPENHAGEN • ZÜRICH • GIBRALTAR • LONDON • HAMBURG • FUENGIROLA

"Since 1984, financial support from the R&D Framework Programmes alone has gone to over 7,000 projects across a wide variety of sectors, involving numerous companies, research centres and universities, as well as thousands of researchers, in all parts of Europe"

SHAPING THE FUTURE:
RESEARCH AND DEVELOPMENT, EDUCATION, TRAINING & CULTURE

BY DR HOWARD MACHIN, DIRECTOR OF THE EUROPEAN INSTITUTE
AT THE LONDON SCHOOL OF ECONOMICS

Can EU common policies be effective, command respect *and* be relatively cheap? The answer for policies in culture, education, training, research and development has to be "yes". The appreciation of those directly involved in these policies – the researchers, teachers, trainers and cultural leaders – as well as the intense political debates when policies are modified, indicate their popularity and importance. Simple indicators of the volume of spending and legislation suggest that these policies are not expensive. Furthermore, these are *important* policy areas. Indeed the issues here concern not only the outputs of firms, schools, universities, research centres and cultural bodies, but also the distribution of power within the EU, between the governments of the member states and the common policy structures, and between the state and the market.

There is no doubt that in relative terms the sums spent on these policies are not great. In a recent report it was noted that the research and development (R&D) spending from the EU budget represented only 3.5% of total spending in the EU; in education, training and cultural affairs the proportions are even lower. In the 1997 EU budget, out of a total spending commitment of 87.65 billion Ecu, 41 billion are devoted to agriculture, 32 billion to the structural and cohesion funds and only 3.4 billion to R&D. For education, training and culture together, spending totals just 489.9 million Ecu; compare this with the cost of "external activities" of the EU (notably overseas aid), amounting to no less than 5.7 billion Ecu. Agriculture consumes almost 48% of the EU budget, whilst R&D takes less than 4% and education less than 0.4%.

Nor is the legislative output from the EU much more impressive in volume and nature. Although, since the signing of the Paris Treaty in 1951, the governments of the member sates of the EU have been attempting to make some common policies in these sectors, the Treaty provisions for legislation in education, training and culture have been small. The provisions for R&D have been more substantial. In 1957, the second Rome Treaty, creating Euratom, was much concerned with research policy, although its promise was largely unfulfilled. The Single European Act added a whole "Title" on research to the EEC Treaty and elevated it to the status of a Community Policy. In the Maastricht Treaty, the responsibilities of the European Union in education, training, culture, research and technological development were redefined in Title II (articles 126, 127, 128 and 130 respectively) of the Treaty. The Amsterdam Treaty will bring yet further changes, including a change to Qualified Majority Voting for R&D Objectives.

Under those Treaty articles some directives and other legislative measures have been adopted. A series of directives have laid down a framework for the mutual recognitition of educational and vocational qualifications. Several policy programmes with inspiring acronyms like Comett, Petra, Lingua, Leonardo and Socrates have been introduced in education and training. With considerably more resources, the EU has adopted a series of four-year "Framework Programmes" for research and development. In 1998 the Fourth Framework Programme reaches its conclusion and the legislation for the Fifth will be adopted. In short, there has been some output of useful legislation but little to compare with the massive legislative productions which underpin the Common Agricultural Policy or the Internal Market.

Microsoft's *community involvement* in **Europe**

Microsoft has grown into a leading global company in just 22 years. In Europe, we have Microsoft subsidiaries in 24 countries and employ more than 4,000 people. We are just as determined today in Europe, as we were 22 years ago in Seattle, to play a positive and active role in the creation of opportunity and employment.

Preparing our children for tomorrow's world

We believe that information technology can enhance and broaden our children's education. When education becomes more interactive and global, it can involve parents, teachers and students to a much greater degree, as they reach out into and across communities around the world. We call this 'the connected learning community' and we have put in place a number of initiatives to help develop it in Europe.

Microsoft provides schools with our products at special low prices, and donates substantial software to pilot projects run by schools. As part of our corporate community involvement scheme 'The Road Ahead Programme', we run 'The Road Ahead Prize', awarding prizes for innovative use of the Internet in education. This year the Prize contests will take place in Belgium, Finland, France, Germany, Portugal, Italy and the UK. The aim of the prize is to highlight models of innovative practice for teachers and students across Europe. In 1997, over 3000 schools from five countries participated.

Skills training and employment

Microsoft's 'European Scholar Programme' is a training programme for unemployed people to become Information Technology specialists. In just two and a half years, over 3000 people have graduated from 11 scholar sites across Europe. One of the most successful programmes has been the Microsoft European Scholar

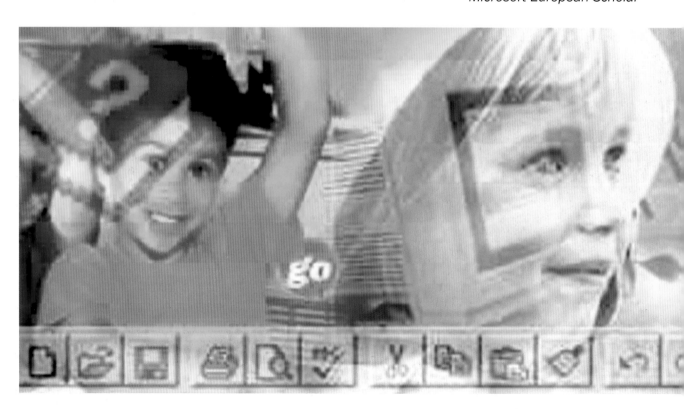

Programme in Ireland, called 'TRAMLINES'. Tramlines is an innovative project run in partnership with the Ballymun Job Centre giving long-term unemployed people from one of the most disadvantaged suburbs in Ireland a chance to become high-level computer professionals.

To date, more than 80% of TRAMLINES graduating trainees have been offered full time employment even though virtually none had previously held a full time job. As one trainee said, 'This is not just changing my life, this is changing my children's lives, and their children's lives'.

Leading the way in research

We founded Microsoft Research in 1991 because we felt that the growth of the PC software industry and Microsoft in particular created a unique opportunity to do basic and applied research in computer science which could make a positive difference in people's lives and set new directions for the field. We started small, with a handful of scientists working primarily in natural language technology and programming environments.

Microsoft Research has since grown to include over a dozen research groups and nearly 200 researchers in areas as diverse as speech recognition, decision theory, 3D graphics and animation. The impact on Microsoft's products has already been felt.

If you use Microsoft Windows 95 and Microsoft Office 97 you have more than likely taken advantage of features which have been enhanced by technology developed within Microsoft Research.

theRoad Ahead *Programme*

With the opening of our Microsoft Research facility in Cambridge last summer, we have committed ourselves to playing a leading role in developing and supporting European talent.

Microsoft®

Where do you want to go today?®

If you would like more information about Microsoft please consult our website:
www.microsoft.com and www.research.microsoft.com
If you would like more information about our corporate community involvement,
please consult: **www.microsoft.com/europe/roadahead**

How then can we account for the importance attributed to these policies in research, education and culture by politicians and practitioners alike? The answers are to be found by examining the policy instruments used, the debates about policy-making, and the outcomes of these policies.

POLICY INSTRUMENTS

The main policy instrument in all these policy areas has been the "incentive programme" which sets downs aims, rules and procedures for EU funding to policy actors. In practice the EU legislates within the Community "pillar" to establish, usually for a fixed period, a set of priority activities for which EU subsidies may be awarded to institutional applicants (firms, schools, research centres or networks of these) on the basis of the merit of their projects, which is usually submitted to peer-group evaluation.

Hence, for example, between 1984 and 1998, the main instruments of research and development policies have been the four Framework Programmes, each of which has been a strategic plan prioritising research activities and phasing funding to support those activities. Since the First Framework Programme (1984-87), development of "technologies for the future" has been a key objective. The Second Framework Programme (1987-91) gave priority to information technology, electronics, materials and industrial technologies. In the Third (1990-94) and Fourth Framework Programmes those priorities were retained whilst the lift sciences, the dissemination of research findings, and the improvement and mobility of researchers were added. For the first time, research in the economic and social sciences became eligible for support.

Funding under the Framework Programmes is largely project based: specific evaluation criteria, which are published, guide the choices made by expert evaluation panels. In most cases the EU supports research projects by providing only "matching funding" to complement the resources of the firm of research centre. There is intense competition for support from firms, universities and non-government organisations from all parts of the EU. Since 1984, financial support from the R&D Framework Programmes alone has gone to over 7,000 projects across a wide variety of sectors, involving numerous companies, research centres and universities, as well as thousands of researchers, in all parts of Europe.

In education, the Socrates programme for 1995 to 1999 focuses on three main activities: improving trans-national co-operation between universities by student and staff exchange programmes ("Erasmus"); encouraging links based on joint projects between schools ("Comenius"); and promoting more and better foreign language teaching ("Lingua"). A parallel programme in vocational training for the same period, "Leonardo", provides funds to employers, non-governmental bodies and public training agencies for a range of training activities including trans-national work placements, pilot projects to develop innovations, and co-operative ventures between companies and universities. In the cultural policy area, the "Media II" programme supports innovation in the audio-visual industries, including the development of new technologies and training.

These incentive programmes usually involve trans-national partnerships or collaboration between public bodies and private firms to solve common problems. Hence, one reason why so many policy actors perceive the importance of these policies is that they have a direct interest in them: thousands of organisations and hundreds of thousands of EU citizens are active participants.

THE POLICY DEBATES

In general the controversies are greater about R&D than about education or vocational training – a consequence of the larger budget and the need to build a very wide consensus as a consequence of the particular methods of legislation for R&D since the Maastricht Treaty. An examination of the enactment of a framework programme reveals the political problems.

Each Framework Programme must be adopted by a Community legislative act. The enacted programme sets out, for its period of application, the objectives of Community R&D policy, specific priorities and research themes, procedures for implementation, an indicative budget and the allocation of funds to the different research themes. These are then implemented by a number of sectoral "specific programmes" which are also by distinct Community legislative acts. The legislative enactment of each Framework Programme is a long process which begins when the Commission is advised by several committees of senior officials, scientists, representatives of industry and experts from the member states, and notably by the Scientific and Technical Research Committee ("CREST" – senior officials); the European Science and Technology Assembly ("ESTA" – 100 top scientists); and the Industrial Research and Development Advisory Committee ("IRDAC" – industrialists).

The Commission sends its proposal to the European Parliament and Council where the process of adopting a legislative act begins. Under the co-decision procedure, European Parliament and Council share decision-making power; legislation can only be adopted under this procedure with the approval of both. The Commission proposal receives two readings in both the Council, where unanimity is required, and the Parliament. In the event of disagreement at the Second Reading between these institutions, the "conciliation procedure" operates. During the legislative process, the Council and the European Parliament may table amendments to the Commission's draft text and the Commission may, or may not, incorporate some or all of these into the proposal on which the vote is taken. Once the Framework Programme decision has been adopted, the legislative process re-starts for the adoption of the "specific programmes", although in this procedure the Council may act by qualified majority vote. After the adoption of each specific programme, a work programme is drafted to detail the research work, as a basis for publishing "calls for tenders" from firms, research centres or networks.

At first sight this procedure seems open and sensible since it allows for a wide consultation of experts, the European Parliament and the governments of the member states in the Council. In practice, however, each member state government, like the Parliament, has a right of veto (though they

"Many young people now undertake part of their studies in member states other than their own as a normal part of their university education"

will lose that right when the Amsterdam Treaty is ratified). However, if the Commission and Parliament seek to advance European science as a whole and to complement the activities already taking place in the member states, many national governments attempt to use their power to ensure that funds are available to promote projects seen to be of particular interest to firms or researchers in their respective countries. This inevitably leads to a great deal of tense bargaining, since the respective powers and the real interests of firms, research centres and governments are at stake.

POLICY OUTCOMES

EU policies for education, culture, training, research and development aim to improve the human capital of the entire EU; to enhance the "life chances" of Europeans in all member states; to reinforce the scientific and technological basis of European firms to enable them to compete more effectively in global markets; to facilitate the free movement of persons (and, indirectly, of services); to promote access to employment for all; to minimise social exclusion; and to enhance the knowledge of both the common European cultural inheritance and the wealth of diversity in the national and local cultures of the EU. In all these policy areas, EU activities are intended to complement and extend the policies and initiatives undertaken in the member states by governments, firms, non-governmental organisations, schools and universities.

One effect of these policies has been to begin to raise the level of investment in research and development in many member states, which was relatively low in comparison to the USA and Japan; and hence to reduce the uneven development of research activities, and of the research communities, in the different member states. Indeed, some progress has been made in research areas like information technology, where the EU has lagged behind developments initiated in the USA and Japan. Another result has been to introduce much greater co-ordination and information exchange between researchers and research centres at all levels in different parts of Europe. The extent of research efforts hitherto wasted in duplication has been reduced. "Critical masses" of researchers, previously not attained in some disciplines and industrial sectors, have been reached, and large-scale facilities, unaffordable by individual governments, have been developed. Serious attempts have been made to increase the comparatively limited capacity to convert scientific innovations and technological achievements into industrial and commercial successes.

The mutual recognition of educational qualifications allows people from any state to move freely to jobs in other member states, and this has involved some harmonisation of standards, at least in education, for such professions as medicine, engineering, architecture and law. Many young people now undertake part of their studies in member states other than their own as a normal part of their university education. Vocational training is also a policy area in which there have been gains by acting together: solutions are being found to common European problems of dealing with rapid technological changes, as well as to specific intense and local problems requiring complements to national policies – for example, by re-training workers in regions suffering sudden and large-scale deindustrialisation. In cultural policy there are attempts to increase both knowledge and understanding of both the common elements in Europe's cultural heritage and the wealth of cultural variety across the member states.

Clearly these policies must continue and develop and many problems remain unresolved. Equally there is a case for concentrating the limited resources on a smaller group of targets – a case which the Commission has acknowledged in its plans for the Fifth Framework Programme of R&D. Nonetheless, what these policies show is that relatively limited resources, employed in a well-targeted way, can mobilise large numbers of groups and individuals in all parts of the EU to work together for their common future. ☆

RECONNECTING EUROPE WITH ITS CITIZENS

BY CHARLES GRANT, DIRECTOR OF THE CENTRE FOR EUROPEAN REFORM

"European governments have to provide the conditions in which jobs can be created. If Continental governments succeeded in shortening the dole queues – and that means doing much more to make labour markets more flexible – it would do wonders for the EU's image"

The European Union, for many people, is a distant, incomprehensible, overweaning and thoroughly unappealing entity. The wave of Euroscepticism which ran over much of northern Europe in the early 1990s has yet to subside. There is scant popular support for the federalist vision of the EU's founding fathers, yet the current set of European leaders has failed to make the case for a credible or coherent alternative.

The roots of this popular antipathy to the Union lie in the mid-1980s, when the combination of the Single Market programme and the Single European Act boosted its powers. Large numbers of people were affected by the dismantling of internal barriers to trade, by the regulation of state aid and mergers, and by the relocation of companies. And then in 1991 the Maastricht Treaty, with its plan for a single currency, promised to touch an essential element of sovereignty.

So it was perhaps natural that many people would resent what seemed an increasingly dominant and remote bureaucracy in Brussels. And that national politicians and officials, who were losing power to the EU, would blame it for unpopular policies they had to implement, such as the lowering of fishing quotas, while taking the credit for popular ones, such as the funding of regional development projects.

A large cause of the Union's unpopularity, however, has been its failure to deliver the goods which most Europeans expect of it, namely peace and prosperity. For example, when war broke out in Yugoslavia in 1991, EU ministers tried but failed to bring about a settlement. And although the Union's policies cannot be held responsible for the relentless rise in Continental unemployment, the ineffectual hand-wringing of its leaders and the inability of governments – especially those of France and Germany – to tackle joblessness have undermined their credibility and that of their goal of European integration.

The exchange-rate crises of 1992 and 1993, which all but blew apart the European Monetary System, tarnished the idea of economic and monetary union (EMU), as did the spending cuts which governments pushed through in an effort to meet the requirement for EMU that budget deficits be lower than 3% of GDP. In the booming Britain of the mid-1990s, the Eurosceptics' strongest suit was that Europe was not working, in any sense of the word.

Europeans would be less suspicious of the EU if they had some respect for its institutions. But the European Commission, the embodiment of "Brussels", has little legitimacy. Its poor image derives partly from its tendency, in the late 1980s and early 1990s, to regulate in too much detail and to grab more power for itself. A bigger problem is the fact that Commissioners are not elected but appointed by governments. Yet even the European Parliament, directly elected since 1979, has failed to win much credibility: at each successive European election, a smaller proportion of the electorate has bothered to vote.

Popular antipathy to Brussels reflects, in part, a wider, global disenchantment with political elites. Consider the rise of the populist Northern League in Italy in the early 1990s, or the more recent success of Canada's west coast, anti-Ottawa, anti-Quebec Reform Party. Many Americans find their capital just as out-of-touch and elitist as Europeans do Brussels. The Republicans exploited this sentiment in the 1994 mid-term elections when, wielding anti-Washington rhetoric, they won control of Congress. It is worth noting that only 39% of the electorate voted in those elections, compared with 57% in the same year's elections for the European Parliament (although only 36% of Britons voted).

Thus the EU's problem is partly geographical: Brussels is inevitably more distant than the national governments with which people can readily identify. So how can popular disdain for EU institutions be tackled? Federalists argue that Commissioners should be elected either directly or by the European Parliament. That kind of change might brighten the EU's image, but it would boost the Commission's authority and so be unacceptable to governments.

In fact there is no simple, easy answer to the problem of the EU's remoteness. That means it should exercise no more than a necessary minimum of functions. In practice, however, there are few centrally-managed tasks that could be devolved to national governments without serious inefficiencies. In 1992, when Jacques Delors was Commission president, he suggested handing back environmental policy to the member states, only to back down when outraged environmentalists explained that pollution did not respect frontiers. The Single Market could not work without central policing from the Commission and the European Court of Justice. Only in two areas could the EU quite easily do less: common rules on workers' rights, which may not be essential to the smooth working of the market but are nevertheless popular, even in Eurosceptical Britain; and the Common Agricultural Policy, which, following future reforms, will probably shift some responsibility for subsidising farmers to national governments.

In the long term, monetary union will mean that EU institutions exercise more rather than fewer powers. The centralisation of monetary policy in the hands of the European Central Bank (ECB) will encourage some harmonisation of fiscal policy. Even if Britain stands aloof from the euro, the ECB's decisions will have an impact on British mortgages. And when – assuming that it does – Britain finally joins, a remote body in Frankfurt will set British interest rates.

REASONS TO BE CHEERFUL
So, is the Union doomed to sink ever deeper into a mire of popular disdain? Not necessarily, for several positive trends may counteract the negative ones. The EU's reputation suffers – and xenophobia flourishes – when its governments engage in acrid disputes, such as, for example, that in the early 1980s between Britain and the rest over budget rebates. However, seen over the long term, most members' economic and strategic interests are probably converging.

Of course there will be rows over allocations of agricultural, regional and social funds. An increased membership will certainly make decision-making harder. But all current and likely future members are now wedded to a similar economic philosophy of free markets, low inflation and budgetary discipline. Even France's Socialist government is, very gingerly, preparing to privatise France Telecom and Thomson.

Politically, too, fundamental interests are starting to coincide. Italy, for so long an oddball country, is moving towards a similar sort of bland, bipolar politics as the others. There are few serious disputes on foreign policy: whether the issue is former-Yugoslavia, Russia, American sanctions on investors in Cuba or the future of NATO, most members have similar views. France's semi-detached status within NATO is an obvious exception, but unlikely to be permanent. Even on the future of the Union itself, there is no longer a huge gulf between a sceptical British government and its federalist foes: most governments now view the EU more as a means of delivering practical benefits than as an ideal to inspire devotion.

The second reason for optimism is that increasing social, economic and cultural integration may eventually rub off on popular attitudes. Labour mobility is greater than many people imagine: at least 350,000 people from other EU countries (apart from Ireland) are resident in Britain, while 400,000 Britons are resident in the rest of the EU, and these figures do not include the hundreds of thousands of people who have not officially registered. Industrial lobbies, trade unions and non- governmental organisations are becoming ever more intertwined in pan-European alliances.

Britain's trade with Europe has grown faster than with any other region of the world: in 1985 its exports to and imports from what are now the other 14 members each totalled £40 billion; by 1996 each had risen to just under £100 billion. The growth of direct investment, in and out of Britain, has been even more spectacular: the annual value of British investment in the EU grew from zero in 1984 to £8 billion in 1995; over the same timespan direct investment from the EU into Britain went from minus £2 billion to £10 billion. Those whose jobs depend on these flows are more likely to think the EU a worthwhile enterprise.

Youth cultures, in eastern as well as western Europe, have tended to converge on similar sorts of music, fashion and lifestyle. The fact that some of this common culture is American does not make it any less of a unifying force within Europe. In any case the English language, rapidly becoming Europe's lingua franca, is doing more than EU directives – or American cultural icons – to bring young people together. The Commission itself helps: its Erasmus programme has, over the past ten years, allowed some 150,000 European students to study in countries other than their own.

Every survey of British views on Europe finds that younger people are the most positive. One of the most extensive surveys, for the 1996 "British Social Attitudes", concluded that "the young, graduates and the salariat are more likely than average to be in favour of integration. For example, nearly half of those with degree level qualifications are pro-integration – compared with less than a fifth of those without such qualifications".

Of course, Britons who feel a cultural affinity with those across the Channel do not necessarily warm to the boring institutions of Brussels. But while these Britons may condemn the institutions for their irrelevance or poor performance, they would be less likely to do so out of visceral xenophobia. They may at least be open to argument about the worth of the EU, if presented with a convincing case.

However, Europhiles should not suppose that all they have to do is wait for the elder generation to fade away, for university education to expand and for the middle classes to grow. For many years to come, cosmopolitan users of inter-rail or the internet will be in a minority. The challenge for pro-Europeans is to explain the EU's relevance to the many poor, ill-educated Britons who do not travel and who fear for their future. They were the sort of people whose French counterparts, in September 1992, almost swung the French referendum against the Maastricht Treaty. In a future British referendum, such people could scupper plans to join the euro.

ALL ABOUT RESULTS
How, then, can sceptical Britons be reconciled to the EU? Talking about institutional reform is scarcely going to help; even many of those sympathetic to European integration yawn at the mention of the "co-decision procedure", "blocking minorities" or

"comitology". Indirectly, however, some of the institutional complexities are relevant to restoring the EU's appeal. For if the EU expanded to more than 20 members without retooling its machinery – for example by cutting the number of commissioners per country – it would become less effective and thus more disliked.

In any case, some reforms may in themselves make the Union a little more popular. Thus the Treaty of Amsterdam allows for greater openness in the Council of Ministers and for national parliaments to have more time to consider EU legislative proposals. Such changes may impress at least a few of those who write for British tabloids, if not their readers.

Further reforms could soften the sense of alienation that many people feel towards the EU. For instance a short, readable, layman's version of the Union's constitution could be extracted from the various treaties. Or the Commission president could be chosen in a new way: the European Council (heads of government) would present the Parliament with a short-list of candidates, each would face televised questioning from Euro-MPs and the Parliament would then elect one of them as president.

In the long run the Union will flourish or perish according to the success, or otherwise, of its ventures, and the ability, or otherwise, of political leaders to communicate such achievements as there are.

The EU has to cope with four challenges in order to win the respect of its citizens. First, it should ensure that enlargement into Eastern Europe proceeds smoothly. That means pushing through the Commission's *Agenda 2000* package of budgetary, agricultural and regional policy reforms. Reconciling the competing interests – Spaniards and Britons will have to accept less regional aid, French and German farmers fewer EU subsidies and inefficient East European firms more bracing competition – without major ructions will be hugely difficult.

Second, EU governments will have to make a better job of co-ordinating foreign policy. With several potentially unstable countries on its eastern and southern flanks, the Union may well have to cope with conflicts of the Bosnian type. Some of the changes in the Amsterdam Treaty, such as the creation of a High Representative for foreign policy, may help it to act decisively. If, as is possible, the Americans pulled out of Bosnia but the Europeans stayed and succeeded in keeping the peace, the EU's credibility would receive a dramatic boost on both sides of the Atlantic.

Third, European governments have to provide the conditions in which jobs can be created. It is true that EU policies cannot make much of a difference, one way or another, to levels of employment. However, if Continental governments succeeded in shortening the dole queues – and that means doing much more to make labour markets more flexible – it would do wonders for the EU's image.

Fourth, and most important of all, monetary union has to succeed. If the ECB and the finance ministers can deliver low inflation, low interest rates and economic growth, public opinion will swiftly latch on to the practical benefits – such as getting rid of the cost and bother of changing money – and back the project. The Union would be seen to deliver tangible benefits to its people and businesses. But if EMU engenders rows, recession, crises and instability, not only the euro but also the whole Union may be damaged beyond the point of repair.

Even achievements on all four fronts will not do much for the EU's reputation unless politicians make an effort to explain and praise them. It is worth remembering that British opinion moved sharply pro-EU in the late 1980s, when Lord Young and other ministers sang the praises of the thoroughly successful Single Market project. Shifting public opinion from its current hostility should not prove an impossible task. Numerous surveys of attitudes to the EU suggests that many people's views are ambiguous – they both like and dislike aspects of European integration – and shallowly held.

There are some positive strands in public opinion that politicians could build upon. A recent survey from Opinion Research Business asked Britons which subjects were better tackled at European rather than national level: the environment and terrorism scored 72%; relations with the rest of the world, 61%; defence, 60%; and organised crime, 57%. But when asked which subjects should be EU priorities, only 5% said EMU and 4% said protecting farmers' incomes. Mark Leonard points out (in *Politics Without Frontiers*, Demos, 1997) that the EU is not busy enough in the areas where people want it to act, but over-busy in areas where they wish it did less.

The politicians' task would be easier if people understood the EU better. A Eurobarometer survey in 1996 found that 89% of Britons wanted schools to teach how EU institutions worked. However, the schools do not; the EU does not even feature in the core curriculum of A-level politics. The Government should ensure that everyone is taught a few basics.

For the last ten years that the Conservatives held power, ministers almost never had a good word to say about the Union. The fact that the new Labour government has already abandoned anti-EU rhetoric seems to have affected public opinion: the European Movement's private polls show that the number of people giving hostile responses to a range of questions on the EU has fallen by about 10 percentage points since the May election.

Business leaders, too, need to be readier to stick their heads above the parapet and explain why the EU is good for jobs. They have been reluctant to do so without political cover. Both they and politicians should be readier to speak out boldly, to face down Europhobic newspaper editors and to support each other.

Tony Blair says that he wants his country to lead in Europe. If he fulfils that ambition – so that Britain sets the agenda rather than reacts to Franco-German plans – it will be easier for pro-Europeans to argue their case. But British opinion is unlikely to shift a great deal unless the Prime Minister is also prepared to use his own authority to argue the case for Europe. ☆

Footnote: The author thanks Caroline Daniel, Ben Hall and Mark Leonard for their comments on a draft of this article.

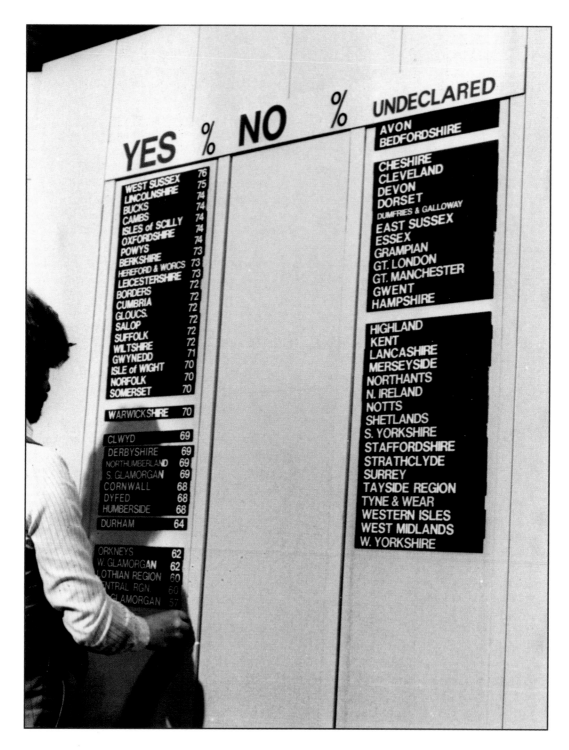

*"From the mid-1970s onwards,
following a decisive 'yes' vote in the
June 1975 referendum, the UK began
to take its place as a normal member
of the Community"*

BRITAIN'S SUCCESSES IN THE EUROPEAN UNION 1973-98

BY ANTHONY TEASDALE, FORMER SPECIAL ADVISER TO CHANCELLOR OF THE EXCHEQUER KENNETH CLARKE AND FOREIGN SECRETARY SIR GEOFFREY HOWE

Britain has become locked into a damaging mind-set of failure about its role and record as a member of the European Union. Too many people have come to see the European experience not as an opportunity or a success, but as either a missed opportunity or a threat. Two views of our membership are widespread. The first is that, as a country, we have repeatedly failed to see the significance of European integration, and consistently underestimated the determination of others to pursue it. The second is that, either because of late entry or differences of interest and institutions, we have been disadvantaged in Europe, unable to shape its policies and structures in a British mould. According to choice, we see ourselves as either having missed the European bus by our own volition, or having been frozen out of the European action by others, in an organisation shaped by and for others. Opinion polls reveal a public equally fearful of being isolated from Europe or being controlled by Europe. Something approaching national schizophrenia is the result.

As a consequence of Britain's low self-esteem about its position in Europe, it now seems counter-intuitive to present the record of our membership since 1973 as anything resembling a national success. The idea that, over the last quarter century, we might actually have shaped the institutions and policies of the Union in a significant way, let alone as much as any other state, seems perverse. Yet this in fact is how many people outside the UK see the history of our involvement. Britain is often viewed as one of the principal architects of the new Europe, especially in the last fifteen years. This essay explores how and why such a perception is almost certainly justified.

POINTS OF DEPARTURE

Few would deny that Britain spectacularly misjudged European politics in the years immediately after the Second World War, repeatedly failing to take seriously moves towards closer political integration on the Continent. The European landscape is still littered with institutions – the OECD, the Council of Europe, WEU and EFTA – that reflected the UK's vain search for an intergovernmental path to European unity from 1948 to 1960. All were to be superseded by events and forced to find new roles in the face of a more successful, supranational rival. The emergence of the European Community, now Union, as the dominant structure in Western Europe confounded British expectations and forced a dramatic reappraisal of the UK position. Harold Macmillan's application for membership in 1961 still ranks as Britain's biggest foreign policy reversal of the last fifty years.

Although de Gaulle vetoed British entry in 1963 and 1967, the stalemate over UK membership coincided with a long period of inertia in the EC's development. The General's own institutional disputes with his European partners in the 1960s immobilised policy formation in many fields. Only in removing internal tariffs and founding a Common Agricultural Policy was serious progress made. By the time Pompidou and Brandt secured British entry in 1973, the European economy was being plunged into recession by the Arab oil crisis, blighting prospects for the rest of the decade. The great leap forward in Europe, which would otherwise have left Britain far behind during these years, never happened.

From the mid-1970s onwards, following a decisive "yes" vote in the June 1975 referendum, the UK began to take its place as a normal member of the Community. Gradually, British successes began to accumulate. The creation of the European Regional Development Fund was the first substantive fruit of UK membership. Roy Jenkins was chosen as President of the European Commission (1977-81). A renewed emphasis emerged in Brussels on making a reality of the European Social Fund. A climate emerged in which the disproportionate share of the EC budget consumed by the CAP was seen as increasingly unjustifiable.

THE THATCHER YEARS 1979-90

After Margaret Thatcher came to power in 1979, British diplomacy in Europe moved into more active gear. During her eleven years as Prime Minister, Britain started to exercise a serious influence on the shape of the evolving Community. Only towards the end of her premiership, when she seriously overreacted to the ambitions of some other heads of government and began to adopt non-negotiable stances, did her leverage wane. The Thatcher effect on Europe can be summarised under two main headings.

Securing Budgetary Discipline in Europe

Soon after taking office, the new Prime Minister decided to confront head-on Britain's impending emergence as the EC's largest net financial contributor (even though it had the third lowest GDP per capita of the nine member states). Christopher Tugendhat, then budget commissioner, has argued that an "act of statesmanship" on the part of Giscard and Schmidt could have solved the British budget problem "before it got out of hand". Instead, they chose to turn it into "a trial of strength" – one which Mrs Thatcher eventually won. Exploiting the UK veto on any increase in the EC's Own Resources (overall spending ceiling), she managed to extract first a series of ad hoc rebates (during 1980-83) and finally, at the Fontainebleau Summit in June 1984, the permanent payment of a compensatory "abatement" which has since reduced Britain's net contribution by some £1-2 billion per year.

The British budget victory delivered shock therapy to a Community reluctant to reopen arrangements of the past, however outdated they had become. Its long-term significance went much wider. Distributional dividing-lines began to develop in EC politics, with a growing sense of solidarity among net contributors. Their ranks (Britain, Germany and the Netherlands) were soon swelled by France when the EC enlarged to include Spain and Portugal in 1986. The budget dispute spilled over into a new, more general climate of budgetary discipline. In 1984, the UK secured acceptance that strict financial guidelines would henceforth limit rises in EC spending, not least on the CAP. Agriculture ministers could no longer pre-empt decisions by budget ministers, by setting excessive farm prices. This was a major political reverse for the farm lobbies in France and Germany, and it had a lasting effect.

Promoting the Single Market and Containing the Single Act

The appointment of Jacques Delors as Commission President in 1985 opened a more ambitious era in European politics.

Delors wished to launch a big new project to demonstrate that Europe counted at home and in the world. Initially he considered action in four areas: completing the single market, strengthening European foreign policy, launching economic and monetary union (EMU) and developing the European social model. Britain responded to the challenge clearly and effectively. It alighted on work being done in the European Parliament on how the single market could generate growth, to offer a liberal route-map to a more integrated European economy. Britain also argued that Europe could indeed benefit from a stronger external identity, provided this was organised intergovernmentally, with the national veto maintained.

Working in alliance with Germany, the UK managed skilfully to channel Delors's energy into his first two objectives, whilst strongly opposing the others. Until 1984, France had been sceptical of action to complete the single market, but now, under Delors's patronage, this idea gained favour in Paris. The contours of the Single European Act, agreed in December 1985, followed this pattern, with supranational deepening largely confined to the removal of non-tariff barriers to trade. Extensions of majority voting in the Council, and of European Parliament power, were limited to the single market and a few other fields, disappointing the Benelux states and Italy in particular. A new intergovernmental foreign policy – European Political Co-operation – was also accepted, along the lines of an early British draft. Despite Mrs Thatcher's subsequent denunciation of it, the Single Act was seen at the time as, and remains, a significant British victory.

The two years which followed the Single Act were to prove the high-water mark of UK-EC relations during the Thatcher era. The 1992 objective provided a new focus for European ambition to which London could subscribe without embarrassment. During the summer of 1988, however, storm clouds gathered. A reappointed Delors returned to the unaddressed agenda items of EMU and social Europe, this time with German support. A re-elected President Mitterrand forged a strategic alliance with Delors to promote both goals. Thatcher dug in aggressively, refusing compromises on either and articulating for the first time explicit opposition in principle to the central institutions of the Community (in her Bruges speech of September 1988). For a while, Whitehall decoy tactics, adopted against her instincts, just about held the line. For example, at the Madrid Summit in June 1989, the EC leaders decided to launch EMU without any firm commitment to complete the project. However, after removing her Foreign Secretary and losing her Chancellor later that year, Thatcher's negotiating position fell apart. By autumn 1990, she was comprehensively defeated at the Rome I Summit and, following the resignation of Sir Geoffrey Howe as her deputy, lost power three weeks later.

THE MAJOR YEARS 1990-97

John Major's tenure as Prime Minister is already widely seen as a wasted opportunity in Europe, coloured by images of Black Wednesday (1992), the Maastricht ratification crisis (1992-93), the Ioannina voting rights struggle (1994), non-cooperation over BSE (1996), and finally a bunker mentality in the Amsterdam Intergovernmental Conference (1996-97). These events certainly created a climate of growing tension, leading eventually to a general perception of Britain as hostile to closer co-operation and semi-detached from the power politics of the Union. However, throughout the six and a half years of the Major government, Britain did in fact continue to exercise a surprisingly strong influence on the EU's development, both policy-wise and institutionally. The concrete legacy of Britain in this period is likely to prove substantial.

Sustaining Economic Liberalism

On the policy front, the achievements of the Thatcher era were consolidated, becoming something of a way of life for the Union. Net contributors came to form a majority, through an EFTAn enlargement in 1995 which the UK did much to promote. The level of the EU budget was effectively frozen as a share of GDP (at below 1.24%), with a continuing shift in spending away from the CAP, itself subject to continuous reform, towards non-farm priorities. During the 1990s, the Union has moved from recurrently overspending to consistently underspending its budget ceiling.

The completion of the single market continued as a central objective of EU policy, matched by action to open up competition in previously protected sectors. By 1994, the EU's total GDP was over 1% higher than it would have been without the single market programme, and average EU inflation over 1% lower. In international trade, the Union played a key part in securing liberal outcomes in several important negotiations. Although Britain could not forestall the social Europe agenda completely, repeated attacks on its intellectual legitimacy did much to constrain the Commission and promote counter-thinking in favour of flexible labour markets.

Shaping the Maastricht Treaty

The biggest single success of the Major government came in the design of the Maastricht Treaty, agreed in December 1991. As with the Single Act, Britain's attitude was critical to defining the contours of the final text. Having resisted the convening of IGCs on monetary and political union, the UK managed to turn both to its advantage by trading agreement to a deal for serious institutional concessions by other states. Drawing on goodwill in the early Major years, when the Prime Minister declared his ambition to be "at the very heart of Europe", the government secured most of its negotiating objectives.

Central among the UK's goals were the retention of intergovernmental co-operation in foreign policy and the acceptance that upgraded action in home affairs should likewise operate on an intergovernmental basis. In both cases, the roles of the Commission, Parliament and Court of Justice were to be marginal and the Council was to act by unanimity. Henceforth the institutional structure of the European Union would be built around three pillars, only one of which (the EC pillar) was explicitly supranational. The principle of subsidiarity was written into the treaty and an opt-out from the new social chapter obtained.

Although majority voting was extended in the Council, it was confined to routine EC pillar activities of a non-threatening kind.

Building a Sound Money EMU

In the parallel IGC negotiation on EMU, the UK also scored a notable success. Without ever saying it would join, and indeed extracting an unequivocal right not to join, Britain played a big role in determining the shape of single currency arrangements. As Kenneth Clarke has subsequently put it:

"Back in 1991, we gave critical support to the Germans in ensuring that the new European central bank would be independent, that price stability would be its goal, that convergence criteria would apply, and that only genuinely convergent countries would be allowed to go ahead and join stage three. We resisted efforts to subject the central bank to explicit political control; to give it other, employment-related, goals; and to allow all countries to go ahead together, at one time, even though they were not properly converged . . .These achievements are not minor matters. They have directly affected . . . the sort of Union which is now emerging" (Speech to RIIA: 18 December 1996).

THE BRITISH OPPORTUNITY IN EUROPE

Despite clear British successes in Europe over the last 25 years, the overriding impression at home is still one of failure. Part of the reason lies in the fact that, except during the Heath government and briefly under Thatcher in 1986-88, prime ministers have been reluctant to promote Europe positively to public opinion. Europe has too often been presented as something to be contained and kept at bay. The election in May 1997 of a new government committed in principle to positive leadership in Europe offers the opportunity to develop a language of British success, rather than failure, in its European endeavours.

Already the satisfactory completion of the Amsterdam IGC negotiation in June 1997 bodes well for the future. As with the Single Act and Maastricht, the new UK government secured nearly all its negotiating objectives, disappointing many on the continent who hoped for a more ambitious result. Now the 1998 British Presidency of the Council comes at a fortuitous moment. It will be the first time for many years that the government of a large country has found itself in the chair with a clear public mandate and without the shadow of an impending election. Moreover, the decisions to be taken, most notably on EMU, are of capital importance.

Today, the Government enjoys a real opportunity to demonstrate to its European partners, and also to the British people, that leading in Europe is a serious possibility for our country. Not only would that be good for Britain abroad, it would unwind the climate of pessimism and failure about Europe which infests the public mood at home. Confidently presenting Britain's past successes in Europe for what they are – the real achievements of one of the Union's most powerful players – might be a good place to start. ☆

APCO **ASSOCIATES**
Public Affairs and Strategic Communications

POLITICAL MONITORING

EU/ MEMBER STATE GOVERNMENT RELATIONS

COALITION BUILDING

GRASSROOTS CAMPAIGNING

INTERNAL/EXTERNAL COMMUNICATIONS

TECHNOLOGY SERVICES

APCO EUROPE assists corporations, trade associations and not-for profit
organisations to develop, communicate and achieve their goals by building
support for their reputations, positions, products and services.

APCO **UK**

Simon Milton
Managing Director

Wells Point · 79 Wells Street · London W1P 3RE
Tel: (44 171) 453 7778 · Fax: (44 171) 453 7799
E-mail: apco.uk@greynet.com
Home-page: http:\\www.apco.co.uk

APCO **EUROPE**

Mark Dober · Brad Staples
Joint Managing Directors

40 rue Montoyer · B-1000 Brussels
Tel: (32 2) 282 48 48 · Fax: (32 2) 282 48 49
E-mail: bstaples@apco-europe.com
Home-page: http:\\www.apco.assoc.com

BEIJING · BRUSSELS · HONG KONG · LONDON · MOSCOW · OTTOWA · PARIS · SACRAMENTO · SEATTLE · TORONTO · WASHINGTON D.C.

A Message from Sir Edward Heath, President of the European Movement

EUROPEAN
MOVEMENT

The Rt. Hon. Sir Edward Heath, K.G., M.B.E., M.P.

HOUSE OF COMMONS

November 1997

Since its foundation fifty years ago in 1948, the European Movement has played a crucial role in explaining to the people of Britain the benefits of joint action with our European partners.

The British Presidency of the European Union, which coincides with our anniversary, is an opportunity to demonstrate the gains that are made through working positively with our European partners. I hope it is an opportunity that the government and others will seize. This publication is a welcome contribution to that process.

In recent years, the European Movement has played a vital role in informing the public about the benefits of being part of Europe, boosting the profile of pro-Europeans at a time when the European debate has been destructively negative. Its work will be vitally important in the coming years.

In particular, if Britain is not, with the single currency, to repeat the mistakes of history by joining a European project long after the rules have been set, those who favour this essential ingredient of the single market - in industry, politics, and across the country - must join together to explain its merits. Those who wish to do so should, in our fiftieth anniversary year, join the European Movement.

Edward Heath

European Movement
Dean Bradley House
52 Horseferry Road
London SW1P 2AF
Tel: 0171-233 1422   Fax: 0171-799 2817
e-mail: info@euromove.org.uk

European Movement of the United Kingdom Limited
Limited by Guarantee Registered in England no. 551817

EUROPEAN
MOVEMENT

The European Movement

The British Presidency of the European Union coincides with the fiftieth anniversary of the European Movement. Founded in 1948 by Winston Churchill and others, the European Movement is the cross-party pro-European campaign.

The European Movement's mission is to communicate to the public the benefits of EU membership and of European countries working together, and hence to provide a climate in which Britain can take the pro-European course which is in both the national and European interest.

The European Movement is a broad coalition. It brings together pro-Europeans of all parties, from business, trade unions, and people from all over the country.

Over the past 3 years the European Movement has expanded rapidly, and has done a great deal to boost the profile and broaden the base of pro-Europeans in this country. The European Movement campaigns in two key areas:

The European single currency

The European Movement has taken a range of initiatives to inform people about the benefits of the single currency. After the Chancellor's statement backing the principle of British participation, the European Movement took up the challenge of turning public opinion around by publishing *The Other Side of the Coin*, a booklet setting out the case for British membership. Benefits include:

- Membership of the single currency offers significant benefits to the people of Britain. It would mean lower interest rates, cutting the cost of mortgages and boosting business investment.

- The single currency would bring greater stability, helping British companies to be more competitive and keeping prices stable.

- The single currency would create jobs, by making it easier for companies to invest and increasing opportunities for business in Europe.

N MOVEMENT

EUROPEAN
MOVEMENT

EU membership is Great for Britain

Membership of the European Union has brought many benefits to Britain: economic, political, social and environmental. The Europe 97 campaign set out "97 reasons for the UK to be in Europe". These included:

- Europe is where Britain sells its products, boosting British companies, winning profits and creating jobs. In 1995, 58% of our exports of goods went to the EU.

- The EU has helped to keep the peace in western Europe for half a century, the longest unbroken period of peace for 300 years.

- Britain has greater bargaining power in world affairs as part of the EU. The 1993 agreement to free up world trade - in which the EU negotiated as one - is saving every British household £500 over 10 years.

- People across Britain benefit from the high environmental standards agreed Europe-wide. Ten years ago half of British bathing beaches failed to meet EU standards. Today nine in ten fly the "blue flag" to show they now meet them.

Getting involved

The European Movement has a network of branches and local groups all over the country. This network has expanded dramatically over the last year. There is also a vibrant youth section, the Young European Movement.

Members of the European Movement and Young European Movement are invited to regular events, and have the chance to become more active in campaigning in their local area.

If you support our case and want to get more involved, you can join the European Movement by filling in the form overleaf.

Pick up a pen and do it today!

What would you say
to an economic policy that...

Lowered interest rates
Reduced inflation
Cut unemployment &
Increased investment?

YES!

Join the campaign to join the Euro

The European Movement, Britain's cross-party pro-European campaigning organisation, is launching a UK-wide campaign to explain the benefits of the European single currency to the public. With all three main parties committed to a referendum before Britain joins the Euro, the European Movement is now putting in place the infrastructure to fight and win a YES vote.

To win the referendum, the pro-Europeans will not be relying just on the support of politicians and the business community. A successful campaign will need thousands of active supporters throughout the country who are willing to put forward the positive European case in their area.

Please fill in the form below or phone
0171-233 1422 (Visa, Mastercard) and join the campaign today!

THE SINGLE CURRENCY: PRACTICAL CONSIDERATIONS FOR BUSINESSES

BY VERNON ELLIS, MANAGING DIRECTOR FOR
EUROPE, THE MIDDLE EAST, AFRICA AND INDIA, ANDERSEN CONSULTING

"Economic and Monetary Union can and should enhance the opportunities brought about by the Single Market. It is a force which, if harnessed correctly, can become a driver of the virtuous circle of European competitiveness"

Economic and Monetary Union will raise issues of fundamental importance to all European businesses, large and small, national and international. Even those not currently engaged in cross-border trade will be affected by changes in the general economic environment and by changes in the marketplace as well as by the narrower issues of currency conversion and transition to the new system.

Although there will inevitably be winners and losers, the overall message has to be a positive one. Businesses will gain from larger markets, reduced uncertainty and lower transaction costs. In this sense Economic and Monetary Union can and should enhance the opportunities brought about by the Single Market. It is a force which, if harnessed correctly, can become a driver of the virtuous circle of European competitiveness. Equally, a failure to grasp the opportunities presented by EMU will almost certainly mean a failure to build competitiveness.

For example, one of the outcomes of a single currency will be increased transparency of pricing. Together with the removal of other constraints on the flow of cross-border funds, this will lead to more open markets. This itself will lead to greater cross-border competition, bringing major economic benefits through lower costs and higher productivity. But in order to succeed in this environment all companies will need to be increasingly competitive. It will be the companies who best exploit the opportunities of the single market who will succeed, and some of this success may be at the expense of others less well placed.

Another positive benefit for businesses of all sizes will be the reduction and in many cases complete removal of long-term exchange rate volatility. Hedging short term fluctuations is one thing but hedging long term investments is much more difficult. The removal of uncertainties arising from movements in European exchange rates will give firms more confidence to rationalise and consolidate their physical assets across borders so that they can take fuller advantage of the opportunities of the Single Market than has been possible up to now. But this too carries a warning message for those companies which fail to grasp these opportunities.

THE FINANCIAL SECTOR

Clearly it is the effects on financial institutions which will be most profound, at least in the short term – and not surprisingly it is in this sector where most work is being done. However, what is particularly interesting here is the impact which these changes will have in increasing competition and driving down costs throughout the financial sector, and the accelerating effect this will have on the virtuous circle of competitiveness. That is not to say that all the impact will be positive for financial institutions: clearly there will be some negatives, at least in the short term. Many traditional sources of income will be reduced as we see simplification of treasury operations, the elimination of foreign exchange conversion and hedging transactions, a move from corporate lending to tradeable debt, and a general convergence in pricing leading inexorably to commoditisation.

To this extent we can expect a benefit to the business sector as a whole, in part at the expense of the banks. But even within the banking sector this may be no bad thing. Arguably Europe has too many banks. For instance Germany has nearly 4,000 financial institutions, Italy 1,000 (of which 750 are single branch banks) and in Spain the number of branches per million inhabitants is three times as high as it is in the UK. What is bad news for banks in terms of lower income is good news for industry in terms of lower costs – a boost for European competitiveness.

There are three other trends which will give a further boost to the virtuous circle. First the move from public to private pensions (and especially to funded schemes partly driven by the requirement to meet the Maastricht criteria) will lead to a vast increase in investment portfolios. Based on a more US-style distribution of household assets, a conservative estimate would show a flow of one and a quarter trillion dollars into pension funds over the next 10-15 years. Secondly, the continuing number of privatisations, again encouraged by the drive for convergence, will further boost both equity markets and equity culture. And thirdly, EMU will enable much more diversification of investment portfolios across Europe as investors make full use of the eradication of exchange rate risk and the wider range of opportunities open to them.

Together these trends will accelerate the move away from long-term bank debt (characteristic of many continental European countries), and towards a more dynamic, equity-based financial markets culture. This will in turn increase pressure on managers to deliver higher financial performance. We can therefore expect companies to accelerate moves to take advantage of the Single Market; to consolidate, rationalise, invest in new "green field" sites; and to initiate new cross-border mergers and acquisitions.

At the same time, there will be even greater pressure on banks by cross-border corporates to rationalise their products and services. Treasury operations will be centralised and we will see a greater use of electronic product and information delivery channels. The net effect of all this will be the rationalisation of basic banking services and an unbundling of products in areas such as liquidity management, risk management and money transmission. In my view the winners will be those banks which can offer "best of breed" cross-border products which can be tailored and packaged to individual requirements and in some cases be delivered or executed electronically.

Barriers to entry in local banking markets will be reduced through the elimination of the need for a local funding base and through price harmonisation. Euro funding will be created initially by the influence of government debt in euro denominations from 1 January 1999 for "first wave" countries. This will lead to significant liquidity in the inter-bank market. Companies will be able to access these markets through any major bank, and dependence on domestic banks, once fuelled by their advantages over foreign competitors in local currencies, will be weakened. The advantage local banks currently hold in pricing risk for higher yield borrowers will be diminished as international rating agencies and benchmark issuers establish more transparent pricing for middle-size corporates. International banks will seek a share of this business as the cost of risk management reduces, especially through syndicated and structured transactions.

As we can see, there will be a huge array of challenges facing banks as monetary union takes hold. But the other side of the coin will be enormous opportunities for those prepared to take them. Debt and equity markets will experience significant growth after 1999, with upside potential of two trillion dollars in each market. I have already mentioned the emergence of a new market in credit-rated high-yield corporate bonds and there is obvious scope for increased corporate advisory services and an increase in trade finance.

The impact on financial services will not be limited to banking. Undoubtedly there will be moves towards a European stock market, cash and derivatives. And the euro will drive substantial changes in the insurance market: investment portfolios will be diversified across Europe and products will start to converge. In turn this

> "Much has been written about the technical issues surrounding the Millennium but the impact of EMU – though less often spoken about – is probably at least twice as large for many financial institutions. For example, for an investment bank there are six rules relating to the Year 2000 which must be complied with, but there are more than 80 rules relating to EMU"

will lead to a sharper focus on core competences and perhaps the unbundling of the underlying components of insurance cover, investment and distribution.

The inevitable consequence of all the above will be the emergence of truly pan-European financial services institutions and an acceleration in alliances, takeovers and mergers.

This is all profoundly important not just for the competitiveness of European financial institutions, but also for the competitiveness of European industry. The truth is that many large financial institutions have only recently begun to understand and assess these strategic options; until now they have been preoccupied with technical and compliance issues.

These are indeed complex and demanding questions and of course many of them centre around Information Technology issues. Much has been written about the technical issues surrounding the Millennium but the impact of EMU – though less often spoken about – is probably at least twice as large for many financial institutions. For example, for an investment bank there are six rules relating to the Year 2000 which must be complied with, but there are more than 80 rules relating to EMU. The Year 2000 issue is a well defined problem with a definite solution. The impact of converting a system to accept the euro is not so well defined.

Larger banks and insurance companies have been assessing the cost implications for themselves: the figures add up to tens if not hundreds of millions of pounds, and that is without including the effect of dual pricing!

THE CONSUMER MARKET

Our view is that preparation, on the compliance and technical side, is quite well advanced, at least in the major banks, although the picture is less clear when looking at smaller banks and the insurance and fund management industries.

The picture becomes even less clear when looking at companies outside the financial arena, or indeed governments. They too will be affected by the euro. Indeed, the retail industry is another industry where the impact and the opportunities given by EMU are significant.

For example, issues like dual pricing, particularly during the transition phase when businesses will need to handle both currencies and display both prices, will have a major impact. This will be exacerbated in the food industry which is already subject to detailed price marking requirements, for example in terms of unit prices and prices per kilo. In addition, receipts for goods will almost certainly have to be in two currencies during a transitional period.

Then there is the whole question of the psychology of pricing. Prices in national currency are unlikely to convert into "attractive" (e.g. £7.99) or "round" euro numbers. Companies will need to decide directly whether to set new pricing points, and if so, which prices should be set at a higher level and which ones at a lower one. Companies will have to weigh the opposing forces affecting this decision – for example whether to set "psychological" prices to increase consumer spending or to set "round" prices to decrease the volume of coins. It may well be the case that we will need a certification process to reassure consumers that the conversion is not simply resulting in higher prices.

Cash handling is another key issue. Retailers handling large volumes of euro notes and coins need to consider how to receive cash and give change. Marks and Spencer has noted that a customer's main source of coins in the early days of the new currency will be from retailers, and so the volume of coins handled by retailers is likely to rise significantly, by perhaps as much as 10%. There will be many other practical questions for retailers such as consumers paying for goods in local currency but getting change in euros. Or how to cater for consumers who want to pay for goods partially in euros and partially in local currency? Certainly the cost implications of the advent of the euro are significant. Even conservative estimates put it at 0.5% of turnover.

OTHER PRACTICAL ISSUES

All industries will face accounting and legal issues like the redenomination of share capital. All of these will need to be thought through in great detail. There are more general considerations too – from the relatively simple yet far-reaching question of how we will enter the euro symbol (the letter C with two horizontal bars) on our PCs when the majority of keyboards do not have the symbol, to planning the practical arrangements for the day that has been set for E day, 1 January 2002. For many businesses, especially retailers, it would be hard to choose a worse day.

Certain countries like Italy and Spain do not include decimals in their currency values, so they will have to confront major logistical issues in converting to the euro.

Other more general issues will arise from the new transparency. For example, companies will need to think through issues of wage differentials across countries; "wage transparency" could result in increasing labour mobility. Arguably this could lead to some form of standard wage policy across Europe. Pensions will need much consideration – for example looking at the effect of the presumed reduction in pan-European interest rates on the value of current pensions. The measurement of inflation, too, will be a significant issue for many companies given the importance of indexation in some price control and tax regimes.

MANAGING CHANGE

We have found little evidence of companies looking at any of these issues or indeed of thinking through the whole change management issue. Staff will need a huge amount of training – not just those in financial services but those at all points of sale. Certainly the advent of EMU and its implications for business needs to be part of a major project, requiring planning and resources. Of course this is not just to do with compliance issues – it is much more than that. The wider impact of EMU has yet to be really thought through. For example, a great opportunity for retailing would be to link the advent of the euro with the idea of introducing "Smart Cards" and other forms of electronic cash. Clearly, at the very least that would help alleviate some of the cash handling difficulties.

The disquieting fact seen from studies carried out by ourselves and other firms is that there is an extraordinary level of complacency about the need to do anything – and that is true inside and outside the UK. Most of the thinking which is occurring is around minimising cost and risk rather than exploiting opportunities. For example, one recent survey showed that a significant majority of companies believed that EMU would *not* affect their international marketing strategies, production strategies, investment plans or supply chain arrangements.

In my view this has to mean that they simply have not addressed some of the key questions. There are major areas of opportunity which the implementation of a single currency can facilitate: for example, moving into new markets, new products and services; new sales channels such as electronic commerce (eCommerce); and mail order or direct marketing to reach new market segments. There are critical issues to think through like widening the supplier base and assessing the impact of the euro on supply chains, distribution and procurement. Small companies have often been reluctant to work with foreign suppliers because of the complexity of pricing calculations, foreign exchange risk and cross-border transactions; clearly most of these barriers should be eliminated. Again, payment conditions may affect the choice of supplier with payment terms currently varying from 19 to 68 days across Europe.

There are major decisions to make about pricing policy. For instance, a Cadbury's chocolate bar (if we are allowed to still call it that) currently priced at 50p may be priced at .50 euro (50 cents) so that it is easier to use vending machines etc. – but then both packaging and weight may have to be adjusted. Pricing policy decisions will be affected by price transparency. Whisky for instance currently varies across Europe by as much as 40% *excluding* tax.

Then there are the even more critical strategic issues around competition and the structure of companies. Will new alliances be forged? Should companies be seeking mergers or acquisitions to enter new markets or to execute their strategy? Companies will need to reassess their decisions about centralisation and/or the relocation of back office services to either lower cost countries or those with a better business environment.

CONCLUSION

In order for the introduction of the euro to lead to a real "virtuous circle of competitiveness" for European business, business leaders need to be thinking about the long-term strategic implications and looking at the opportunities EMU can bring, as well as making sure that they meet the short-term compliance requirements. Currently at least it would seem that thinking is a little behind schedule.

Business will not make or break the single currency. That responsibility must lie in the hands of politicians. But – assuming that the macroeconomics are broadly right – the business community has a huge opportunity. If we make the right strategic decisions – about cross-border alliances, about investment, about relationships with customers, all enabled by the creative use of technology – we stand to achieve a sea-change in European competitiveness. ☆

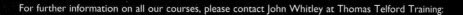

IN THE MARKET FOR FLEXIBILITY

BY ADAIR TURNER, DIRECTOR-GENERAL OF THE CONFEDERATION OF BRITISH INDUSTRY

"The Chancellor has rightly identified that the UK as well as other EU member countries must work to ensure that labour markets in Europe are flexible enough to support, and so not undermine, EMU"

" Employers have a responsibility to ensure that they improve the 'employability' of their staff, which means developing a broad base of skills, so that employees can, if necessary, move easily to new jobs"

The Chancellor's statement on EMU to the Commons in November included reference to "flexibility" as one of the key conditions if Monetary Union is to be a success. The CBI, which has come out in support of the principle of UK membership of EMU, but only if and when the conditions are right, certainly believes that flexibility (particularly flexible labour markets) is among the most important of those conditions.

What the Chancellor has rightly identified is that the UK as well as other EU member countries must work to ensure that labour markets in Europe are flexible enough to support, and so not undermine, EMU. This should not be seen in terms of where labour markets are run better or worse, nor in terms of a simplistic contrast between "Anglo-Saxon" and "Continental" models. What matters is simply that the required actions are now taken. And these actions are important for Britain, even if we stay out of EMU – since in or out we have a clear interest in EMU's success

The CBI has long recognised that across Europe there is a "patchwork quilt" of differing practices; what is needed is the adoption of the best practices and elimination of the worst. The challenge is to find ways of tackling problems at national level, learning from the experiences of others, whilst avoiding the dangers of blanket European legislation.

There are still some sizeable obstacles in the way of achieving this. Not least is the idea that "labour market flexibility" equals employee insecurity. It is vital therefore to define clearly what we mean by flexible labour markets and the challenges and opportunities that they create. A flexible labour market is above all where *people and their skills are flexible*. This skills flexibility is essential in a world where the skills needed by industry continually change and where a job for life is increasingly the exception rather than the norm. To flourish in this changing labour market, people have continually to retrain and reskill, throughout their lives.

A flexible labour market also means *flexible patterns of working*. Old patterns of working – continuous, full-time employment – are becoming less common. Part-time employment, meanwhile, is increasing rapidly. But, all too often, part-time employment is regarded as in some sense second-rate. This can only have a demotivating effect on many people who positively want to work part-time because it better suits their needs.

The most contentious aspect of flexible labour markets is the freedom of companies to lay off staff when the competitive circumstances demand. It is right to ensure that companies are governed by laws on redundancy and unfair dismissal. These laws are required to defend individual rights to fair treatment and to smooth labour market transactions. But if they are pushed too far or seen as measures for "defending jobs", they can deter new job creation. Companies faced with high costs of shedding labour will either not expand or opt for high investment in automation to limit staff cost exposure if business turns down.

If there is a problem with flexible labour markets, it is one of image. Outside the business community, flexibility is often viewed, at best, with suspicion and, at worst, with outright hostility. What we need to get across is that flexible markets offer opportunities, but opportunities with *responsibilities*.

On the one hand, employers have a responsibility to ensure that they improve the 'employability' of their staff, which means developing a broad base of skills, so that employees can, if necessary, move easily to new jobs. And employees meanwhile have a responsibility to work to develop new and transferable skills throughout their careers providing themselves with the opportunity to find new employment in different areas if one job market disappears. In a world where on average 80 per cent of the existing technologies will be obsolete and replaced in the next ten years, such opportunities will be absolutely vital.

It is important across Europe to recognise and develop different solutions to the different problems being experienced in each EU member country. That need will increase with EMU. It is not true that continental Europe has it all wrong and the Anglo-Saxon economies all right: several countries have interesting lessons for the others. But it is true that there are many things wrong with several European markets and that change is essential. Different labour markets have different strengths and weaknesses. There are many different paths to success, but they all lead in roughly the same direction – towards a flexible labour market. ☆

ACCELERATING DRUG APPROVAL IN EUROPE

BY FERNAND SAUER, EXECUTIVE DIRECTOR,
EUROPEAN AGENCY FOR THE EVALUATION OF MEDICINAL PRODUCTS

"The EMEA is designed to co-ordinate the existing scientific resources available in the member states. Rather than create a new 'Food and Drug Administration' for Europe, the EMEA acts as an interface between national competent authorities without dismantling their existing structures"

PUBLIC HEALTH IN THE SINGLE MARKET

Based in London since January 1995, the European Agency for the Evaluation of Medicinal Products (EMEA) is one of a number of the new so-called "decentralised" bodies of the European Union. The decision to locate the EMEA in London was taken by the Heads of State and Government of the EU at the end of 1993, recognising the United Kingdom as an international centre for pharmaceutical research and development.

The EMEA is designed to co-ordinate the existing scientific resources available in the member states. Rather than create a new "Food and Drug Administration" for Europe, the EMEA acts as an interface between national competent authorities without dismantling their existing structures.

As part of the completion of the internal market, the EMEA is a new way – through a single European procedure – of having medicinal products for human and veterinary use authorised throughout the EU. Instead of 15 separate applications to the national competent authority of each member state, companies with an innovative product have the possibility of a single application and scientific evaluation leading to the granting of one marketing authorisation.

Before a new medicine can be placed on the market, all industrialised countries require a complex series of tests to determine the quality, safety (via toxicity tests on animals) and efficacy (via human clinical trials) of the product. These public health requirements have often differed from country to country, adding to the cost of development and significantly delaying the moment when a product is placed on the market by anything up to four to six years.

There are essential public health reasons for such requirements, but within the context of a European Single Market for pharmaceuticals there is also clearly a need for harmonisation of these rules to ensure the highest level of public health protection throughout Europe and free movement of medicinal products.

During the past three years the EMEA has worked hard at streamlining this single evaluation process and making it user-friendly – speeding access by patients and users to new and better medicines, benefiting patients and pharmaceutical research in Europe.

EUROPEAN PHARMACEUTICAL AUTHORISATION: HOW THE SYSTEM WORKS

The European authorisation system is based on a partnership between the national competent authorities and the EMEA. Oversight of the EMEA is assured by a Management Board, made up of two representatives from each member state, from the European Commission and from the European Parliament.

The evaluation work of the EMEA is undertaken by its two scientific committees: the Committee for Proprietary Medicinal Products (CPMP), and the Committee for Veterinary Medicinal Products (CVMP), both of which are composed of two members nominated by each member state. The work of these scientific committees is assisted by about 2,000 European experts covering the full range of expertise needed to ensure the best possible quality of the EMEA's scientific opinions. Their scientific competence is guaranteed by the member state which nominates them and their integrity assured by a public declaration of interests. When acting for the EMEA, they act independently of their nominating authority. The work of the committees is supported by the EMEA Secretariat of about 185 scientific, technical and administrative members of staff.

Applications for biotechnology medicinal products and other innovative medicines are submitted directly to the EMEA. In this "Centralised Procedure", a single evaluation is carried out leading to a single Community marketing authorisation for the product within one year, valid throughout the whole of the EU.

Babies born in the 21st century

may still develop diseases like asthma,

diabetes and multiple sclerosis.

But they may not have to live with them.

As the millennium approaches, we stand at the threshold of a dramatic turning point in the history of medicine.

It's the genetic era. And within the lifetime of our children, its developments could provide us with the keys to conquer many of today's most threatening diseases. The reason for such optimism? The genetic era signals a quantum leap in our understanding of the body and of disease.

Until recently, medical research has taken three main directions: to develop treatments that kill disease-causing microbes; to chemically influence diseased tissues; or to develop surgical techniques to remove or repair damaged organs and tissues.

For the most part, we haven't been able to fully overcome our disease enemies.

The great exception is our victory over many infections through antibiotics.

What we have learned is how to manage or treat illness, allowing people with diseases like hypertension and diabetes to live longer, healthier lives.

Now, with our first real understanding of the human body's genetic programming, comes a real chance at real cures.

At Pfizer, a world leader in biomedical research and development, the excitement is palpable. "We are entering a truly revolutionary period in which insights derived from genetic research will shine a powerful light on the root causes of disease," says Dr. Arthur Franke, who heads

Pfizer's molecular biology research in neuroscience. As high school biology students learn, genes determine

1347	1600s	1796
Bubonic plague blamed on vapors rising from earth	**"Royal Touch" thought to cure tuberculosis; monarchs mobbed**	**Discovery of smallpox vaccine**

such physical characteristics as hair and eye color, height and weight range. We now know that genes also determine whether we are likely to develop a range of dangerous and potentially fatal diseases. Our genes play a role in deciding whether we will be susceptible to colon cancer, despite eating low-fat diets and exercising until we drop. Or whether we will be able to gorge on ice cream, chain-smoke and die in our sleep at 90.

Today, an important portion of Pfizer's $1.7 billion R&D budget is spent on genetic research. The reason is obvious: **If genetic coding can cause disease or encourage it to develop, genetic therapy could prevent or cure disease.**

At Pfizer laboratories in the U.S., Europe and Japan, genetic research focuses on understanding the genetics of disease processes — exactly which genes give instructions that create or enable disease, how they do it, and how they might be stopped. "The way we can really use the genetic revolution is to study the genes that are expressed in diseased tissue, compare them to gene expression in normal tissue, and develop a medication to block the actions of the genes found only in the diseased tissue," says Michael Fogliano, Manager of Molecular Sciences at Pfizer.

Genetic research is pointing Pfizer scientists to the types of therapies that once might have seemed like science fiction. Some examples? Cancer treatments that will turn off the genetic mechanism instructing cancer cells to divide, without poisoning healthy cells nearby. Antibiotics that will specifically target bacterial genes necessary for disease survival. It's real hope for real cures. To families who have watched generation after

1842	1918	1920s	1928	1929	1944
Ether's introduction allows surgery without torturous pain	Flu pandemic kills more Americans than any war before or since	Average U.S. life expectancy is 54	Alexander Fleming discovers penicillin in a moldy lab dish	DNA identified in cell nuclei	First ever mass-produced penicillin, from Pfizer, protects WWII GIs

generation of children give themselves daily insulin shots, **it is the promise of liberation from a life-threatening cycle.** To sons whose fathers fell to heart attacks in middle

age, it means new hope. And to people living in fear of congenital multiple sclerosis or cystic fibrosis, it's the dream that their fears will end.

Medical progress is the source of all these hopes. And what makes it possible is a tremendous commitment of time and resources from Pfizer and other leading research companies. "We are driven by the knowledge that our work

today could end or prevent suffering for millions of people tomorrow," says Dr. Ian Williams, who heads

molecular science research at Pfizer. "Pfizer researchers go to work each day knowing that they are contributing to an effort that could change the world for their own children and for the generations to come."

Pfizer

We're part of the cure.

www.pfizer.com
AOL keyword: pfizer

1955	1970s	1990s				
Polio vaccine makes iron lung obsolete	First report of **AIDS** and Ebola	Top 8 killers of 1920s cause few if any deaths today	Average **U.S.** life expectancy is 76	Cancer is target of 215 drugs in development	First time scientists crack full genetic code of a disease organism	Pharmaceutical industry invests nearly $2 million an hour in research

> **"The EMEA seeks to promote public health by providing health care professionals and patients with the same improved information throughout the EU in all 11 official languages"**

The EMEA seeks to promote public health by providing health care professionals and patients with the same improved information throughout the EU in all 11 official languages. This means the same product name, labelling and package leaflets for all patients and – particularly important for health care professionals – the same indications and product information. Regular meetings are also held with representatives of consumer and patient groups, industry, and health care professional bodies.

The "Decentralised Procedure", applying to the majority of conventional medicinal products, is based on the principle of mutual recognition of national marketing authorisations allowing for the extension of a national authorisation to one or more other member states selected by the applicant. Where mutual recognition is not possible, the EMEA is called on to give binding arbitration.

In the three years since the EMEA was inaugurated, about 70 positive opinions have been adopted for human and veterinary medicines within the tight time-frame set down in legislation, leading to the granting of nearly 55 pan-European marketing authorisations. In addition, some 350 maximum residue limits have been established for veterinary substances used in food-producing animals.

Even several years before an application is submitted, the EMEA can assist European research and development-based pharmaceutical companies in giving scientific advice – for instance, on the conduct of clinical trials, where the EMEA has advised in some 45 cases. Companies are also helped in their export activities with export certificates issued by the EMEA for access to major markets in the world.

Funding of the Agency comes from two sources: a subsidy from the budget adopted by the European Parliament and Council of Ministers; and fees paid by industry for applications. The 1998 budget amounts to about 32 million Ecu, of which nearly 20 million Ecu is expected to come from fee revenue. It is expected that fees will account for about 75% of the EMEA's revenue by the end of the millennium. The national competent authorities to whom scientific evaluation services are sub-contracted by the EMEA currently receive half the application fees paid to the Agency.

NEW CHALLENGES

The EMEA, like other European bodies, is trying to place itself closer to the citizen; careful attention is paid to considerations of transparency and openness. The EMEA has used the growth in Internet technologies to communicate and disseminate information on its work (http://www.eudra.org/emea.html). The EMEA is exploring how its work can be opened to the wider scientific community and to learned societies in Europe and across the world.

Internationally, the EMEA makes an important technical contribution to the EU's external relations in the field of pharmaceuticals, both with international organisations and third countries. In particular, the EMEA plays a key role in the tripartite EU-Japan-US International Conference on Harmonisation (ICH) initiative and the veterinary counterpart, VICH.

> **"Internationally, the EMEA makes an important technical contribution to the EU's external relations in the field of pharmaceuticals, both with international organisations and third countries"**

International activities are increasingly important for the EMEA. The first half of 1998 sees the direct participation of Iceland and Norway in the work of the Agency and the EMEA has been requested to offer technical assistance to Central and Eastern European countries as they prepare for closer association and possible accession to the EU. There is also an increased role for the EMEA in the direct management of pharmaceutical aspects of mutual recognition agreements between the EU and third countries, including Canada, US, Australia, New Zealand and Japan.

During the UK Presidency important new proposals will be discussed by the Council of Ministers and the European Parliament which are of particular significance to the future development of the EMEA. These proposals include the reform of fees payable to the Agency which, combined with performance reviews, will lead to improved service for users and a more effective structure for the EMEA better adapted to discharging its responsibilities. The EMEA is giving its full support to a number of other proposals directly aimed at patients, including the proposed EU "orphan drugs" policy, which should help encourage companies to develop medicines for rare diseases; better protection for patients involved in clinical trials; and improved supervision of starting materials used in medicines. ☆

cancer research campaign

Making Cancer History

**by Professor J. Gordon McVie, FRCP,
Director-General, Cancer Research Campaign**

Next year marks the 75th anniversary of the Cancer Research Campaign. It is now the largest of 600 cancer charities in the UK in terms of voluntary income, and as those charities account for 90% of cancer research funding (only 10% from government), the Campaign is a major player.

The charity has an outstanding record in drug discovery and development, dating back to the synthesis of stilboestrol for breast and prostate cancer before the War to temozolomide – probably to be registered in our 75th year – for brain cancer. We are Europe's leader in this area, and the mechanisms applied by us are now adopted throughout Europe.

In the last 15 years alone, we have taken over 50 compounds from the lab into the clinic. The spectacular success of our drug carboplatin, now used worldwide for the treatment of various kinds of cancer, prompted the establishment of our technology transfer company, Cancer Research Campaign Technology. This company transfers all its profits back to the Cancer Research Campaign to fund further research and currently its activites generate around £4 million a year extra revenue to our pioneering researchers. In contrast to carboplatin, which was not patent protected by the Campaign and therefore earns us no money, temozolomide has already produced £2 million of revenue for the Campaign and royalties are secured for the next 10 years.

The Cancer Research Campaign raises its money through a network of one thousand local committees, some dating back over 50 years. Added to this is a chain of 250 shops which deal exclusively in donated goods and which earn more per shop than almost any other charity in the country. Legacies are our major source of income, as with other large charities, but increasing income is derived from corporates and trusts.

The Cancer Research Campaign works together with others on a co-ordinating body called the United Kingdom Co-ordinating Committee on Cancer Research which ensures lack of duplication or competition of spend and particularly facilitates collaboration in the field of large clinical trials. Cross-membership of scientific committees ensures that projects are not replicated and international poor review is standard for all our large programme grants in medical schools and universities.

The most significant achievements over the last year or so include the cloning of the breast cancer susceptibility gene – $BRCA_2$. This extraordinary feat was a major morale boost for British science as it was the first major gene associated with any form of ill health to be cloned by any British team. Cancer Research Campaign Technology has patented the gene and has now licensed the information to an American diagnostic company, Oncormed, to provide a kit to assist in the prediction of risk in breast cancer amongst those with cancer in thier families. A unique clause in the contract provides assurance that this kit would be made available to the National Health Service in due course at a not-for-profit price. In this way we hope to ensure that those who have paid for the research, supporters and volunteers throughout the country will not be disadvantaged by pricing out the benefit of the discovery. It is our plan to take the $BRCA_2$ discovery into the realms of therapy in the next five years.

We already cure four out of ten people with cancer and six out of ten children. We expect to improve those statistics considerably by 2010.

MONT BLANC

*In times that are changing ever faster,
we need things which preserve the moment.*

*Meisterstück Solitaire Sterling Silver
925 sterling silver with pinstripe guilloche;
hand-crafted 18 K gold nib
with platinum inlay.*

THE ART OF WRITING

MAN'S BIGGEST ENEMY.

(Magnified approximately 30,000 times.)

This is the bacterium which causes tuberculosis. Every year diseases, such as tuberculosis, account for 9 out of every 10 deaths worldwide. Glaxo Wellcome, working with universities and hospitals, spends £1.2 billion a year and employs 9,000 researchers in the fight against disease.

GlaxoWellcome DISEASE HAS NO GREATER ENEMY.

WHY EUROPE MATTERS

BY THE RT. HON. LORD HOWE OF ABERAVON, FORMER DEPUTY PRIME MINISTER

"The 1998 UK Presidency offers an important moment to relaunch Britain's profile in Europe as an active, engaged and successful player, one determined to carve out a big role in the power politics of the continent"

1998 marks the twenty-fifth anniversary of the United Kingdom's accession to the European Community in January 1973. It is 40 years since the fledgling Treaty of Rome launched the world's first serious experiment in democratic, supranational governance in January 1958. The first half of this year also marks the fifth British Presidency of the now European Union, and the first under a Labour government committed to finding a place for our country in the mainstream of European politics. In short, 1998 marks both a coming of age for Britain in Europe and a great opportunity for Britain to draw on this new maturity to attempt to offer serious leadership in Europe. After the awkward stand-offs which came increasingly to characterise the last government, there is a chance of a new beginning in our relations with our Continental partners. It is a good moment to assess why Europe matters to Britain, what Britain can offer to Europe and how Britain can make the most of Europe as we approach the turn of the millennium.

Over the last quarter century, Britain has never fully reconciled herself to membership of the EU. A less happy anniversary this September – ten years on from Margaret Thatcher's Bruges speech – provides a telling reminder of the tendency, at any given time, for at least one section of our political establishment to challenge some of the basic assumptions of entry. Having finally converted Labour to membership by the late 1980s, Conservatives began to spin off in an increasingly Eurosceptic direction, with Mrs Thatcher investing most of her remaining political capital in shifting the centre of gravity in her party on this issue. She succeeded in this task, but only at the cost of losing the support of her most senior colleagues, and indeed herself losing power.

Ten years after Bruges, Euroscepticism is sufficiently powerful in Britain to curb the confidence of a new government with a large parliamentary majority, a clear electoral mandate and a heart firmly in the right place on European issues. Those of us who believe, whichever party they inhabit, that our country's future lies as a central player in European politics know from hard experience that the case for Europe has constantly to be argued and restated at the bar of public opinion. This is just as necessary today as at any time in the past twenty-five years. Indeed, in the context of EMU, it is perhaps more necessary than ever before.

A VEHICLE FOR ENHANCED POWER

Ironically enough, despite public misgivings, the actual record of UK membership since 1973 has proved remarkably positive. After a late start, we have become increasingly adept at shaping the policies and institutions of the EU. The Single Market, budget discipline, enlargement first to the EFTAn states and now to the East, reform of the Common Agricultural Policy, the development of a European foreign policy, the pillared design of the Maastricht Treaty, the legitimacy of intergovernmentalism, the importance of a monetarist EMU: in area after area, Britain has been able to impress its priorities and identity on the development of the Union. Influencing others, persuading others, and acting with others, Britain is finding that the EU is something which we can help to mould in our national interest.

Europe matters to Britain, above all else, as a vehicle for enhancing our influence in the world. A strong, united Europe offers Britain the chance to participate in and influence a larger, continent-wide enterprise, and thus to offset the decline in independent power, both economic and political, which Britain has suffered since the war. Commanding only one per cent of the world's population and four per cent of its GDP, the UK is no longer in a position to call the shots on the international stage. We would be unable credibly to maintain our status as one of the five permanent members of the UN Security Council, for example, if we now operated outside a common European framework. The fact is that *scale matters*: the 370 million-strong EU is the world's biggest and richest integrated marketplace, and its largest trading bloc, representing some 40 per cent of international trade. With five of the ten richest countries as members, the EU is a global player by any standard. When Britain speaks alone, her voice often goes unheard; when Europe speaks as one, the world listens.

Enhancing British influence is not just a question of maximising our voice in the world beyond Europe's shores – whether in foreign policy, development co-operation or trade relations with the US or Japan. It is also, and quite crucially, a matter of influencing important, essentially domestic, European decisions which our partners will be taking anyway, whether or not we are there with them. The internal rules of the single market, for example, or environmental and safety standards, or mergers and competition policy, or employment and equal treatment law are all things in which Britain has a direct interest, so long as we wish to sell our goods and services into the European market, and to buy firms and employ people across the Continent. We need to have a say in the day-to-day European choices which are going to affect us one way or the other, whatever we do. Ten per cent of all UK jobs now depend directly on this country's trade with the EU. A number of major UK multinationals – British Telecom and Commercial Union, for example – now employ as many people in other EU countries as they do in Britain.

THE REALITY OF INTERDEPENDENCE

Since we joined the Union, our economic interdependence with the rest of Europe has risen rapidly. With tariff and non-tariff barriers falling faster within Europe than globally, the UK's trade with other EU countries has increased twice as fast as with the rest of the world. Today over 60 per cent of British trade in goods, and more than half of total trade, is transacted with our European partners. The most striking illustration of this is the fact that Britain's visible exports to Germany now equal those to the US and Japan combined. Likewise, we export more to France than to the whole of the Commonwealth, more to the Netherlands than to South-East Asia and China together, more to Sweden than to the whole of Latin America, and more to Ireland than to Canada, Australia, New Zealand and South Africa combined.

Just as Britain's economy has been boosted by membership of a growing, prosperous single market – widening choice for consumers and keeping prices down – so our position in Europe has allowed Britain to emerge as the main magnet for inward investment, drawn to and servicing that very same single market that we have done so much to promote. Britain has now been Europe's largest recipient of non-EU inward investment for several years. During this decade, we have received as much as Germany, France and Italy combined. A total of over £170 billion worth of such investment has brought 700,000 jobs to the UK. In the process, Britain has become Europe's biggest net exporter of televisions, computers and microchips. Already 40 per cent of British exports are manufactured by foreign-owned companies.

In the last two decades, the UK has become a truly international economy, using the new, large home market it has acquired in the rest of the EU as a motor for growth. Compared with other G7 economies, we trade a higher share of GDP, we generate larger flows of cross-frontier investment (in both directions), and we have a bigger financial services sector. These are the hallmarks of a country that has chosen to compete and succeed by looking outwards, not inwards, and by responding to the needs of others. Economic interdependence and political independence make poor bedfellows. If we are serious about maximising our economic success – and there is strong reason for believing that we are – then real political consequences follow. Foremost among them is that the key political choices made by Europe – over the single currency most notably – are of growing importance to Britain's future.

THE OPPORTUNITY FOR BRITAIN

Fortunately, the opportunity for Britain to influence the central choices facing the EU, if we play our cards right, has never been greater. This is partly to do with economics. Because the enterprise policies of the last two decades have built a strong UK economy, capable of taking full advantage of the Single Market, we have gained credibility and moral authority in our dealings with partners. For the first time perhaps during our membership, the British experience is now seen on the Continent as something of a national success. Some even regard it as a model to follow. Our flexible labour and product markets, our large and efficient capital market, our privatised utilities, our shrunken state sector, our low personal and corporate taxation, as well as our effective control of public expenditure, are all now viewed as important sources of competitive advantage for Britain. We have not been alone in pursuing such